Six Years 'til Spring

A Polish Family's Odyssey

Teresa Mikosz-Hintzke

To Rose

With best wishes, & many thanks for taking interest in me

Fondly

Teresa

Authors Choice Press

San Jose New York Lincoln Shanghai

12-9-11

Six Years 'til Spring
A Polish Family's Odyssey

Authors Choice Press
an imprint of iUniverse.com, Inc.

For information address:
iUniverse.com, Inc.
5220 S 16th, Ste. 200
Lincoln, NE 68512
www.iuniverse.com

ISBN: 0-595-17720-4

Printed in the United States of America

To my husband Edward, without whose support this book would not be written, to my son Richard, who dedicated much time to put the manuscript into printable form, and to Gigi, our granddaughter, so she would know the past.

Contents

Preface

A number of years ago I decided to write down the saga of my family during World War II, much of which we shared with thousands of Polish families who followed a similar path but whose hardships and privations now are forgotten by all except those still living who experienced them.

I celebrated my fifth birthday on August 1, 1939; one month to the day later, September 1, 1939, my world and that of millions of Poles, indeed the entire Polish nation, was shattered by the German and subsequent Soviet invasions, and was never to be restored. That world is gone forever.

Having heard my father's recounting of his wartime ordeals for many years after the war, I after a long delay tape-recorded him telling his story. My subsequent research in family letters, papers and stories from my aunt and cousins, as well as my own recollections, brought me to the point of being able to put it all in written form so that the memory of it will not be lost.

The book traces the six-year ordeals of my father and of my mother and I, following different and widely separated paths, from the outbreak of war when we left Chobielin, my grandfather's estate in Poland, to the day when we were finally reunited. Our wandering took the family through eight countries and three continents.

I have written this book with two purposes in mind. First, I wanted there to be a record of these years of travail for the sake of history as well as for the family. Second, to show present and future young generations that people who have the will to do so are capable of surviving great upheavals and subsequently lead normal lives, not blaming the past but learning from it, in order to insure a better future.

List of Photos

JUNE 24, 1939-CHOBIELIN
Aunt Maria's wedding. It was the last time the family was together. Within a few
months many would be dead. dead

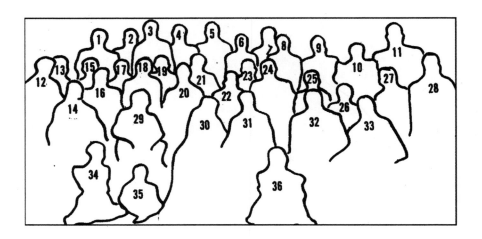

1. Anna Reysowska-Mikosz (my mother)
2. Jan Slawinski ("uncle Jas", aunt Helen's husband)
3.

4. Stankiewicz (uncle Wacek's youngest brother)
5. Maks Reysowski (mother's brother)
6. Maryla Miller (grandfather's niece)
7. Friend of uncle Wacek
8. Alexandra Wityk (Josef Muslewski's niece)
9. Janusz Slawinski (aunt Helen's son)
10. Irena Diedzinska (a friend of aunt Maria)
11. Stanislaw Mikosz (my father)
12. Lucja Reysowska-Muslewska ("aunt Luta", mother's sister)
13. Bernard Reysowski (mother's brother)
14. Col.Heldut-Tarnasiewicz (father's commanding officer)
15. Alfons Reysowski (mother's brother)
16. Stanislawa Zwierzchowska
17. Helena Marchlewska (grandmother's niece)
18. BarbaraReysowska (uncle Maks's wife)
19. Judge Prange
20. Helena Reysowska-Slawinska (mother's oldest sister)
21. Josef Muslewski (aunt Luta's husband)
22. Maria Marchlewska (grandmother's niece)
23. friend of uncle Wacek
24. Maryla Prange (mother's cousin and wife of the Judge)
25. Mrs.Stankiewicz (uncle Wacek's sister-in-law)
26. Jadwiga Gapinska
27. Capt. Josef Cetnerowski
28. Mr.Stankiewicz (brother of uncle Wacek)
29. Mrs.Stankiewicz (uncle Wacek's mother)
30. Maria Reysowska-Stankiewicz (mother's sister)
31. Cpt.Waclaw Stankiewicz ("uncle Wacek", aunt Maria's husband)
32. Julian Reysowski (grandfather)
33. Father Sobocinski (cousin and officiating priest)
34. Barbara Muslewska (my cousin Basia)
35. Teresa Mikosz (myself)
36. Maria Slawinska (aunt Helen's daughter)

SUMMER 1939-CHOBIELIN
From left to right-uncle Alfons, aunt Maria, aunt Barbara and her husband uncle
Maks, mother, father and grandfather Reysowski.

1935 GRUDZIADZ, POLAND
Father (far right) on parade.

1937 GRUDZIADZ, POLAND
Father as an instructor in Officer Cadet School.

SUMMER 1939-GRUDZIADZ, POLAND
Mother, father and I.

SPRING 1939-GRUDIADZ, POLAND
Playing with my friends in a park.

SEPTEMBER 1939-LWOW, POLAND
Under Soviet occupation. Mother and I on one of our walks into town.

SEPTEMBER 1939-GROSSBORN, GERMANY
Father's POW ID photo.

1943-WOLDENBERG, GERMANY, OFLAG II
Father third from the left (with cap). Uncle Jas center front.

MAY 1942-TEHERAN, IRAN, Camp #1
First Communion of children released from the Soviet Union. I am circled.

1942-ISFAHAN, IRAN
Group photo of some children and personnel of the Polish schools. Back row-mother second from right, Mrs.Berdowska third from left. I am in the middle in my Polish national costume.

1943-ISFAHAN, IRAN
Cousin Basia (left) and I with a friend of hers and my dog Zuzu.

1944-ISFAHAN, IRAN
My tenth birthday with my playmates.

1945-TEHERAN, IRAN
In the garden of our apartment house with a friend.

MAY 1945-MURNAU, GERMANY
Father's first photo after being liberated.

SEPTEMBER 1945-CINGOLI, ITALY
Father in his British uniform.

JANUARY 1946-EL QANTARA, EGYPT
Visiting aunt Maria on the way to Italy.

JANUARY 1946-EL QANTARA, EGYPT
My parents' first photo after being reunited.

Part One

1939

Chapter 1

Chobielin, Grudziadz, Bydgoszcz, Gorki, Wiele

AUGUST 13,1939
CHOBIELIN

It was a hot Sunday afternoon. Everyone was relaxing on the veranda that spanned the rear of my grandfather's sprawling country house, Chobielin, in western Poland about twelve miles from the German border. The tall trees cast their shade upon the house, giving some much-needed relief from the sun. In the distance, at the foot of the hill upon which the house was situated, the river flowed rapidly, cooling the air somewhat. Grandfather was half-sitting, half-lying in his lounge chair, puffing on his ever-present cigar, while father, 35 years of age and a career cavalry officer in the Polish army, was reclining nearby. They were engrossed in conversation that, as always in those days, constantly returned to the political situation. The world around us was in turmoil, but no one perceived the closeness of the oncoming war. There already had been partial mobilization, but it was regarded as only a precaution.

The tranquility of the afternoon was interrupted when the maid walked in to announce that she had a telegram for father. Grudgingly, father extended his hand to take the message from her and ripped the envelope open. The message was from the Headquarters of the Cavalry Training Center in Grudziadz, where father was stationed, ordering him to report there immediately; general military mobilization had begun. The telegram, considerably delayed, had finally reached him here in Chobielin where we were vacationing, and abruptly shortened our stay, since mother and I were to return to the city with him.

Within an hour we were ready to set out for Grudziadz, about sixty miles to the north. After saying our farewells, my parents and I climbed into the seat of grandfather's chauffeured Opel and departed for home. The ride was uneventful but dusty, over unpaved country roads that in a few hours brought us to the doorstep of our apartment in Grudziadz.

By this time, both mother and I were tired out but glad to be home. Mother was looking forward to a quiet evening, while I was ready for bed. Father, on the other hand, could not indulge himself in such peaceful thoughts, since he had to follow the orders set forth in the telegram and leave mother and me at the apartment and proceed immediately to Headquarters.

Reporting to his commander, Colonel Bor-Komorowski, who was in charge of the Training Center, father was informed that he was being transferred to a new regiment, the 16th Lancers at Bydgoszcz, and having been a captain of cavalry for a year, he was now to be given a command of a company. The reassignment orders were effective immediately, but since there were additional matters of pressing military business, his actual reporting to his new unit was delayed for several days while armaments from the Center were being relocated to Garwolin, southeast of Warsaw.

AUGUST 25,1939
GRUDZIADZ

Having accomplished the formal transfer of his functions at the Training Center, father came home to pack his personal belongings and say good-bye to us all.

"Wake up…Teresa, wake up…. say goodbye to your Daddy."

I awakened resentfully and hesitantly from a deep slumber. As I looked around the familiar bedroom, above my bed stood my mother, gently nudging me into consciousness. Behind her was father in his officer's uniform, fondly smiling at me. His uniform always evoked a chivalrous fairy-tale-like aura. Even then, at the age of five, I had a romantic attachment to a uniform. This seems to have been inherited from my mother, who has always had a weakness for a man in uniform. Father bent over my bed and tenderly hugged and kissed me goodbye, I sleepily responded and promptly returned to my slumber...

AUGUST 26,1939
GRUDZIADZ

Next morning there was great activity in the apartment. Mother was in charge of seeing that all our furniture and belongings were packed, since the apartment was to be closed and she and I, together with our housekeeper Victoria, were to return to Chobielin as father wished, there to sit out the "unrest" that was anticipated.

Meanwhile, father had boarded his train for a short ride to Bydgoszcz, arriving there in the early morning of August 26th.

AUGUST 27,1939
CHOBIELIN

The following day, packing accomplished, the three of us, together with our personal belongings, departed by train for the short journey of sixty miles to Chobielin. I was looking forward to again seeing all my cousins, who always indulged in childish teasing since at five years of age I was the youngest of them all.

At the railroad station in Naklo, grandfather's Opel was waiting to take us back to the house. As we settled ourselves in our seats, I peered anxiously through the window for my first glimpse of the big house. As we passed fields being readied for harvest, working people would stop and wave to our passing car and I would happily wave back. The car turned off the main road onto a narrower cobblestone road lined on both sides with cherry trees and began to descend rapidly, signaling that we were almost there. As the road started to level out a row of red brick cottages appeared in front of us—the houses for the people that worked on the estate. The car made a sharp turn to the right and then to the left, and the light gray stucco house of Chobielin came to view. It was a two story late classic style structure built toward the middle of the nineteenth century, facing west, with an additional wing added at the turn of the century. Across the rear of the house was the magnificent veranda, with french windows leading to the main salon. The back of the house was sheltered by a small park abundant with age-old trees and a much used tennis court. The car stopped. We were once again at Chobielin.

Aunt Maria was rushing towards us. She was my mother's youngest sister and was also married to an officer, uncle Wacek. Her wedding, at which I was a flower girl, had been only two months ago.

Maria was an attractive woman of twenty-five with a well endowed figure, a provocative smile, and an exuberant personality. As she reached me she stooped down to smother me with embraces and kisses; attention that I enjoyed greatly, she being my favorite aunt. The exchange of greetings continued for some time, since most of my aunts and uncles and cousins were already there. The large house was buzzing with activity.

But this was not the same happy place that had witnessed many other joyous family gatherings, the last one being only a few weeks ago when we intended to spend the summer together. Now the adults were preoccupied with getting ready for possible evacuation in case there was an invasion by the Germans.

After a few days of extreme tension and apprehension, everyone began to relax, thinking that maybe there had been undue alarm. The radio was broadcasting Hitler's speeches and commenting that "these things will be worked out...." Nevertheless, several days before the month's end a detachment from the army corps of engineers arrived to prepare the nearby bridges for eventual demolition.

AUGUST 26,1939
BYDGOSZCZ

Father reached the city in the early morning hours and from the railway station headed straight for regimental headquarters where the mobilization officer, Capt. Dmochowski, assigned him the 3rd company. Father was to take it over from Capt. Wojaczek, who was not present since he had already been transferred to a different unit. Capt. Wojaczek's second in command was in charge of the actual change of command procedure; he was 2nd Lt

Salmonowicz, whom father knew personally as a former student officer-cadet. Father was given a personnel list of his company. Scanning the names on the list, he found to his disappointment that most of the officers were reservists who were unfamiliar to him, and to make it worse he did not know any of the regulars personally. It was the same story with the noncommissioned officers; he knew only the Sergeant-Major. There was nothing he could do about it, however, so, having overcome the disappointment of not being acquainted with the men whom he was to command, he plunged into the task of quickly putting his group into a combat-ready position.

The company did not look promising, because in addition to being an uncohesive unit, some of its equipment had been taken away. Many saddles had been taken and in their place the supply depot issued new saddles which required assembly and fitting; all that required time, which they did not have. Since actual mobilization was not being conducted in Bydgoszcz due to precautionary measures against air raids, father's company was to assemble in a village called Rynarzewo, situated a few miles to the southwest.

So, when around noon orders came for his company to move out, the unit's equipment was not ready. Therefore, father ordered the unassembled saddles to be loaded into carts and the lancers led the horses or rode bareback, while the officers constantly kept an eye on the equipment so none would be lost. The Sergeant Major stayed behind in order to get a supply of ammunition as well as fodder for the animals.

After an hour's march, father arrived at his company's mobilization center in Rynarzewo, where he was able to complete the task of equipping the company before orders were received to be ready to march out at 1800 that same day; however, due to the chaotic state of the forces the march-out time was postponed to 2300 so they could join up with the rest of the Regimental column in Bydgoszcz.

Having accomplished the difficult task of organizing the concentration and readiness of his polyglot company, father's troops were ready for the march. In the darkness of the night a loud "mount your horses!" was heard, and more than a hundred men in unison executed the order. A few minutes' pause, then another order: "Company forward!" and the mounted column started to proceed slowly—father leading his company, with his staff of six officers following him. Then came the three combat platoons in order of numerical sequence, followed by the support platoon which consisted of field kitchen, ammunition supplies and the administrative unit.

The now orderly column proceeded back toward Bydgoszcz, with the horses slowly trotting under the burden of their combat-ready riders. The tower clock on the church of Saint Klara was striking midnight when in the silence of the night the regimental companies trotted north on Gdanska street, leaving behind the city with which the 16th Regiment had close ties. They marched into the unknown; occasionally they came upon some passersby who looked at them with concern. There was silence in the ranks, as if all perceived that there was something ominous about the night march.

The destination of the marching unit was the small village of Wiele, a vacation spot during the summer situated about 20 miles northeast of Chojnice, 10 miles north of Czersk, and some 55 miles from Bydgoszcz. It was here that the Pomeranian Brigade, to which father's regiment belonged, was grouped.

AUGUST 29, 1939
GORKI

After hours on the march, the company reached the village of Gorki in the early hours of the morning. The village was near Wiele, and was the quarters assigned for the 3rd Company while the Regimental Headquarters was quartered in Wiele, with the rest of the regiment's companies closer to the German border.

After a day's rest and a restful night, father began the actual preparation of his company for combat, which consisted of a first battle drill, as well as inventorying the equipment and completing the unit's armament, which included new anti-tank guns. The new guns were accompanied by instructions stating that for security reasons they were not to be unpacked. Father's own instincts of security told him that he could not rely on arms that he had not tested or was not familiar with himself. To the astonishment of his Sergeant, father ordered the weapons to be unpacked and told his officers and a few selected noncommissioned officers to start using them on a secluded range.

AUGUST 31, 1939
WIELE

General Skotnicki, the commanding officer of the Brigade, called a staff meeting for the afternoon. All officers were briefed on the general apprehension concerning the clearly oncoming crisis. After the briefing, the general turned to father and asked him to remain since he had special orders for him.

"Your assignment, Captain, is to take your company to relieve the 4th company of Captain Zarembicki, and then to organize as defense as fast as possible. "But," he added, "you know that there is not going to be a war, since England and Germany are in touch with each other and Britain has convinced Hitler to change his mind about invading Poland."

Having received his orders, father bade good-bye to the general and proceeded with preparations for his unit's departure. Since he wanted to see the position that he was to take over during daylight hours, father requested a regimental vehicle and drove there.

Capt. Zarembicki, a detail-minded and conscientious person, had the entire post well organized and secured. He had all necessary information ready for father, as well as guides, so the relief of the 4th company by the 3rd could go smoothly and without a hitch. Captain Zarembicki informed father that in the woods to the west, which were already in Germany, there was an unusual amount of activity with periodic flashes of light.

Upon returning from his reconnaissance, father came back to his company's quarters in Gorki and began to issue his orders for the upcoming march. The preparations did not take long and the company was ready and mounted by late evening.

"Proceed forward!" was heard and the troops of the 3rd company got on the move again.

Chapter 2

Vicinity of Lesno Lakes, Chobielin

SEPTEMBER 1, 1939
VICINITY OF LESNO LAKES

It was close to 1 a.m. when father's company reached its position. He took over command of the post from Capt. Zarembicki, who departed; father was left on his own in a place relatively little known to him and which he had not had sufficient time to adequately check out during daylight hours.

The position was situated between two lakes and was about seven miles from the German border, which ran generally north-south at this point, Germany being to the west. The actual border crossing was at Konarzyny to the southwest, but placing the main defensive position here, where the road ran east-west between the two lakes, made for easier defense. Father's defensive position was on the west side of the lakes, while the horses and supplies were on the east side. As the platoons situated themselves quietly and quickly in their positions, father went to find the border checkpoint on his flank in order to meet with its commander, who was under father's overall command.

This particular checkpoint was manned by some 50 soldiers belonging to the Frontier Defense Corps, under command of an officer. Beside their rifles, the armament of the troops of the border station was reinforced by two machine guns. The entire patrol was housed in two rectangular red brick buildings that were situated near the road and served not only as quarters but also as offices for the border patrol.

In addition to the border patrol, attached to father's command at this time were several sappers who had just completed preparations for the demolition of the bridge between the lakes; a precautionary measure in the event of a retreat becoming necessary.

Upon arriving, father informed the border patrol commander of his orders to assume overall command and then proceeded in the darkness of the night back to his company to check the progress of their positioning. Within two hours the task was accomplished, with the heavier equipment, such as machine guns and anti-tank guns, burrowed into a ditch. The border patrol troops were assigned to man the right (north) flank of the defensive alignment. The horses were tethered in the rear.

After bidding goodnight he headed into the village from where he was able to contact his regimental command through the village post office telephone (he had no radio communications equipment) and report that his position was secured. Father headed for a village roadside house where he quartered himself. He paused a moment before opening the door…listened…everything was quiet. The air was pleasant but still unseasonably warm for this time of the year. Father took a deep breath, inhaling the aroma of the late summer harvest that filled the night air. "Another warm day tomorrow," he thought to himself as he scanned the sky before entering the house.

As father opened the door he was greeted by his orderly, who was patiently waiting for him. The orderly already had made some coffee, which was a welcome treat after a long and tiring day. It was now about 4:00 a.m. After taking a long sip of the brew, father removed his side arm and unbuttoned his jacket without taking it off. He sat at the edge of the bed and begun to remove his riding boots with the orderly's help.

Suddenly the silence of the night was shattered with thunderous explosions that made the ground shake. Evenly spaced salvos of German artillery fire were quickly answered by the spatting of Polish machine guns. Father jumped to his feet, leaving the stunned orderly sitting on the floor. As father ran to the door he saw that the sky was ablaze with explosions from gun fire…it was coming from the direction of the border patrol post.

Hastily, father buckled his side arm back on and headed for what passed for his communication center next door in order to report the German artillery assault to his Headquarters but, being unable to make contact, went back to check on the status of his unit.

He walked over toward the nearest entrenched platoon while his platoon leaders scurried back to trenches that they had left only half an hour ago. The tension was mounting. There was now complete silence among the troops while they strained their sights towards the border, ready to open fire. The early morning fog that enveloped the region was now getting thicker, obstructing even further the line of vision. Nothing was advancing towards them; the light wind blowing eastward occasionally would bring a sound of revving motors intermingled with the spattering of machine gun fire from the direction of the German border.

Father sent out one patrol to go forward to the border ditch and to remain there for an hour while the second patrol went to the border post. The second patrol was led by a corporal who had been there with father just a little while ago, so he knew the way. The time passed slowly; minutes seemed like hours, as father waited to hear from the patrols he had sent out. He saw flares being shot into the air from the vicinity of the border patrol station. Germans were signaling their position…they had occupied the border station!

The patrol which had been sent to the border post returned confirming the German occupation of the buildings there; several men were wounded, with one fatality. Before the Corporal could go into the details of his report, father spotted figures emerging from the shadows. He recognized the men, bloodied, with ragged uniforms, leaning on each other for support. They were the men of the border patrol, trying to escape to safety. Seeing these embattled figures, the men of father's 1st platoon hastened to give assistance to their wounded comrades and to drag them to the safety of the nearby ditch.

The border patrol men were in a very bad state, not only physically but also psychologically—they were in a state of shock and not fit for further combat.

Questioning the shaken border patrol commander, father received a report of what had occurred.

"The Germans invaded and attacked the border patrol post without any warning and machine gunned most of the men…what you see here is what was able to escape…" he related while trying to hold on to his wounded arm, which was covered with a tattered cloth that once was a uniform and now was revealing bloody flesh. "They are now occupying the building." Exhausted, he sat on the ground, shaking his head in disbelief.

"Sergeant" father called, "get some men to assist the wounded! Take them to the rear and have them taken care of." With that, he turned his attention to the ongoing shelling, in anticipation of an imminent attack. But no attack came, although the artillery fire was becoming more severe. The exchange of fire continued without any further advance from the enemy side.

The dawn came enveloped in the heavy fog, making the vigilance of the troops continuous and nerve-racking. The inactivity and anticipation also strained the nerves. The weather situation slowly improved; the fog gradually dissipated, making visual reconnaissance possible.

As the sunlight illuminated the terrain, there was an abundance of smoke visible to the west on the German side of the border. Father took out his field glasses and scanned the area—it was a German village on fire that had been hit by Polish artillery support.

"That's lucky!" he thought to himself. The Germans were not lifting their shelling, but neither were they advancing.

It was now full daylight and once more father was trying to assess the situation; he climbed a low hill nearby in order to have a better vantage point. Peering through his field glasses, father made a visual sweep of the area. To the south he spotted a rising cloud of dust…the cloud was moving east.

Without hesitation father returned to his group and quickly gave orders to mount a patrol to investigate the source of the movement. Within twenty minutes the mission was accomplished, and the patrol confirmed father's suspicion that it was indeed a German panzer column moving east in the direction of Wiele, where the regimental HQ was located. By this time the German panzers had bypassed father's position, and by so doing were cutting him off from his regiment.

Father's first thoughts were to contact regimental HQ in order to inform them of the German advance and at the same time to request updated orders for his unit. Relinquishing his command momentarily into the hands of his senior lieutenant, father headed into the village where the telephone was. But, as he feared, the telephone lines had been cut, leaving him with only the alternative of sending a mounted messenger with the hope that he would get through. The messenger he sent never returned.

When it was evident that the messenger would not come back, another effort was made to reinstate communications with the regiment; this time an officer was sent with the message to HQ in the hope that he might succeed where the earlier messenger could not.

Meanwhile, the battle continued with intensified vigor. The battlefronts were to the north and west of the village; father's unit was on the north end of the Polish defense line, which extended far to the south. Father, complying with his orders, held his position. The Germans were not showing any activity on the perimeters of his company with the exception of sending out an occasional patrol which, after being fired upon, quickly disappeared. On the other hand, south of father's position was an ongoing continual battle that systematically moved east. Time was running out—it was past noon and there was no sign of the officer he had sent, nor had he received any further orders.

"I can't just sit here and wait forever," father was thinking to himself, while trying to evaluate the situation. His thoughts centered on a strategic road crossing which was to the rear of his position.

"If the Germans capture that crossing, we won't be able to retreat when the orders will arrive. They will come.... something must come."

Having considered several different alternatives, he reached a decision— half of the company, reinforced by a machine gun, was sent to the crossing with orders to head off the advancing Germans and to hold that position.

The shelling continued without relief as the day dragged on into the late afternoon. At about 4 o'clock, two lancers from the 2nd platoon returned bearing the unhappy news that the German tanks, of which they counted seventeen, had come upon their position and just rolled over them. The unfortunate lancers were no match for the heavily armored tanks. The two soldiers had managed to evade the German column and return to report the discouraging situation.

Now came a realization of the entrapped position in which father found himself. It was time to take matters into his own hands, since it was evident that no new orders would be coming through. Father knew that he would have to retreat into the depths of the countryside; not an easy maneuver in his present condition, with a company that at present consisted of about 125 lancers and the same number of horses, an armored vehicle and several machine guns, 10 sappers and a few soldiers of the frontier guard. Such a column was too long, and as it was on the move it would be unable to dig in to defend itself against tanks.

The heat of the afternoon still lingered and the air was permeated with dust and the smell of smoke when father called for his officers, who were joined by two more from the border patrol, and informed them of his plan as follows:

"Gentlemen, we have no contact with the regiment and we are surrounded by the Germans. Therefore, as soon as it gets dark we are going to start to retreat; we will prepare for this maneuver without drawing any attention to ourselves by the enemy. That will be all...Proceed!"

The officers saluted smartly and returned to their positions in order to get preparations for the move under way. Father sat down in the safety of his trench and began studying maps of the terrain, as well as orchestrating in his mind the sequence in which to move his men, while the distant exchange of fire continued unabated around him.

With the fall of darkness the German shelling ceased, and around six o'clock the long awaited orders from Regimental HQ in Wiele arrived. The were brought by a communications officer, who came by car and handed father orders to immediately abandon his position and join the regiment, which was on its way to Czersk. The officer added:

"The Regiment left Wiele at 1400 and is on the march south-east. I could not get to you sooner since I was twice detoured by German tanks."

The company began to ready itself for the withdrawal. Upon a pre-arranged signal the platoons, one by one, started to depart from their positions in foxholes and to mount their horses. There was some difficulty in getting the soldiers manning the machine gun that was closest to the German line out of their positions, since their departure from the trench had to be executed without arousing any suspicion on the part of the enemy. But even that was eventually accomplished, with some luck, and now all were ready to proceed.

Father mounted his horse and, having seen that the column had safely begun its march under cover of night, pulled his mount to one side and headed towards the bridge where the sappers were still on guard.

"Sergeant," he called in a low voice, "detonate the bridge!'

"But Sir, I have been ordered not to detonate the bridge unless brigade headquarters has authorized us to do so," replied the sergeant.

"I said blow it up," snapped father.

"Yes, Sir!" was the terse answer as the sergeant quickly began to execute his orders for demolition of the previously wired bridge.

Within seconds, the solid concrete structure went flying into the night sky with a thunderous blast, scattering debris everywhere. Pieces of flying cement and the noise of the sudden explosion startled father's horse, causing it to rear.

"Down, boy..' he patted the horse's neck gently, soothing the frightened animal, as he turned to take a look and make sure that the job was accomplished. It was. The bridge was gone, and with that knowledge came a sense of relief that the enemy could not pursue them. The road from Germany, at that point at least, was severed.

However, the coast was far from clear. The German panzer column that had devastated the 2nd platoon only a few hours ago was heading east, in the same direction as that in which father's company was to retreat. Consequently, he gave an order to avoid the roads and to proceed through the forest. Furthermore, as a precautionary measure he sent out another patrol to double-check the status of the road-crossing. As father suspected, the patrol returned with news that two German tanks remained there guarding that position.

Having thus been alerted of the enemy's situation, by staying off the roads and proceeding through the woods the company was able to avoid a possibly fatal encounter and to retreat unnoticed in an eastward direction in order to join the regiment. This was not an easy maneuver, since the darkness of the night and the density of the woods added more elements of danger to an already difficult situation.

After several hours' march the company finally emerged from the cover of the woods onto a dry dirt road that led into a nearby village. Gingerly proceeding in the hope of seeing some familiar face, they trotted forward. There was no movement from the settlement, only the eerie silence of the night; everything was dark. Passing several darkened houses by the roadside, the lancers kept moving forward when, out of the shadows, a woman's voice was heard:

"Oh, my God, oh my God...you...you are our lancers!" A stout peasant woman with arms outstretched emerged and was running towards father. Everyone halted. As she reached father she held on to his booted leg, as if to find solace and safety in the presence of an official representative of her native people.

Father calmed the woman and began to inquire as to what had occurred in this village. The frightened woman related that a few hours ago a multitude of Germans had passed through heading east. This was not welcome news, since now father had enemy forces not only behind but also ahead of him.

Having considered this information, he realized that a change of direction in the company's march would have to be made and he needed some time to study his position. As father proceeded into the woman's house, he gave orders for the troops to dismount and take a few minutes' rest.

Under the lamplight in the woman's farm house, with his maps spread out in front of him, father concluded that the only possible way to reach his regiment would be to head southeast for Czersk not on main roads, since that would be too dangerous, but through the countryside; fields and woods. He knew that this march would bring added hardship to his troops because of the difficulty of the terrain, but at the same time, being under cover of darkness, ft would also be safer. Father took out his compass and, having calculated the bearings, gave his instructions to the officers who were to head the company.

"Mount up!" once again came the order, and in the darkness the column proceeded out of the village, through the harvested fields, and into the nearby woods, heading in the direction of Czersk.

SEPTEMBER 1, 1939
CHOBIELIN

It was morning. As I came down for breakfast, I saw most of the family at the dining table. There seemed to be a dark cloud hovering over the gathering. They were listening to the radio blasting the latest communiqué——'THE GERMANS HAVE ATTACKED OUR BORDER POSTS!" Even at this news, the view of the majority of people gathered there was that the Germans would be repelled and that the attack was only "an incident".

A few hours into the morning, an officer from the engineer corps unit stationed nearby informed grandfather that the bridge on the Notec River that flowed nearby would soon be detonated. At this announcement, the decision was made to leave Chobielin and to go east where it would be safer—away from the invasion. But still there was no great hurry, until uncle Josef, husband of mother's older sister Luta who was still vacationing here with her children Romek and Barbara, arrived on horseback from his nearby home dressed in his army uniform (he was a reservist) and covered with dust.

"German tanks are crossing the fields of Kraczki [his home] and I barely got out by darting out the back way! They are coming...tanks and all!" he blurted out the news as he sat down, trying to catch his breath.

The news of uncle Josef's arrival passed swiftly through the house and in a few minutes everyone was gathered in the salon. While uncle was being calmed down and given a stiff drink to compensate for his mad and dramatic horseback ride, grandfather was asking pertinent questions.

Since the distance from Kraczki to Chobielin was only about twenty miles, it was apparent that the Germans could be here within a few hours. Realizing the gravity of the situation, it was decided to pack the already prepared provisions and head east to Garwolin, southeast of Warsaw, where aunt Maria's husband, uncle Wacek, had been transferred to be attached to the armies' supply center—away from the approaching battle zone. This was to be just a temporary situation, until the "battle" blew over.

Since it was the 1st of the month, aunt Helen, who was in charge of the payroll for the people working on the estate, had to pay them this afternoon. This delayed the departure for several hours while the hundred or so field hands, domestics and the rest of the staff lined up at the administrative building that stood at the entrance to the grounds of Chobielin. Here, each individual was handed cash by aunt Helen as Miss Gabrysia, the bookkeeper, checked them off in her book.

In the meantime, the family's evacuation plan began to take shape. The Chobielin Opel was being readied, as well as the Chevrolet pickup truck. Into the truck went both luxuries and necessities—several oriental rugs, oil paintings, some silverware and the food supplies. The rest of the valuables which were impossible to take with us were stored in the house, as well as some silver which was buried in the park behind the house. The house servants were told to go back to the village to their families. Only a few stayed in order to close up the house. Then the stable hands and stock hands were instructed to release all horses and cattle into the pastures where the animals could fend for themselves. The only person who refused to leave his post was a slow witted swine herd—this was his domain and he decided to stay with it.

As for the rest of us, our caravan was beginning to form. The lead car, grandfather's Opel, was driven by Hildebrandt, chauffeur for Mr. Poll, grandfather's neighbor and good friend. The passengers included uncle Alfons, who because of his weak health (he had a heart condition) was not in the army. He was a quiet man in his late thirties, not the sort of a person that would leave one with a clearly etched impression of himself. He had a disastrous marriage which ended in a divorce. His health was failing him, and one could see that in his pale complexion and drawn physique. Together with uncle Alfons, our vehicle's party was comprised of grandfather, aunt Maria, mother and I. Grandfather, who was to have his 69th birthday in few days, was a typical picture of a distinguished and prosperous country gentleman. His portly form was distributed over a six foot two inch frame. He sported a walrus mustache and carried a walking stick that added to his genteel aura. Even in this hour of commotion, he was dressed casually in a pair of beige trousers topped with a tweed sport coat over an open neck shirt. Our car was followed by a large horse drawn landau which carried the Muslewski family—uncle Josef, his wife aunt Luta, their children Romek and Barbara, and their children's governess, Miss Flora. The Muslewskis were a good looking family. Uncle Josef, who had changed out of his uniform, on this day looked more as if he was going on a sporting spree rather than the successful industrialist that he was. He was a tall and well built man on whom jodhpurs and a sport shirt looked dashing. In contrast to his sporting casualness was aunt Luta, who was the epitome of elegance even in this hour of distress. Her blond hair was meticulously coiffed in the latest fashion. The blue silk dress fitted over her slender frame with easy elegance, and of course the perfectly matched shoes and bag finished off the ensemble. As usual she did not omit to wear some exquisite jewelry, of which she was lavishly fond. Their two children were the pride of their parents, who lavished great affection upon them. Romek was then twelve and tall for his age. He was my favorite cousin, who always came to my rescue and always took time to play with me when the rest of my cousins did not want to have me tag along. His sister Basia was a year younger, a shy and slender girl who resembled her mother. They were pampered children, not only by their parents but also by Miss Flora, a proper middle-aged woman who tutored them and looked after all their needs.

Following the Muslewski's Landau was the third vehicle of the entourage, a navy blue Opel, with the Slawinski family. Uncle Jan Slawinski was not here. Being a reserve officer he had been recalled to active duty and, unknown to us then, was at the same front as my father. Aunt Helen Slawinska, mother's oldest sister, was a down-to-earth practical person whose only real concern was her family. She now had her hands full with her four children, three of whom were teenagers. Janusz, the oldest at sixteen, saw the political turmoil as a liberation from schoolwork, which he found to be a bore. The two girls, pretty teenagers with naturally curly mops of hair, were helping their mother with last minute arrangements. The youngest, Andrzej, was holding on to his mother and peering through his thick horn rimmed glasses—he was only nine years old. With them was Miss Gabrysia, the Slawinski's bookkeeper, who through being in their employ for many years had become one of the family.

The Chevrolet pickup truck with the provisions and valuables followed at the tail. The driver of this vehicle was grandfather's chauffeur, Walkowiak, who took his wife and children with him. After hasty and frantic last minute packing, the oddly assorted caravan started on what was for some of us to be a worldwide odyssey. What was in store for us was unknown and unimagined. For the majority of us it was to be the last view of our home, our roots. Some, like aunt Helen and her four children, would be back within a few months. For grandfather and uncles Josef and Alfons, it would be the final goodbye, for they would die within a year, never to rest in their native soil. As for the rest of us, we would be scattered over many parts of the world with our roots cut short but always hoping that our absence was only to last a few months. Everyone believed that this chaos would not last long. It was just a matter of surviving a few months—'til spring....

By two o'clock on the afternoon of September 1st the caravan started to proceed up the hill away from the columned portico of the house. From the hill top the last glimpse of the river and the mill could be seen. As the road turned to the left, the workers from the cottages gathered at the bend looking at our exodus. At this point the road graded upwards for a few hundred yards, leading the way into the tree lined road that would take us to Labiszyn, about 30 miles away to the southeast. At Labiszyn was grandfather's mill, managed by his son, my uncle Maks, and since we had a rather late start this seemed like a perfect place for our first stop. By this time the roads were beginning to fill up with people fleeing from the line of battle. Our vehicles proceeded at a snail's pace, with only the hope of reaching our destination before dark. The journey to Labiszyn, which under ordinary conditions would take at most an hour, dragged out now into six, making our arrival there a welcome relief for us.

Uncle Maks was expecting us, since grandfather had managed to telephone him before we left and before the telephone lines went down. Maks Reysowski was the oldest son who, after a very colorful as well as costly bachelorhood, married his bookkeeper, and settled down into running part of the family business. His wife Barbara, who was fifteen years his junior, in the short years of their marriage had two children, a son Marian, aged two, and a daughter Danuta who was only two weeks old.

The house was full of people who, like us, were trying to distance themselves from the war zone. That evening as we sat down for supper, many things were being sorted out at the table. One memorable decision was reached; the two week old Danuta was not yet baptized, so this was to be accomplished immediately. As it happened, one of the people that was seeking haven with the Reysowski's was a Catholic priest and a relative, father Sobocinski from the nearby Samoklenski parish, who would perform the ceremony. After the supper dishes were removed, we moved to the living room where aunt Maria and uncle Josef were godparents in this middle-of-the-night ceremony officiated by the priest who in a few months would lose his life in the concentration camp of Buchenwald.

For me it was the end of an exhausting day and after being tucked in some corner, totally exhausted, I fell asleep, leaving the adults to ponder the next days' strategy.

Chapter 3

Czersk, Dworzysko

SEPTEMBER 2,1939
CZERSK

The town of Czersk is interestingly situated in the center of a sprawling forest complex, with two main roads running toward it from Gdansk to the north and Bydgoszcz to the south. In addition, through Czersk ran east-west railroad tracks that in 1939, when it was in the so-called "Polish corridor", connected greater Germany with German East Prussia, making the town a strategic transportation center.

As the night was coming to its end with the march of father's company still in progress, a reconnaissance patrol which had been dispatched some time before returned and rode up to father to report:

"Captain, a military column is moving towards Czersk along the railroad tracks." At first the thought crossed father's mind that it might be part of a Polish infantry force which was supposed to be in this vicinity, but the corporal, continuing with his report; stated "They are bicyclists".

The Poles had bicyclists, but so did the Germans. Although his force was tired and hungry, father did not want to take anything for granted. Leaving the company in the shelter of the woods, he rode out toward the edge of the forest where he began to study the situation intensively through his field glasses.

It was now early dawn and the autumn mist was rising from the ground, obscuring visibility and making positive identification impossible for the moment. From his vantage point about a mile away, he indeed could see a column moving along the embankment on which the railroad tracks ran in the direction of Czersk. As he strained his eyes to see more clearly, a ray of light pierced through the silver-gray morning mist, reflecting a sudden flash from the soldiers' helmets and confirming his suspicions that the troops might not be Poles.

He took the binocular from his eyes, trying to wipe away the weariness and to rest for a moment. Then, as often happens at dawn, the mist lifted suddenly and the sun came out, giving a full view of the mysterious column. It now was a mystery no longer.... it was a German unit of bicyclists consisting of approximately 300 men, marching along the railroad tracks and pushing their vehicles beside them, heading in the same direction as father's company.

Being apprehensive of the extent of the enemy's advancement, father sent a reconnaissance patrol to Czersk in order to find out who held the town. This gave the troops a few moments of much needed rest while still remaining in the shelter of the woods. As they were resting, the patrol returned hastily, galloping and out of breath: "Captain..." the soldier started talking while trying to catch his breath "...we could not get to Czersk...as we approached we were shelled." He finished his report and dismounted, waiting for further orders, but there were none to give.

It seemed that they were once again surrounded by the enemy, with no place to go. Nevertheless, before making any further decisions, father decided to send another patrol to reconfirm the situation, hoping that there might be some slight chance of a way out.

"Hoffman!" father called to an NCO who was resting under a nearby tree. The man jumped to his feet, brushing the pine needles from his trousers, and approached father. Hoffman was well acquainted with father, since he had served under him as an enlistee several years previously and now, as a reservist, had been called back to active duty during the last month's mobilization.

"Hoffman," repeated father, "take another patrol and this time try to approach the town from the left in order to find out what actually is happening there....hurry!" Hoffman acknowledged the order and rode off with two other lancers whom he chose to accompany him on the mission.

Twenty minutes passed before Hoffman and the patrol returned, galloping back to the shelter of the woods where they were awaited anxiously. "Captain!" Hoffman shouted, grinning from ear to ear, as he rode up to where father was standing. "I'd like to report that it is our cavalry in Czersk!" Hearing the good news, everyone started to stir, anticipating the continuation of the march with the hope of linkup with the rest of the regiment. Orders were given, the company mounted and was ready to emerge from the cover of the trees when the silence of the woods was shattered by the sound of gun fire coming from the direction of the road leading into town.

"Halt!" resounded a command to the company, already on the move. Taking two officers with him, father galloped to the edge of the woods to investigate the source of the sounds of battle. Standing still in the cover of the woods, he raised his field glasses and, looking in the direction of what seemed to be a confrontation, was able to clearly observe what was occurring.

There was indeed a battle being waged, between the German bicycle column which was marching towards Czersk and the Polish light tank company that was defending the town. The tanks were rolling from the town and heading in the direction of the marching Germans, with their guns continuously spitting out fire on the enemy and inflicting the desired results. Debris was being scattered from the German column and some men who were not directly hit were trying futilely to run for cover.... Without any effective opposition the Polish tanks continued forward, rolling over anything and anyone that stood in their path—then silence; the battle ended and the defenders of Czersk headed back for town, leaving the battleground behind them.

With the road cleared of the enemy and the final dust clouds from the tank trail settled, father and his company were able to leave the protective cover of the forest and proceed to the town unobstructed. Wearily, the men and horses trotted towards a place that held the promise of much needed rest and replenishment.

Once in town, father sought out the regimental headquarters and reported to his commanding officer, Col. Rusocki, who was startled to see him and his company since according to all reports they had been written off as lost in action.

"Captain, how did you manage to get out from your position with your whole company and reach this destination when the whole area is under the

Germans?" inquired the colonel, wanting to know the details that father in due course provided concerning the happenings of the past two days.

"So, staying off the main roads was your saving element, since the German offensive concentrated on these main arteries," concluded the colonel, adding that the enemy was unfamiliar with the terrain and thus very hesitant about venturing through the woods with their armored vehicles. The Germans preferred to keep their offensive to the main roads, so in this particular instance a horse proved to be more maneuverable and evasive as a troop carrier than an armored vehicle. Unfortunately, this episode was an exception and not the rule of that war.

Having concluded his report, father requested quarters and food for his men, explaining that they had been on the march all night and were in need of rest. Col. Rusocki responded that it would be impossible to stay in Czersk since the brigade, or the remnants of it, was readying itself for the defense of the city. He gave father directions to continue the march one mile further to the rear. Here, in a specified village, father and his men would be quartered and would finally get some rest.

Reinforced by the hope of rest shortly to come, father's company headed for the assigned village. But before even reaching the village, a messenger from the brigade overtook father's marching column with orders not to quarter in the previously assigned place, but to retreat further back!

"The whole regiment is retreating," he added, as if it would console the disappointed troops.

It was now noon on September 2nd, and both the lancers and their horses were exhausted since they had been in combat all the previous day, followed by a full night's march which now was being extended into another day. The situation was not getting any better; now, in addition to the ground attack of the roving panzers, the column was periodically swooped down upon by German fighter planes. Fortunately, the German air force at this stage of the war had not yet acquired the precision for which it was later to be known. The company managed to scatter before any heavy losses could be inflicted upon them, but in order to avoid any further encounters the march was now to continue in the periphery of the Tuchola forest, in order to obstruct the visibility of the enemy pilots. The scattered brigade continued its march through the pine forests of Tuchola, making a slow and difficult but relatively safe retreat from the enemy.

About 15:00 the column stopped for what they hoped would be two hours, in order to feed the horses and for a much needed rest. No sooner had the 3rd company dismounted when a dispatcher arrived on a motorcycle with orders for father to report immediately to Brigade HQ. Before leaving, father cautioned the platoon commanders and master sergeant that their rest might be shortened and therefore to hasten the feeding of the horses. Father's precautions turned out to be accurate.

The command post of the Brigade was situated in Bramka, a nearby small village, where father reported to Col. Zakrzewski. The colonel was sitting in front of a village house with maps of the surrounding terrain spread out in front of him. He inquired about the condition of father's company and the events of the first day and his march from town. After listening attentively to father's report, the colonel briefed father about the present situation.

At this point the brigadier general in command, General Skotnicki, evaluated the manpower of his unit, which was still reassembling and whose ranks were gradually swelling. Unfortunately, its losses had been very heavy. The remains of the demolished brigade now consisted only of 2 1/2 regiments of cavalry and 1 1/2 batteries of artillery. The 18th Lancers regiment had perished completely. The 2nd. regiment that was to have come from Gdansk never reached its destination. Out of father's 16th Lancers regiment, the company of Captain Grudzien, as well as the company of bicyclists, had been wiped out.

As the situation was being evaluated by the general, a report reached him that the Germans were already ahead of the brigade in Chelmno, which made the planned crossing of the Vistula river at that point impossible. Again they were boxed in by the enemy! The fast moving German motorized division had overtaken the mounted Polish regiments and was now surrounding them on all sides. General Skotnicki decided that the only possible solution to this virtually hopeless situation was for the brigade, or what was left of it, to try to break through to the south with the hope of reaching Bydgoszcz. With the general's decision came father's orders:

"Captain, you are to take your company to the village of Dworzysko where you will dig in and try to hold off the Germans as long as possible, thus securing the left flank of the unit by keeping the road to Bydgoszcz open. You are not retreating with the rest of the brigade, but may do so only when your mission is accomplished. As you see it is about 6 miles away; march out at 16:00."

The situation appeared dismal at best, but armed with those orders father set out in the appointed time for Dworzysko.   His own losses so far were not too great; he still had all four platoons, although they were slightly diminished in strength. The company now numbered about 120 men, two cannons, numerous machine guns and two antitank guns.

For the first mile and a half they moved slowly and laboriously since they had to forge through formations of various marching military units going in many directions, all of whom showed fatigue and wounds from heavy battles. In addition, in many places the road was cratered from bombardment and was blocked by masses of civilian refugees trying to flee from the battle. The 3rd company had to get off the road and maneuver through the fields nearby. The situation then changed; the infantry disappeared, there was no sight of refugees, and the company swiftly moved forward in order to make up for lost time and to be able to reach the designated destination before dark.

That was done easily. They did not encounter any Germans on the route, but as father was nearing Dworzysko, his reconnaissance patrol reported a German motorcycle unit in the village which, seeing the advancing company, quickly moved out.

Father speedily organized the security of the place by putting a machine gun post next to the road. At the same time he had to arrange for the feeding of mounts and men, since the village was able to provide some bare essentials of much needed provisions for the men as well as the horses. Here father was able to leave some of the more seriously wounded men, who were unable to continue with the march, in the care of the village schoolmaster. The other wounded men who were still able to ride were given medical attention and rest.

Night fell; it was totally black. The men were in their assigned positions waiting apprehensively for the sunrise, when they knew the Germans would launch their offensive. The enemy were now signaling their positions by means of flares that illuminated the warm autumn sky. Father stood outside of his village quarters observing the German light show. The night was passing peacefully while the company was resting. A patrol that father had sent out in order to make contact with the brigade clearly was not coming back.

Then, around midnight, the silence of the night was abruptly interrupted by the sound of an approaching vehicle -it was coming from the direction of brigade headquarters. A moment of apprehension; then relief.... it was a "jeep" from the command post bringing Col. Jatrzembski, the commander of the 8th regiment. Having exchanged brief cordialities with father, the colonel revealed the purpose of the mission that had brought him to Dworzysko in the middle of the night.

"Captain, the brigade is going to start its retreat due southward for Bydgoszcz this morning at dawn and you are to hold off the enemy as well as provide support for the left wing as you were previously ordered. Then, when this has been accomplished, you and your company are to proceed and join the brigade."

"Sir, how will I know when the brigade has accomplished its withdrawal?"

"You are to use your own judgment and evaluate the progress of the battle."

What he meant (and father comprehended it) was that father was on his own; the battle was to be a do-or-die situation. With that the colonel departed, and in view of the upcoming encounter father put his unit on full alert.

SEPTEMBER 3, 1939
DWORZYSKO

With the rising of the sun came the first sounds of the battle that soon resounded all around them; the basso sounds of artillery gun fire were intertwined with the whining engines of the German planes that came like buzzards for the kill. The blue autumn sky was splattered with smoke from exploding shells and the rising dust that they stirred when making contact with the ground. The fighting was being waged all around Dworzysko.

Around 06:00, as father was discussing strategy with his officers, the sound of a motorcycle engine was heard coming from the southward. Alerted, everyone turned their attention toward the direction of the approaching sound. In a few moments, in the dawn light appeared a motorcycle, trailed by a cloud of dust, bearing the liaison from Brigade HQ.

As it was nearing them, the vehicle began to reduce speed and finally came to a stop when it reached the group of standing officers. The rider shut off the engine, dismounted, and, saluting father proceeded to deliver orders:

"Captain…by order of the General, you are to follow the brigade; immediately." Unfortunately the officer could not explain where the units were, but added:

"All units are moving toward Bydgoszcz along the Vistula. On one of these roads you will find your regiment."

After pulling in all his platoons from their positions and forming a column, father proceeded in the stipulated direction.

Soon the company once more was on the march, heading south across the terrain rather than on the open roads, which with the coming of daylight came under continuous fire. The march was painfully slow and full of obstacles, as the company tried to reach the brigade without being spotted by the enemy. The day was sunny and the terrain was familiar to father from previous years when he had been here on maneuvers. Nevertheless, it was hard on horses and difficult to pull the light cannons and supplies.

Father was proceeding in the right direction and anticipated that soon he would meet up with his unit. Then, when entering a village perched on a hill, from where he had good visibility, came machine-gun fire and artillery salvos. The fire was not aimed at father's company but at some invisible unit that was hidden from view in the rolling terrain about half a mile away. Then, along the perimeter of the trees, a German tank column was seen moving east at full speed. These tanks soon were engaged in a battle with some unidentified Polish army contingent. The tank column was preoccupied with the battle at hand and did not spot father's company, which was now under cover while he tried to determine its next move.

Then, as the last salvos of the tank guns were fired, a herd of riderless horses stampeded from the woods heading east towards the river. Looking through his binoculars, father recognized the insignia on the animals-they were the spare horses of the 8th SPK regiment, which was the spearhead of the Brigade marching formation. He surmised (and it was later confirmed by Capt. Pacewicz of the 8th SPK, who was stationed here) that indeed it was the 8th Regiment, which had formed the left wing of the army that had been badly hit by the panzer column and had sustained great casualties, both in men and horses. Having completed their devastation, the panzers continued on their course east to the Vistula, still oblivious of the presence of father's company nearby.

The situation was clear; they could not march south, since the road was cut off by the German panzers. After a short deliberation with Capt. Pacewicz, the they decided to change the direction of their original south destination of march north where they saw various Polish units retreating.

When the dust of the horse stampede subsided, father's company proceeded on its course in the unseasonable heat of the September sun. The weary soldiers, burdened by their heavy equipment and tired of the endless march, feared that it would never end...

The first town that the company reached was Przechowo, located about 2 1/2 miles from the banks of the Vistula— it was free of Germans, but with evidence that the occupants had left in haste. It also bore evidence of fierce fighting that must have gone on there not long before. The road that cut through the settlement was strewn with the debris of shattered vehicles, intermingled with the mutilated bodies of men and horses. From looking over the equipment and scanning the insignia of the fallen soldiers, father came to the conclusion that his brigade had come through and engaged in battle in this small hamlet. "Well, at least we are following the brigade...but where are they now?" he pondered.

After stopping for a couple of hours to rest and water the tired horses, but still not making any contact with his unit, father decided to continue on the same road, which upon reaching the Vistula turned south and wound beside the river bank.

The picturesque road was sheltered by a high cliff on the west side, while below it the wide and deep waters of the Vistula were overgrown with tall rushes; it was not feasible to cross the river here. The only thing to do at present was to follow the road south and take advantage of the natural cover of the embankment above. Unfortunately, the idyllic road soon ended its low lying course and abruptly began climb up the high embankment, taking the company out of the river bed.

As father reached the top of the embankment on the climbing road, a burst of gunfire rocked the ground beneath them and brought the march to a sudden halt.

"Take cover!" came the instant order, as the company retreated to the lower part of the road awaiting further instructions; the fire was coming from the direction of the nearby village of Topolno.

Having encountered this unexpected cut-off of his retreat, father sent out a patrol in order to verify the position of the enemy as well as its strength. The men soon returned with the unwelcome report that the village was indeed held by the Germans, with the help of heavy artillery and machine guns. The patrol also brought back with them the tattered remnants of a company from the 8th Cavalry regiment led by 2nd Lt. Zak, who reaffirmed the patrol's report that a German motorcycle unit together with a reinforcement of tanks was holding the strategic road crossing at Topolno, only a mile due south. Furthermore, the German cycle unit was proceeding parallel to father's unit, on the same southward course, thus blocking any chance of retreat in that direction.

It was now 1600. The sun began its descent westward, leaving only a few hours of daylight in which to complete any intended maneuver. Fortunately, at present the Germans were only exchanging fire and holding their positions without advancing forward, thus giving father some precious time.

Wanting to personally reassess his position in order to make a proper decision, father rode up to the crest of the rising embankment to determine the gravity of his predicament. To his astonishment, there was on the west bank a wall half a mile long created by a German tank column that was blocking his retreat to Bydgoszcz!

The thought ran through his mind that if he was together with the rest of the brigade they could have been able to get through, although probably with heavy losses. Now, however, he was out off from the main force with no possibility of retreat, since the enemy was also advancing on the road behind him. "You can't just raise your hands and surrender, and fighting against such odds would be suicide—the only way out is to chance it and cross the river!" He evaluated the situation and began to proceed with preparations for the hazardous river crossing. The crossing would not be a simple matter, since the horses were tired out from the almost continuous marching of the past several days and would probably drown under the added burden of a rider. The only feasible way to accomplish the task was to do it the old tartar way—the Tabun style! The tartars had successfully used the method of unmounted horses led by a leader for water crossing throughout the centuries.

The immediate need was to establish cover for the upcoming maneuver. The high bluff next to the river created a favorable terrain which gave cover against the machine-gun fire of the enemy. To hold off any advance by the Germans, two anti-tank guns together with several machine guns were strategically placed on the crest of the embankment and for the time being were holding the enemy at bay. But there was no illusion that this position would last indefinitely; time was of the essence since the situation was very volatile. Also, dusk was descending rapidly, thus making the oncoming crossing still more difficult.

Then, a stroke of luck. Among the rushes of the marshy riverbank, two old fishermen's boats were found and promptly put to good use. The larger boat was designated to carry equipment, saddles and the majority of the lancers to the opposite shore, while the smaller fishing boat was to take father and the crew that was providing fire support after the main company's crossing was safely completed. As a precautionary measure, father left one of his corporals to guard the second boat, which was left hidden in the nearby rushes.

As the crossing began to proceed in earnest, so did the German offensive, which opened with a heavy artillery barrage on the embankment, giving support to their slowly advancing infantry which was encroaching upon father's position; however, father held them at bay with his own machine-gun support.

Squatting low in the boat among the saddles and an assortment of other equipment, under a cloud of exploding shells, the dismounted lancers completed the painfully slow first phase and reached the opposite shore, where they were ready to receive the horses that were about to follow the same route. Lt. Salmonowicz was designated to accomplish the delivery of the animals.

The remaining lancers who were to lead the animals, and who of course had to be good swimmers, having stripped themselves to their shorts, were now proceeding into the cool and rapid river waters with their assigned groups of ten horses per man. The first lancer walked briskly between the two lead horses, holding them tightly by the reins until he submerged himself with only his head above the water and began to swim toward the opposite bank. The remaining horses with their respective leaders followed, but some persuasion of the reluctant animals was needed in form of a few slaps on the rump. Group after group followed and in turn were received on the opposite shore by the waiting lancers—the completion of the crossing took about forty-five minutes.

All during the time while the crossing was in progress, father was personally overseeing the cover support that he had positioned on the bluff, as well as keeping an eye on the progress of the crossing his company was making. He was hoping that his cover would be able to hold back the ever-advancing enemy long enough for him to execute the company's river crossing without loss. When at last he saw the last group of horses nearing the opposite shore, he blew his whistle, signaling the gun crew to abandon their positions and proceed to the hidden boat for the final crossing.

Without hesitation the crew, which consisted of about fifteen lancers, and father scurried down the hill to the reeds where the second boat was hidden. To their astonishment, when they reached the designated spot there was no boat, nor the corporal that had been left to guard it! The shock of being trapped was reinforced almost immediately as the German infantry, taking advantage of the abandonment of the covering position, had now reached the edge of the embankment and was showering father's group with fire from its high vantage point overhead.

The rapid approach of dusk, as well as the high-growing thick foliage of the riverbank, temporarily provided much-needed cover for father and his lancers. Father, huddled together with the lancers, began to move through the reeds hoping to find another abandoned boat and thus be able to cross the river and join the rest of his company. Since it was impossible for father to retaliate, he only hoped that the failing of darkness would put a temporary halt to the German assault long enough for him to regroup and cross the river at some further point, thinking that the Germans were only along the road above.

But to no avail. The enemy was persistent in their efforts to flush out father's group by constantly spraying the river rushes with blind bursts of gunfire. Between the bursts of spattering machine-guns, the Germans were shouting commands to their troops.

In this confusion and under cover of darkness, father was left with only a handful of his lancers at his side and tried to move southward through the thick foliage of the river bank. Moving slowly, their boots singing in the soft mud of the river bed, groping for firmer ground yet cautious so as not to give away their position, the men kept on advancing well into the night without any results. The group had now spread out, but still kept its course. Father could no longer see where his men were, but could only distinguish their position by the slight sound of a reed cracking under a nearby boot or a splash of the water.

Hungry, tired and constantly under enemy fire, father's small group managed to be on the move south for the next two days, catching rest whenever they could. The situation was bleak.

SEPTEMBER 6, 1939
During the third night, as they resumed their maneuver and once more were on the move, still under artillery fire, father suddenly was thrown to the ground from the shock of a shell exploding nearby, losing consciousness.

Chapter 4

Labiszyn, Ludwikowko

SEPTEMBER 2,1939
ON THE ROAD FROM LABISZYN

On the next day we were to start bright and early in the hope that by doing so we would avoid the road congestion that was building up. After a hasty breakfast and even more hasty goodbyes our group, with the addition of uncle Maks, aunt Barbara and their children, including the infant Danusia, set out in the direction of the town of Inowroclaw. In Inowroclaw lived some cousins of grandparents, the Kemnitz, who hopefully would put us up for a night or two.

Mr. Kemnitz, the administrator of the Baharcia estate near Tarnowko, was most hospitable to our rather large group. We were put up in the guest house, which made our stay a little more comfortable for everyone although the news that were reaching us were not encouraging—the Germans were pushing forward.

Here in Baharcia, we had a surprise visit from uncle Jan Slawinski, aunt Helen's husband, who was able to leave his post in nearby Bydgoszcz in order to say goodbye to his family. But the visit was very brief; just a couple of hours, since he had to return immediately.

After uncle Jan's departure another decision was made—aunt Barbara and uncle Maks decided to return to their home in Labiszyn with their children, since they could not endure traveling with an infant. So we said our goodbyes to them. For uncle Maks it was a final one; he was to be arrested by the Germans, and then released in such a physically abused state that he was only able to die in his home.

SEPTEMBER 5,1939
ON THE ROAD

The morning started out as had our previous days on the road, as we continued toward the east, in the direction of Warsaw. Our earlier apprehensions seemed to disperse and everyone began to think that we would be able to reach Garwolin, near Warsaw, in safety, since so far we had not seen or heard any signs of battle except for the radio broadcasts that were reporting casualties. The choice of going to Garwolin was made because uncle Wacek had been transferred there with his unit and had rented a house where we were to sit out the "short" battle.

We passed fields on which peasants were putting their last touches before the onset of winter. The scattered fires from the burning of the remnant potato foliage emitted blue-gray smoke that slithered over the fields like a giant snake. For the most part the fires were unattended, but occasionally a keeper was seen, raking the surrounding ground and replenishing the dying embers. Lazy cows by the roadside were chewing the grass that was under their feet and ignoring the commotion of the people passing on the road.

As the hours passed, travel became more physically demanding. The roads became a sea of people, all going in the same direction—away from the oncoming German invaders. Around noon, with the sun blazing in the clear early autumn sky, from the distance came the sound of aircraft engines. In minutes airplanes were above; then they passed over us. I peered through the car's open window in amazement, thinking that it was the last I would see of the planes—-there were only two of them. Then, as I continued to watch them, the planes a made swift circle as they lowered themselves towards us. The panic-stricken multitude of people begun to dart off the road, taking cover in roadside ditches and under the trees. Uncle Josef was shouting for us to get out of the cars and to take cover. The shouting was drowned out by the sound of machine gun fire.

The German planes descended nearly to tree top level—all I could see was the black insignia painted on the side of the plane and then there was a burst of gun fire, screams, the fading roar of the engine motors and then the moans of the wounded. Mother lay on top of me trying to cover me with her body. I could not comprehend what had happened. Were we all going to die?

After several minutes which seemed like eternity, people begun to stir. The dust begun to settle. Uncle Josef was on the other side of the road and began checking to see whether everyone in our group was alive and all right. By some miracle we all came through this attack unharmed, but with dirty faces from hugging the ground in desperation. As I stood up, I could see that on the road lay unmoving bodies of the people that did not reach safety in time to escape the spray of bullets. They lay in awkward positions with their blood-covered limbs spread out. Their families, too stunned to apprehend what had happened, were trying to revive them, with no hope. Now the war had come to us and we had to move faster. Kutno was only a few hours away, so we quickly gathered together and proceeded onward, hoping that the planes would not come back.

It was autumn, harvest time. But the fields that usually would be full of working peasants and sweet smelling haystacks were now for the most part empty, except for scattered debris that someone could no longer carry and had to leave along the roadside. Here and there lay cadavers by the road-side; some remnant of a corpse would hang like a gruesome ornament from a nearby tree, quiet testimony to the violence that had passed through here earlier. Nobody paid much attention to such sights anymore, having quickly become accustomed to them. Everyone was seeking their own survival and unconsciously tried to ignore what they saw but could not succeed in doing so. To me, since at age 5 I knew how to count, these new visions became a game of counting that helped to pass the time by.

As we were drawing near Kutno the destruction seemed to lessen, and that gave us a false sense of security, thinking that we had left the worst behind. But as we passed through the outskirts of the city and were getting closer to the center of town, the wail of air raid sirens broke into the rou-tine humdrum of city noise. People began darting from the buildings and shops and air raid marshals with armbands and helmets seamed to materi-alize from nowhere, directing everyone to the closest shelters. By the time we oriented ourselves and headed for the nearest shelter, which was in the cellar of a nearby house, the shelter was filled to capacity and so we were back on the street again. The warning sirens were still giving out their piercing wail. Across the street we spotted a sign indicating another shelter so we scurried there, but once again there was no room for a large group such as we were. The warning time was running out, so the decision was made that the best thing was to get away from the town as quickly as possible. We headed out of the city, continuing in the same direction as before, but this time without any obstacles since the streets were almost empty except for some stragglers.

Within a few minutes, when we were almost out of town, the roar of aircraft engines was heard. Our caravan stopped, and everyone started to scramble out of the cars and the truck. Hildebrandt was standing at the back of the truck, trying to help the children who were jumping out of it. Then came Miss Gabrysia's turn and she jumped into Hildebrand's outstretched yet unsuspecting arms, toppling him over under her weight. The picture of the fallen man with Gabrysia landing on top of him brought a burst of spontaneous laughter from the children. As uncle Alfons and others came to rescue the fallen couple, the kids were chastised for laughing at their misfortune.

Within minutes composure was regained, and our focus was upon the imminent danger from enemy aircraft and the need for shelter. As it turned out, a cemetery near the roadside became our shelter for the moment.

As I lay down between grave-mounds, with my face in the dust, mother's protective hands covered me. I could hear her whispering prayers, offering ourselves into Divine protection as the falling bombs exploded on the nearby town. The eerie whistle of the falling bombs was rapidly coming closer and the planes seemed to be upon us. I thought "the next one is going to fall on us..." but my cousins told me that "you don't hear the bomb that hits you!" So, between praying for God's protection and listening for the shriek of the failing bombs, I did not immediately notice that suddenly there was no sound. There were a few seconds of silence, and then the "all clear" signal of the sirens pierced the air.

From among the grave mounds and monuments, members of the family started to reappear. We all were shaken and dusty, but unhurt. As my gaze turned towards the city, all one could see was pillars of fire and smoke surrounded by destruction and people trying to climb out of the rubble…cries and screams for help were coming from all directions. On the road just beyond our abandoned cars lay an overturned colorful gypsy wagon; the horses were mutilated by the machine guns of the aircraft but there was no sign of the occupants.

As we began to move and shake the dust from ourselves we realized that the resting place for the dead had sheltered us and given us a chance for life. As we slowly began to emerge from our places of shelter and head towards the cars, it was noticed that the Muslewski family was not with us. Since they had been in the last vehicle, it was presumed that they must still be in town, and this forced us to return there in order to find them. Now the roads were crowded, making it difficult to maneuver, and since it would take too long to negotiate them by car, grandfather, aunt Maria, aunt Helen and the girls started to walk in the direction of the town square where all roads seemed to come together.

Several hours passed before our small family reconnaissance group was sighted heading toward us. They had found the Muslewskis all intact, having been able to find shelter in town during the air raid. Reunited, and relieved that all were safe, our group was on the move again.

It would have made no sense to return to town for the night, since the bombing had left many inhabitants homeless and accommodations would be impossible to find. In addition, the air attack left the roads difficult and sometimes impassable. Several detours and side roads had to be negotiated before we were able to reach the next town, Lowicz.

It was already dark when we arrived there. Precautions had been taken by the town in order to camouflage it against enemy bombing raids; the streets were not illuminated and were almost deserted. The windows of the houses were shaded so as not to have any light escape through them, giving the town an eerie quiet atmosphere.

Uncles Josef and Alfons were assigned to find us some lodging for the night. As they went knocking at several doors, inquiring for accommodations, I was dozing off in mother's lap; it had been a long and tiring day for the sturdiest of adults, but for a five year old like myself it was above endurance. I could no longer keep my eyes open...

Within an hour we were all finally settled in various houses where people had rooms to let and give us much-needed rest.

SEPTEMBER 6,1939
ON THE ROAD

It was early morning when we left Lowicz after a night's rest, heading for Garwolin via Warsaw. Our hopes were high, thinking that we were almost at the end of our journey. The radio communiqué the night before had not been very encouraging—the Germans were advancing and Warsaw had been heavily bombarded.

By now our family group was well drilled in an efficient routine; we would start in the early morning in order to get as much mileage as possible during the day. The youngsters asked to change some of their sitting arrangements; the idea was well accepted by all since this request broke down the tedium of continual travel. With some negotiating, the new arrangements were completed within a few minutes and we were on the road once more.

It was a clear autumn morning with no visible clouds in the sky, foretelling another hot day; under normal circumstances, a welcome prospect. But now it meant perfect visibility for attacking planes and easy roads for the advancing enemy troops.

Because of the early morning hour highway traffic was still very sparse, which made progress swifter, but our movement left a trail of dust on the well trodden road. As we proceeded we soon encountered military traffic also heading in the direction of Warsaw, and we had to give way.

It was around 8:00 AM when we reached the outskirts of Warsaw. The city was silent and there was hardly any movement in the streets—at first it appeared to be deserted. As we meandered through the streets, the image of its devastation begun to emerge. The bombed out buildings cast their skeleton-like shadows on the empty streets. Here and there, from among the rubble, thin wisps of smoke appeared, giving evidence that these were recent ruins. Some buildings that had not been totally destroyed had makeshift boarded-up windows, making them still habitable. The trees that once bordered the streets and would by now have started to assume their autumn color were just burned stumps.

As we penetrated deeper into the city we were confronted by a military patrol which stopped our family column. The sergeant in charge requested identification and, after scrutinizing our papers and eyeing the cars, announced in an authoritative voice that the vehicles were to be surrendered for military use to help transport the wounded.

"That is all very well," sputtered grandfather, "but what are we to use for our transportation in order to reach Garwolin?"

"That is not my problem!" responded the sergeant, shrugging his shoulders.

At that, aunt Maria, mother and uncle Josef surrounded the sergeant, producing documents in order to convince him that we were military families trying to reach our destination of Garwolin and that, if necessary, the cars would be surrendered there. The sergeant, either tired or resigned, after twenty minutes of "negotiating" realized that it was futile for him to argue and agreed to let us through. Hurriedly, everyone climbed back into the cars, trying to leave before the fellow changed his mind.

Our group proceeded north on Marszalkowska Avenue and then turned east into Jerozolimskie Aleje, trying to reach the bridge which would take us across the Vistula river. As we came closer to the center of the city, the destruction was greater and the once elegant palaces and buildings bore the brunt of the bombardment. People, including the military, were now everywhere, making our progress slower, but with patience we reached the Poniatowski Bridge. Again there was a checkpoint. Fortunately there was no problem this time, just a warning to stay off the roads since this area was preparing for a battle, and we crossed the bridge to the east side of the Vistula.

Finally around noon we reached Garwolin, which by now had become the center of the military command for the defense of Warsaw. It seemed that there were more army personnel than civilians. Uncle Wacek was relieved to see us and took us to the house that he had found for us. This was marvelous; we all sighed a sigh of relief, thinking that we were safe for the moment.

The house that uncle Wacek had rented was a pleasant place, but not large enough for the whole entourage that had descended upon it. Though we were cramped, we were happy to be in our "own " place. The house was made even more inviting by the fact that some of the furniture from our apartment in Grudziadz had been shipped here, in anticipation of the growing scope of the battle.

Miss Flora, the Muslewski's governess, took charge of the domestic arrangements, allocating parts of our limited quarters to various members of our family group. Aunt Maria was beaming from happiness because she was able to see her husband. I was overjoyed that I was able to romp in the backyard with my cousins and we did not have to pack into the car again! It took us only a few hours to make ourselves at home and for a while not to worry where we would find lodging for the night.

In the evening uncle Wacek joined us for supper but he came with bad news. Since Garwolin had become the point for centralization of the military forces, all civilians had to leave. The military was a anticipating a heavy offensive by the Germans. In spite of the grim situation, we were able to stretch our stay for two more days, giving us some much-needed rest.

SEPTEMBER 8,1939
ON THE ROAD

With daylight came the first sounds of not-very-distant battles, and we began to pack into our vehicles for the next leg of our journey. As an addition to our group came Mrs. Przeracka, wife of an officer friend of father, who had her own car, a red convertible. Uncle Wacek was able to lead the group to the village of Stoczek, about 15 miles east of Garwolin. By the time we were able to reach Stoczek, Garwolin was being heavily bombarded. In Stoczek there was no house or inn in which we could stay and it was too late in the day to make further progress, but we were able to find a hay-barn where we could stay for the night.

As night fell and darkness enveloped the village, we sat outside the barn and watched the illuminated western horizon where Garwolin was ablaze from the day's bombardment. Uncle Wacek had to return to his regiment, so he said his goodbyes and departed for his headquarters. The parting was especially hard on aunt Maria, who was very disappointed that we were not able to stay there. It was the young couple's last farewell, since uncle Wacek was eventually captured by the Soviets and was executed by them, along with thousands of other Polish officers, at Katyn forest in April 1940.

The night was restless as we tried to make ourselves comfortable on the hay. The sound of nearby explosions made us apprehensive. Nevertheless, we all managed to get some rest in preparation for the next day's trek.

SEPTEMBER 9,1939
ON THE ROAD

As we kept heading east, the days merged into one another and ours became a nomadic way of life as we grew accustomed to stopping in different places for the night. Although we kept moving, the war was always just on our heels.

Because of the constant bombing, shelters became the home of the moment. When the roar of a plane was heard, everyone instinctively went for cover, but unfortunately not always in the safest place.

I learned to pray very rapidly while lying in a roadside ditch with my face in the ground. Between the repetitions of the same prayer, I would listen to the whistle of the failing bombs; what a relief it was when the bomb finally exploded, because I knew that once more I was safe—till the next time.

The days were warm and sunny, a perfect early autumn and one could easily forget that there was a war going on when one stood in the glow of the sun looking at the golden wheat fields interlaced with colorful wild flowers. It was a on day like this that the euphoria of fall was interrupted by the hum of a distant plane. Reluctantly we took cover in small patch of woods that was separated from the road by a large field of harvested wheat. In the middle of the wheat field a small fire was set up by a peasant, probably Ukrainian, clad in loose white pants, topped with a white tunic tied at the waist with a rope-like belt. On his head was a straw hat and his weather-beaten feet were bare. He continued to tend the fire as he observed us taking shelter in the trees, ignoring the signs of oncoming danger.

As we took further precautions in our newly found shelter by lying down and covering ourselves with earth-colored clothing, two German planes came. They circled the woods above us as we held our breath. Then the roar of the engines began to diminish, signaling the planes' departure. Gingerly I lifted my head from the ground to see whether the coast was clear and noticed the peasant still standing in the middle of the field. He was looking into the sky with his hat in his hand, waving it at the planes and pointing to our wooded shelter! I did not comprehend what was happening; there was consternation among our group as what should be done. Before any action was taken, however, there was a burst of machine-gun fire that sprayed the woods. The assault came from one of the planes that had decided to return and answer the peasant's signal. I felt mother's hand pushing me back to the ground and sheltering me with it. In a few minutes the attack was over. The pilot probably took this precautionary flight because of the "signal" and. not finding any target, continued to his primary destination. Of course, by the time we recovered there was no sign of the peasant, just a dwindling fire.

SEPTEMBER 15,1939
LUDWIKOWKO

By noon our family caravan, still in full force and miraculously unhurt, came to the small village of Ludwikowko which lies about 100 miles north-east of Lwow. This eastern part of Poland was mostly populated by people of Ukrainian and Byelorussian origins who were hostile to native Poles. it was tranquil here, with no visible signs of war; people were going about performing their everyday tasks. But we soon found out that the village of Ludwikowko was totally Ukrainian, with the exception of one farmer who was a Pole and was willing to lease his house to us while he and his family took up lodging in their hay-barn.

Our lodgings were in a small white-washed house that consisted of several rooms. Behind it was a yard filled with the last of the summer flowers, beyond which was an orchard with its dwarf-like trees that extended into a field with haystacks of neatly stacked hay. The front of the house was adjacent to a road, across which was a small private airport that still had two single engine planes on the ground. The planes had been left behind because of lack of fuel.

By evening everyone was settled down and we gathered around the kitchen table for supper, thankful that we had found a corner of peace and tranquility and that all of us had survived the last chaotic days. The news gathered from the local people was exchanged among us, and as we began to disperse for the night into our assigned places everyone was optimistic that the situation was going to be settled soon. Nevertheless, uncles Josef and Alfons were more practical and did not accept all the news of "all is well"; they unloaded only the most necessary luggage. They also took precautionary measures by hiding the guns, pistols and most of the silverware around the property—most of the items were in the haystacks at the back of the house.

Almost instantly I assimilated myself into the new surroundings; it was a pleasant and enjoyable interlude. There were no thoughts of bombings, killing, shelters and air raid sirens. This was like a holiday, with my older cousins playing hide-and-seek with me among the haystacks. There were special games which involved going across the road to the abandoned airplanes and being able to sit in the plane's cockpit, pretending that we were on bombing missions: Polish, of course.

SEPTEMBER 17,1939
LUDWIKOWKO

The radio announced that Soviet armies had entered Poland. Then came leaflets from the Reds proclaiming that they had "liberated the peoples of Western Ukraine and Byelorussia from Poland". This news was received by us with gloom and apprehension. Grandfather advised us that we were to keep a low profile and by so doing we should be safe in this secluded corner of the country. Nevertheless, to his consternation, grandfather found out that cousin Janusz had stowed away among the oriental rugs several hunting rifles and sabers. This discovery created panic among the family group, since possession of arms would bring instant and severe punishment from the Russians. But no problem arose thanks to our host farmer, who kept his peasant "cool" and quickly and efficiently buried the equipment in his nearby field.

SEPTEMBER 27, 1939
LUDWIKOWKO

It was mid-morning when a group of Soviet soldiers led by two officers arrived in the village and headed directly for the house in which we were lodging, accompanied by the newly appointed mayor of the village and his followers. The Ukrainian villagers were eager to be informants of our existence to the Soviet occupying authorities, who in turn were eager to pursue the lead. Our family represented a social group the Soviets intended to stamp out; grandfather and my uncles were large landowners and my father was a career officer, which in their ideology constituted two strikes against us! Therefore, mother instructed me what to say should I be asked about father. I was to tell the interrogators that father was a postal clerk and I didn't know where he was now. Fortunately, I was not asked, since the soldiers were much more interested in the booty they found than in thorough interrogation. Though their main objective was to look for guns, they did not find ours since the arms were well buried in the ground. Everyone of us tried to look undisturbed, which did take some acting on our part. I tried to play with my doll and pretended that the soldiers were not there, having been previously well tutored by my older cousins as to what would happen to people who got caught possessing arms.

After several hours of searching the Soviets were ready to leave. No amount of bargaining or pleading by grandfather and the uncles could persuade them to leave us some of our major possessions. The victorious conquerors departed with the loaded truck, some of the oriental carpets and anything else that appealed to them. The two cars, one of which was Mrs. Przeracka's, were left behind but they promised to pick them up the next day.

As we began to put away and repack all that remained to us, which of course had been overturned by the searchers, the realization struck that we were stuck in this out-of-the-way village without any means of transportation. Since, as grandfather said, we couldn't stay in Ludwikowko because the villagers would probably create more trouble for us, we should try to get to Lwow. Grandfather had some friends in Lwow and, it being a large city, we would not be so conspicuous.

The farmer whose house we occupied was approached, and he was willing to rent to us his wagons so that we could take the remnants of our possessions to the nearby town of Dubno, from where we could get a train to Lwow.

On the day before our planned departure from Ludwikowko, cousin Danka Slawinska came down with a very high fever. Therefore, so as to not to postpone our departure, it was decided that aunt Helen, with her children and Mrs. Przeracka (wife of Col. Przeracki, who also was later murdered in Katyn, and with whom we had been traveling from Garwolin) would stay behind with her and join the rest of us as soon as Danka got better. The parting was very emotional and sad.

Chapter 5

Bank of Vistula; Germany-West Fallenhof, Grossborn, Itzehoe

SEPTEMBER 6, 1939
ON THE BANK OF THE VISTULA RIVER

When father opened his eyes dawn was breaking; it was about 0500. As he began to come to, father heard voices around him; they were indistinguishable.

"Where am I...what happened?..." he thought.

The contours of faces started to materialize before him; a hand shook his shoulder.

"Hauptmann?" the voice inquired. At once, as if startled from a deep sleep, father jerked himself into full alertness.

The morning sun was rising into the autumn sky. Father was lying on the edge of the river bank with his feet submerged in the water, and above him stood three German soldiers.

Two of them were pointing their rifles at him, while the third one was shaking father's shoulder vigorously.

The soldiers, seeing father revive, helped him up and quickly disarmed him, taking from him the side arm which he never had a chance to use. The German repeated his question:

"Hauptmann?" to which father replied "No, Rittmeister." (Rittmeister is a captain of cavalry, as opposed to Hauptmann, which is a captain of infantry.)

"Ja, ja " replied the ruddy-faced soldier, shrugging his shoulders with indifference and motioning to father to follow his comrade, who began to walk in the direction of the higher ground. Looking around, father realized that these men were part of a division that supplied cover for the German engineering corps that was in the process of building a pontoon bridge across the Vistula in order to enable the German armies to cross the river.

His captors led father to their commanding officer, a captain, who was in charge of directing the construction of the bridge. One of the soldiers gave his report to the captain, who after hearing it looked father over, paying specific attention to his insignia and then, without a word, extended a cigarette pack to father.

"No, thank you." replied father in Polish. One of the soldiers acted as translator between the two officers.

"Captain," said the German officer as he lighted his own cigarette, "I will send you to our command headquarters, since I have no time nor facilities to take care of prisoners of war." With that he gave father a salute and turned to his sergeant, giving him instructions as to where to take father.

So, on this early morning of September 6th, 1939, father began his captivity, which was to endure for many years.

As father stood waiting, guarded by his captors, a small military car pulled in and a soldier motioned to him to get in. Here, the guarding German soldier relinquished his duty to two other sergeants that had come with the car.

The car reached the main road. Father, looking over the terrain, got his bearings and came to the quick conclusion that he was on the road leading to Swiecie, the same road that only a few days ago, on the 3rd, he was trying to use in the opposite direction in order to reach his destination of Bydgoszcz to the south. After an unobstructed ride, since it was evident that the Germans held this territory, the car reached Swiecie and headed for a building above whose doorway flew a German flag. A sentry was posted at the entrance.

The car stopped. One of the sergeants proceeded to lead the way into the building and reported to another NCO who took them into an adjoining room. Here, father was brought in front of a German colonel, the commander of the unit which occupied that area.

"Sir!" saluted the sergeant. "I brought Rittmeister Mikosz, captured near our station."

"Thank you sergeant, that'll be all" replied the colonel, who then, turning, addressed father.

"Captain, from which direction did you march?" he inquired. Father did not answer. With that the colonel motioned to father to sit down, pointing to a nearby chair. As father sat down, the door opened and there entered another German officer, a younger one, who saluted his superior and after exchanging a few words with him turned to father and started searching father's pockets. taking out his ID and removing his side pouch, which held his maps.

As the officer was putting the papers and maps on the desk, the colonel was examining the contents of father's pockets and of the map-pouch.

"Oh, I see," said the colonel, with a thin smile crossing his face and looking at father, "Pomeranian Cavalry Brigade."

Having completed the preliminary search and interrogation, the colonel turned to father once more:

"Are you hungry, Captain?" Father understood German but did not answer his captor. But the colonel, not waiting for an answer, gave the sergeant instructions to bring some coffee and then to find a place where father could clean himself up.

Coffee arrived almost instantly, and father drank it with great gusto, not having had any warm substance to eat or drink for the last several days. As the warm drink was finished, the sergeant returned and motioned father to follow him. His rifle slung over his shoulder, the sergeant led father to the nearby house of a Polish villager and gave orders to the startled occupants to take care of father while he positioned himself by the door.

"How can I help you?" asked the robust, stocky woman who seemed to be relieved that this was all that she was wanted for. With her was a young boy, crouching in dimly a lit corner of the room and trying not to be noticed.

"Well…I want to clean myself up and shave." replied father, putting his hand in his pocket and taking out some money which the Germans had not confiscated.

"Here, young fellow, could you get me a razor and maybe some soap?" father motioned to the lad. The boy extended his hand gingerly, looking at the guard, who just nodded in consent.

In the meantime, by the large stove that occupied a large portion of the sparsely furnished room, the woman had begun to fill a basin with steaming hot water. Taking advantage of the opportunity, father shaved and cleaned himself of the dirt and grime of the past several days. Feeling refreshed, he sat down at the table where the woman managed to provide some soup for him. There was no exchange of conversation, since everyone was tense about having the ever-present armed German sergeant sitting by the door.

Some time elapsed before an officer appeared in the doorway and informed father that he was going to be taken to a prisoner of war relocating center that was not far away. Without response, father followed the officer into his car and continued on the next leg of the journey.

The road signs were pointing to Koronowo, a small town nine miles from Swiecie. The short and uneventful ride brought father to the relocating center that indeed was on the outskirts of Koronowo.

Again father was searched, this time more thoroughly—besides his ID and maps that had been taken before, his money was now confiscated. A German sergeant was executing the search while a captain was looking on; the sergeant in his zeal was ordering father to take his wedding band and a diamond ring off.

"No!" interrupted the captain and turning, addressed father:

"You had better put these rings away in a safer place, since there are all kinds of people in the army."

"Thank you." responded father, relieved that he did not have to lose his personal possessions.

As it happened, father at this time was the only officer prisoner in this compound, so in accordance with the Geneva conventions, the Germans had to intern him separately from the enlisted POWs. Not having any suitable quarters available, a sergeant was ordered to take father to a nearby small white-washed house that was nestled by the roadside and presently unoccupied.

The two men, the captive and his captor, unhurriedly crossed the dusty road heading toward the designated house. The door gave way under a shove from the sergeant and they entered the main room, through whose dust-covered small windows the nearby road could be seen. The guarding sergeant, a nondescript individual in an ill-fitting uniform, seated himself on one of the several chairs that were in the room, leaned his rifle against the wall and made himself comfortable by taking off his helmet and unbuttoning a couple of the top buttons of his uniform jacket. Judging from the sergeant's preparations, father presumed that he would be kept here for some time, so he sat down and stretched his legs. After some time of prolonged silence the sergeant started up a conversation:

"You know I am only a reservist." the sergeant began as if to apologize. "I am from Berlin, and I have a small store there."

Father gave the man a look with a faint smile, and replied, in German, "Oh, how nice..."

Not discouraged by father's lack of enthusiasm for his conversation, he continued:

"This war won't last long you know. I just can't wait to get back home.... You know, Captain, when this is over, why don't you come and visit me when you are in Berlin?" Then without waiting for father's reply, he took out a piece of paper and a pencil and wrote something.

"Here..." he extended the paper to father, "here is my name and the address of my store. I'll be looking for you."

"Thanks." replied father, taking the paper and putting it in the top pocket of his jacket.

"By the way," the sergeant continued, "did you know that the Fuhrer is coming through here?"

"What? What do you mean...Hitler?"

"Yes, Hitler. He will be just passing, on the way to inspect the troops." stated the sergeant, pleased that at last he had caught father's interest.

With that announcement, the sergeant moved towards the window and started to wipe the dust from the glass with a circular motion of his palm, while father moved towards him, wanting to see what was happening. With their faces to the window, they watched as the SS arrived and began to station armed soldiers in a solid line along both sides of the road with their back to the highway and rifles held in front of them; eyes protectively scanning the scene in front of them. In addition to the armed guards, there were several machine guns placed on both sides of the route, also pointing away from the road.

No sooner had the guards positioned themselves when from the west rolled two tanks, followed by a column of several armored vehicles carrying more troops. They all come to a stop beyond the house where father and his captor were peering gingerly through the window pane. On the heels of the armored column came a large limousine that stopped almost in front of the house, where there had gathered a hastily organized reception committee from the German Military Center, consisting of army and SS officers. All stiffened to attention. Out from the front door of the car jumped an officer, heading to the back door and opening it. There emerged a smallish man with a mustache who was extending his arm in the Nazi salute.

"It's the Fuhrer!" the sergeant exclaimed, nudging father in the ribs with his elbow.

"Yes…I see." Father replied, recognizing the man that he had often seen in newsreels throughout the last several years.

The two adversaries, father and the German sergeant, kept their faces glued to the small window, observing Hitler talking with the local commanding officers. After some time had elapsed, Hitler turned on his heels and jauntily walked up and down the road exchanging words with the guarding soldiers while followed by his entourage. Then, with the same abruptness with which he had come, Hitler raised his hand in the party salute, returned to the limousine and departed in an easterly direction, the way his troops were advancing. The entire visit was short, lasting approximately twenty minutes. With Hitler's departure, the SS gathered up the guarding retinue of soldiers, loaded them into trucks and left to follow the visiting entourage.

The commotion of Hitler's surprise visit having subsided, the German post resumed its normal activities and another corporal was sent to where father was detained with an order to take him to a group of other Polish prisoners that was forming in front of the house.

The Germans having gathered their prisoners, father among them, they began to march the group westward to another prisoner relocation center. The small, tired and dejected group of Poles proceeded through the nearby settlements that were inhabited by a large German population that made them their home. The inhabitants come out to watch the march and as the column of prisoners moved along the road, the civilian Germans armed with horse whips, started to beat the helpless men, shouting "Polische schwine!" (Polish pigs)

The cruel and sadistic behavior of the Germans who lived in Poland and were citizens of that country went unchecked by the guards, who watched in amusement and just kept the column moving. By the time they reached their point of destination, it was late afternoon.

Once again father was searched, and this time his helmet was confiscated. Then he was handed over to the SS men who were in charge of this operation. The guard led father out of the building into a nearby open field that was strewn with prostrate Polish soldiers.

Here, in what once had served as a meadow for pasture, were men lying with their faces to the ground, not daring to move since any movement was answered with a burst of machine-gun fire that ripped the air above their heads; the guns were positioned at such a height that their fire would hit the raised head of a prone prisoner. The perimeter of the field was encircled with several of these machine-guns, manned by guards who intermittingly were shouting obscenities at their helpless captives, and several armored vehicles.

Upon reaching the encircled prostrate group, the SS guard gave father an order to lie down and at the same time reinforced his command by pulling father's cap off and shoving the butt of his rifle into father's back. Stunned, father fell.

The afternoon autumn sun warmed father's back as he lay face down on the cool grass; he was exhausted and, lying there, helpless thoughts began to run through his mind:

"So much happened in just a few days…the world has turned upside down…this can't last too long…no, no, this is only a bad dream."

But then his thoughts would be dispersed by the constant spattering of the machine-guns and reality would set in.

As the evening fell the bursts of gunfire as well as verbal abuse of the captives became more frequent. The situation had become dismal since by now the guards were noticeably drunk and, having got their hands on alcohol, were ready to amuse themselves with the prisoners.

Here an SS man would at random select a victim from the sprawled group and drag him to his comrades, where the Germans would take turns beating the prisoner with their rifle butts.

After pounding the helpless captive senseless, the guards would throw the bloodied and mangled prisoner back into the field and then look for the next victim.

The evening extended into the night while the Polish prisoners, both officers and enlisted men, were forced to lie on the damp ground without any food, water or medical attention and were continuously abused by their German captors. The cries and moans of the wounded and beaten, pleading for help, were answered only with an occasional burst of machine-gun fire.

Father lay there, expecting the worst, listening to the cries for help and the groans of the suffering, while the drunken guards continued their beatings:

"Am I next?" he thought.

SEPTEMBER 7, 1939

Dawn began to filter through the darkness but no relief came for the prisoners. Some of the wounded were relieved of their agonies by death that came to them during the night, but were left lying among the rest of the prostrate prisoners.

With morning arrived a new group of Polish prisoners and though there was no visible room, the Germans shoved the newcomers into the already over-crowded space, making the unbearable conditions even worse. People were almost on top of each other, enduring the situation without protest since any move would provoke the wrath of their captors upon them. This bizarre situation continued throughout the day; it was at dusk when two military trucks with additional German personnel arrived to change the command and sort out the prisoners.

Since it was impossible for the Germans to identify the officer prisoners in this mass of prostrate people, the order was bellowed out for officers to get up and line up in a designated area. Hesitantly heads, then bodies began to move and rise from the ground, apprehensively waiting for a burst of machine-gun fire...but no sound came, except for the constant barking of commands by the captors.

"Schnell! Schnell!" the guards kept shouting.

Father, stiff from lying on the ground for such a prolonged time, moved with difficulty from the spot where he had been immobilized for almost thirty hours to a designated area outside the perimeter, within which hundreds of prisoners still remained on the ground. This time the segregated officers were left standing while their ranks grew. Then, seeing that no more officers were left lying down, the Germans ordered father's group, which numbered around eighty officers, to load into two nearby waiting trucks.

Again, push, push, shove; one could hardly breathe in the close confines but at the same time felt relief at leaving the meadow. Finally, when all the prisoners were packed into the trucks, standing up, the tailgate went up and before the tarpaulin was lowered in order to cover the back opening, a warning was sounded by the German captain:

"Gentlemen, let me give you a word of advice. Do not try to open the covering or tamper with it in any way. The guards have instructions to shoot anyone who attempts to disobey!"

This warning given, the tarpaulin came down, sealing the prisoners in the dark confines of the truck. The engine started and slowly the vehicle with its sealed cargo began to move to an unknown destination. The truck would stop every few hours and voices outside would be heard, but no one in the vehicle had no idea where they could be. The ride continued through the night with the weary prisoners propping up against each other, trying to doze off.

Finally, after what seemed like an endless trip, the truck stopped once again, but this time the tarpaulin was lifted, letting fresh air and sunlight into the depths of the vehicle. The sudden light blinded the captives momentarily; a gust of fresh air entered, bringing relief, and everyone started to inhale the open air as if to make sure that there was enough of it to go around. The tailgate was lowered by armed guards who began to shout:

"OUT! OUT!"

One by one, father among them, the officers, obeying the order to come out, started to jump off the truck, which was now encircled by armed soldiers who then marched the prisoners to a nearby compound. The compound was a railroad yard surrounded by barbed wire that already held hundreds of Polish prisoners from different regiments and ranks, both officers and enlisted men.

Surveying the surrounding area from behind the barbed wire, father became aware that he no longer was in Poland; the night ride in the truck had taken them onto German soil.

Under the open sky of this rail yard prison, father stayed till evening when once more soldiers came and weeded out the officers from the group. The officers then were marched a distance of approximately a mile to what used to be a work camp for Germans. The camp was Westfallenhof.

SEPTEMBER 12,1939
WESTFALLENHOF, GERMANY

After days of being marched, driven in a closed truck, and beaten, this camp appeared to be a welcome relief, since for the first time the Germans gave some food to the prisoners. This nourishment consisted of only some meager soup that was brought out in several kettles to the starving men, who were not provided with any utensils, thus forcing the hungry prisoners to regress to primitive tactics, slurping from the common kettle. In order to get a gulp of the soup, some tipped the kettle trying to get their fill of the watery substance and then passed it to the next fellow until, too soon, none was left while the pangs of hunger still lingered.

In Westfallenhof father stayed two more days and there had a chance to be reunited with some of his former acquaintances and friends who, like him, were brought here as prisoners. They had news of further Polish defeats and the generally dismal situation.

On the morning of the third day of his stay there. and still without any organized system, the prisoners were milling around the camp when, through loudspeakers, came orders to assemble in front of their barracks. The dejected and tired POWs trudged to the designated spots and waited for orders; within an hour the Germans again began to divide them into groups and walk them toward the camp gates where awaited city busses of the town of Schneidemuhl (today's Pila, Poland) which they boarded.

Having been assigned to bus transport, father consoled himself with the idea that at least this time he did not have to walk. Bus after bus was loaded to capacity and armed guards were positioned next to the driver and the front door, keeping a watch on their captives. As the bus doors closed, the convoy began to head out of the camp, forming a long, winding column that headed west, further into German territory.

Several uneventful hours passed before the bus convoy came to a stop at the German army training camp of Grossborn (now Wielkie Bory in present-day Poland). The large sprawling camp with its numerous three-story, red brick barracks looked very impressive. Several of these structures were separated by barbed-wire fence from the rest of the camp and designated for the prisoners of war.

SEPTEMBER 15, 1939
GROSSBORN, GERMANY

Upon arrival in Grossborn, the first item on the German agenda was to segregate the officer prisoners from the NCO prisoners. Also, for the first time since having been taken prisoner on September 6th, father received a hot meal which could be eaten with the use of utensils, which until now only a few men who had managed not to lose their mess kits had possessed. Things began to look even better when, after the meal, the POWs were led into showers and were able to wash off the accumulated dirt of many days.

Thus, having revived themselves with a basic cleansing, the prisoners were assigned to their barracks, which even contained beds; unfortunately, there were not enough for all. Many therefore were forced to sleep on the floor, but after the last weeks of bare ground under the open sky, even this was a luxury. Furthermore, here in Grossborn, the POWs were under the jurisdiction of the German army, which conformed to the Geneva Conventions, and not, as previously, at the mercy of Hitler's SS which answered only to the Nazi party.

The stay here again was rather brief, but it gave father a chance to find some of his military friends who were among the prisoners. which not only helped to pass the time but also gave them the chance to reinforce each other morally. He and his friends tried to stay together, so when on October 10th the announcement came that officers were, once again, to be transported to different camps, they maneuvered in such a way that they managed not to be separated.

OCTOBER 10, 1939
ON THE ROAD, GERMANY

By early evening the officer POWs started their new journey, which this time was to be by train. The train convoy, consisting of nine 3rd class passenger cars that were clean but sparse, soon was filled over its capacity. To each car was assigned one armed guard who positioned himself at the already locked end entrance. The "all aboard!" whistle sounded and, amid clouds of steam, the train began to slowly roll out of the station.

As the train sped westward, its passengers were trying to determine the route and the destination of the journey. Here, they passed through land untouched by the devastation of war; people were going about their everyday tasks oblivious of the destruction that their nation had brought upon its neighbors. Through the dusty window, father observed the names of stations that flashed by as the train passed; towns and hamlets seemed to melt into one large continuous metropolis. The monotonous ride continued through the night and into early morning, when the train started to reduce its speed as it entered Hamburg. Then the train wound its way onto one of the numerous sidetracks, came to a halt, and the engines were shut down. The sudden stoppage of the train's chugging noises had awakened the still sleeping passengers.

Father opened his window and observed the daily bustle of the station where the commuter trains were shuttling working people to and fro. The late autumn sky above the city was streaked with rising smoke from factories that were diligently engaged in war production, but there was no sign of war except the constant visible presence of assorted military units and personnel waiting on the platform.

As it turned out, Hamburg was not to be a point of disembarkation, but just a stop during which all the POWs remained confined to the train. Finally, after almost three hours, the train engines were restarted and the train lumbered out of the station while slowly gaining speed.

Once out of the city the engines were at full speed; only the names of the stations flashed by: Pinneberg, Elmshorn, Gluskstadt…then the tracks veered abruptly north. By evening the convoy train came to stop in Itzehoe.

OCTOBER 12,1939
ITZEHOE, GERMANY

At the station waited a new detachment of German guards who immediately boarded the newly arrived train, giving orders for the POWs to leave the cars. The unenthusiastic prisoners started to disembark and assemble in their designated places and form a column, while the guards marched up and down the length of this formation barking orders to fall in. Finally satisfied that all prisoners seemed to be accounted for, the Germans gave orders to march.

The prisoner column proceeded out of the station heading for the outskirts of town toward a large German military complex that, as was evident from the remaining signs and insignias, had at one time housed the 20th Panzer Division. The camp consisted of solid, modern three story, red brick barracks that were neatly planted in long rows and presently served as a German "boot camp". The prisoners were led through the camp, past the barrack buildings toward two sprawling structures that were once used by German cavalry as riding galleries. Here, tired and weary prisoners were hurled in and enclosed to spent the night sitting on the bare ground. The only comforts they had were the availability of drinking water and toilets.

Through the high aboveground windows of the former riding stables, the morning light began to creep and with it came the shouting of orders for the prisoners to assemble outside.

Once more the POWs filed out to be counted and this time segregated according to their officer rank. So, the groups of 2nd lieutenants were separated from the lst lieutenants, then came the captains and lastly, of which there were the least, came majors together with lieutenant colonels and colonels. The groups were then in turn led into the barrack buildings, which were separated from the rest of the German military camp by a barbed wire fence.

Here, the quarters were adequate and consisted of rooms which contained six bunk beds that accommodated twelve officers. Furthermore, on each floor there were showers and toilets and in addition the building was heated. In accordance with accepted military codes, the maintenance of the Polish officers' quarters was done by Polish enlisted prisoners of war.

Chapter 6

Dubno, Lwow

SEPTEMBER 29, 1939
DUBNO

The carts were lazily rolling over the bumpy road toward the railroad station. Evidence of the disorder of war and the recent battle was strewn all around the streets. People moved with caution, trying to resume their everyday activities, but impaired by the intimidating and ever-present Soviet militia. Uniformed and armed soldiers were everywhere, in addition to the constantly patrolling military police.

The railroad station came into view, with yet another checkpoint at the entrance. This was composed of a large contingent of soldiers, scrutinizing the documents of everyone who was entering or leaving the station. Those who did not satisfy the occupiers' scrutiny were shoved into a covered truck standing nearby. Since there was no way of avoiding the Soviet inspection if we wanted to get to a train, we continued forward toward the entrance of the station building, where the carts stopped. Before anyone could get off the wagons, armed guards with their rifles slung over their shoulders surrounded us, demanding to see our papers. The routine check continued with standard questions as to our destination, occupation, etc., When the soldier questioning us reached Hildebrandt, the chauffeur, he looked over the document Hildebrandt handed to him and hesitated. Then the soldier's suspicious gaze rested upon grandfather.

"Do you work for him?" the guard addressed Hildebrandt, while pointing at grandfather.

"Yes".

"Chauffeur? His?" gesturing again at grandfather.

"Yes."

"Where is your car? Surely you are not employed to drive a cart?"

"The cars were… were… requisitioned a few days ago by your military" replied Hildebrandt, trying to be calm in an uneasy situation.

"Ah…" the guard nodded his head in approval.

"This man", again pointing to grandfather, "he is a bourgeois. Did he pay you for your work? Don't be afraid to tell the truth! We know how these people exploit the working people. So, did he pay you for your work?" haughtily demanded the soldier, by now puffed up with his self-importance.

At that instant all of us were still and waiting for Hildebrandt's answer, which would decide our fate in a moment.

"Yes, of course he paid me," Hildebrandt answered, with indignation that such a ridiculous question should have been put to him.

With that the interrogating guard snapped the papers shut and shoved them back to Hildebrandt, with obvious disappointment that he had not found a pretext to perform his "duty". The rest of our papers continued to be checked, but without any deterrence. Other guards prodded the contents of our baggage, but without much interest or enthusiasm. Finally, the OK was given that we could proceed. The remainder of our possessions were unloaded from the carts, and our group proceeded to the rail platform to catch the first available train for Lwow.

SEPTEMBER 30, 1939
LWOW

The train ride to Lwow was short and uneventful, but the tranquility of the journey was disrupted on arrival when we were greeted by shouts from soldiers demanding to see the passengers' documents. Having passed this inspection, we were allowed to disembark and unload our baggage. We were fortunate to find a corner in one of the overcrowded waiting rooms where we settled with our belongings. Now, the problem was where to go from here, and how. Since we had no place to stay, grandfather decided to go and look up a distant acquaintance of his, taking uncle Josef with him. In the meantime, mother and aunt Maria would look for lodgings. The rest of us would remain in the waiting room until a place to live could be found.

Within a couple of hours grandfather returned with news of finding his friends, who were living not too far from the train station and were able to rent him a room. Unfortunately, however, there were no accommodations available for the rest of us, since they only had a small apartment. Hence, we waited for mother's and Maria's return with nervous anticipation.

It was well into late afternoon when they returned, after literally going from door to door searching for a place to stay. Lwow was overcrowded with refugees who had fled from the west of Poland to get away from the German onslaught, only to be caught by the Soviets. This situation created a critical scarcity of living space, but the two women were able to rent a place for us, located on the outskirts of town.

Hildebrandt managed to find a taxi for grandfather, whom he took to his lodgings, and was also able to stay with him. Meanwhile, uncle Josef rounded up a horse-drawn wagon into which our baggage were loaded and we all piled on top of that and proceeded towards our future home.

Having spent most of the day in the railroad station waiting room, we had not seen any signs of battle, but as the wagon moved through the city the scarred buildings as well as many casualties were visible in the streets. The corpses of Polish policemen and other government employees executed by the Soviets were strewn in roadside ditches on the outskirts of the city. There were so many of these bodies that although the massive Soviet killings had taken place several days ago, the burial detachments could not catch up.

It was still light when we arrived at the house on Zielona Gorna Street which we were to occupy. The house was located on the fringes of the city adjacent to the grounds of a brick factory. The building itself was very picturesque with large forested grounds. In addition to the main house, there was a small cottage which housed the caretaker and his family.

Our hosts and benefactors were Mr. & Mrs. Domaszkiewicz, who were friends of one of grandfather's acquaintances and took pity on our circumstances. They relinquished half of the house, which filled up very fast with eleven of us. A large room that had been a sitting room became a bedroom and living quarters for eight of us, and uncles Josef and Alfons shared one of the small bedrooms. Ours was a cheery sunlit room with french doors which opened unto a spacious veranda that overlooked a wooded garden. Besides the usual living-room furniture of sofas, chairs and end tables, the room contained a grand piano.

There were no beds, but by this time we knew the routine of rolling out the carpets and the bedding on the floor, so the furniture was moved to one side of the room while we prepared sleeping places against the wall, one next to each other. Miss Flora and Miss Gabrysia took charge of preparing our meal with the help of the housekeeper that our hosts had, and that became our system for the duration of our stay there.

We seemed to feel safer here than we had in any place since our journey started on September 1st. It was away from bombing and battle and we had a roof over our heads. Therefore, within two days grandfather sent Hildebrandt back to Ludwikowko to bring back aunt Helen with her children as well as Walkowiak and his family, who had stayed behind with her. The thought was that we would sit out this time of turmoil together here in Lwow, and when it settled down we would return home to Chobielin. Everyone believed that the war would be finished within a few weeks, or perhaps months, because England would prevail and would not permit the occupation of Poland.

A day after Hildebrandt's departure there came a telegram from him with news that aunt Helen and her group had returned to Chobielin and he was unable to go back to his employer, Mr. Poll, so he would be back with us as soon as he was able. This news was greeted with mixed emotions. There was concern about aunt's safety in crossing the (now) German-Soviet border (*Germany and the Soviet Union had divided Poland between them*) and how she would manage with four children. On the other hand, this meant that the new border was open and we might all be able to go back home. That idea was soon dispelled, since in order to leave the city we had to get proper papers and that would take some time; or so we were told by the Soviets.

With the hope of returning home, grandfather wrote a letter in the naive belief that he might get his cars back.

OCTOBER 5, 1939
To War Procurator for the County of Luck
A request from Mr. Julian Reysowski residing in Lwow regarding the return of the 2 confiscated automobiles.

Therefore I am turning to you Mr. Procurator with the following request of account to me and my family which is comprised of five men, 6 women and 6 children from Pomorze. My son in law, Jan Slawinski from Chobielin, lent me two automobiles. One is a truck with plates "Mlyn Chobielin" owned by Jan Slawinski, Chevrolet registration nr. B61-149, model 1881400, engine nr. 6808055 and a passenger car Opel-Olympia, engine nr 37-1703, license plate 297-68521 which is also the property of my son in law Mr. Jan Slawinski from Chobielin, county Szubin.

With these cars I evacuated the whole family and property to a place called Ludwikowko, municipality Mlynow (county Dubno). The truck was taken on September 24, 39 and the car on September 25, 39 by Soviet military and temporarily placed at the military command in Mlynow. I did not receive any compensation for these vehicles or any receipt. But I have witnesses that can vouch that they have been taken: temporarily appointed mayor of Ludwikowko Mr. Jan Paradowski as well as his brother Mr. Pawel Paradowski and the chief of the municipality of Mlynow, whose name I don't know.

Since these vehicles were new and for which I am responsible, therefore I ask you Mr. Procurator in taking steps in order that the above mentioned cars be returned to me. Notify me at the address in Lwow.

Needless to say, no reply to this plea was received.

The next few months became a round of constant searching for family members, such as my father and uncle Wacek, and trying to get permission to return to our home. In addition, in order to make ends meet, personal belongings had to be sold or bartered.

The warm autumn came to an end and the December cold settled in, and with it crept in a new concern—fuel for heating. Most of us survived the cold without any side effects, except for grandfather. His cold developed into pneumonia and he had to be hospitalized on the day before Christmas in a private clinic of Dr. Rudziecki, who was a friend of his. Here he was to remain almost five weeks.

CHRISTMAS 1939
LWOW

It was a far cry from the festive and warm holidays we had enjoyed in Chobielin, but for me as a five-year old child it did not feel much different since, being the youngest, everyone was giving me attention in the hope that I would not experience the hardships they endured. My cousins Romek and Basia, though teenagers, were my constant playmates. The favorite game that they would play with me would be "house", where I was a mother and they my children. They also introduced me to stamp collecting, and it became a passion for the three of us and helped us to pass the time.

On Christmas Eve all of us gathered in the living room for the traditional "Wigilia", which took many hours of preparation on the part of all the women in the household. There was even a small Christmas tree that stood on the piano and was decorated with ornaments that the three of us had made. The Holiday wishes exchanged were all for the end of the war and that we would be together next year in Chobielin; a wish that would be expressed again and again by all of us for many years following.

The year came to an end without any changes in our situation except that grandfather was still in the hospital. Weather permitting, mother and I would make daily treks to see him. Sometimes aunt Maria would come with us, but since she was pregnant she was not often up to it. In addition, there was still no word from aunt Helen, although many letters and telegrams were sent to let her know our whereabouts.

Chapter 7

Germany-Itzehoe

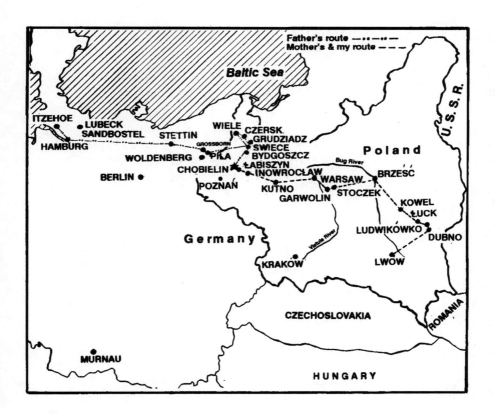

OCTOBER 12, 1939
ITZEHOE, GERMANY

Today father began to settle into what turned out to be his 5 1/2 year=long captivity. Having now a permanent address, his first thoughts were of mother, who he presumed must have returned to Chobielin. After obtaining an official postcard, he wrote his first news to her at that address:

> *OCTOBER 12, 1939*
> *ITZEHOE-GERMANY*
> *My beloved Aniusia!*
>
> *I am in captivity, together with Jas. We are well. I am very worried about the lack of news from you. Please Beloved, don't worry, everything is in God's hands. If you could, please send me two sets of underwear, a few collars and socks, slippers, a scarf and to complete the package, something to eat. I long for you Niusienka and for Terenia. I think of you all of the time.*
>
> *Ending, I kiss you tenderly and also little Terenia. Embraces for your father, a hand kiss for Helen and Maria as well as sincere regards to all.*
>
> *Your Stach*

In the meantime the camp administration systematically began to register the officers, who by now numbered 1050, giving them a photographed ID that was to be worn around their necks at all times. Now, father had his POW number as well an official address that read as follows:

Oflag Xa. Blok 2, Kamp 3

Deutschland.

A few days passed when father again dispatched another postcard to Chobielin. Almost identical to the previous one:

> *OCTOBER 16, 1939*
> *ITZEHOE-GERMANY*
> *Beloved Nusienko!*

l am a prisoner of war. I am well, and together with Jas. I am worried about the lack of news from you.

I already have sent two cards [they evidently did not reach Chobielin, since nothing was found] but all without any answer. After you receive this card, I beg you for an answer. In previous cards I have asked you for a response. In previous cards I have asked you for underwear, if of course you could send it, and if I receive a card from you then I will repeat the details. I kiss you tenderly Nusienko, as well as Terenia, hand kisses for Helen, Maria, and Luta, regards for father.

Your Stach

[There is a brief postscript from uncle Jas, mother's brother-in-law who was married to her older sister Helen. He came to the POW camp with the ever-swelling ranks of prisoners. Uncle Jas and father were to spend their imprisonment together until almost the end of the war.]

Organization of the camp facilities continued for several more weeks, but unfortunately day to day life did not improve. Though the accommodations were adequate in that no one had to sleep on a bare floor and toilet facilities were available, the food was barely the minimum necessary for one to survive. Morning and evening meals consisted of only a glass of herb tea, while the main "eating" event, around noon, was a bowl of soup. In the first days the camp kitchens were staffed by German women who came from the nearby town, but they soon were replaced by cooks from the Polish army who were also POWs.

Every noon the companies of prisoners were marched to the mess-hall and their rations of soup, whose consistency varied with the daily availability of produce on hand, were doled out to them. Since in the first days no one possessed eating utensils, the bowl was passed around during mealtime and then left in the mess hall. Then, after several weeks of marching daily to the mess, the camp command issued each prisoner a mess kit and from that day on the soup kettle was brought to each floor of the barracks

where the officers lined up for soup and returned to their room to con-
sume it.

The days passed slowly, and the camp's inhabitants began to eagerly
exchange the few items of news that began to reach some individuals who
were fortunate enough to make contact with relatives and friends. Father's
concern for mother and me grew and so he dispatched another card in the
hope that this one would bring some response. Like the previous postcards, this one was also sent to Chobielin, since he presumed that we all by
this time had returned there after the fighting was over.

> OCTOBER 20, 1939
> ITZEHOE-GERMANY
> My beloved Aniusia,
> I am in prison, healthy. Jas is with me. I wrote to you several
> times, but no answer. I am very worried about you, please answer.
> Don't worry, all is in God's hands. In previous postcards I asked for
> underwear, scarf and gloves, if it is possible.
> I kiss you tenderly, and Terenia. Hand kiss for Helen and
> embraces for father and all.
> Your Stach.

Like the previous cards, this one did not reach mother, but it did arrive
in Chobielin, where Victoria, our housekeeper, had stayed behind and
kept the mail which had arrived there in the hope that the family would
return. By now Chobielin had been taken over by the Germans and put
under their administration, while retaining the house-servants and field
workers.

In the meantime Oflag Xa was swelling in ranks; Polish officer-prison-
ers were sent here from several different camps, filling up the three buildings that now housed over 5,500 prisoners. With the influx of prisoners
came the problem and danger of informers. Taking advantage of the situation, the Germans planted their people among the POW ranks; they
were Germans that had lived in Poland for several generations and were
Polish citizens, but now were gathering information for the Germans.

Some of the information gathered was insignificant; such as who had not turned over all their currency to camp authorities, since the POWs were forbidden to possess it. But more serious and dangerous was the constant German search for officers who the authorities believed to have reprimanded or executed Germans for saboteur activities during the defense of Poland. Furthermore, the Germans were looking for Polish chaplains who held officer's rank but were reservists. The camp had 25 chaplains and the German command extracted 21 of them from the ranks and sent them to concentration camps such as Dachau, Buchenwald, etc. Only four remaining priests who were captains were spared and stayed as POWs.

It was almost three weeks after his arrival at Oflag Xa when the long awaited response to father's cards came. It did not come from mother but from aunt Helen who, after being separated from the rest of us, had managed to return to Chobielin with her four children, enduring a hazardous journey of several weeks.

It should here be noted that after we left Ludwikowko for Lwow, aunt Helen, who had stayed in Ludwikowko was told that the Soviets were not allowing any people to go to Lwow, but that they should go instead to Wlodzimierz, 80 miles northwest. Therefore, after a couple of days, Mrs. Przeracka, and aunt Helen, with the four children, hired a horse drawn cart from a Ukrainian peasant who was to take them to their destination. The weather had changed; it was getting cold, and they all huddled in the back of the cart. Aunt Helen still had a bottle of cognac that she passed around for all to take a swallow; then the cold became unbearable. At night, the cart driver would search for a place to spend a night out of the cold. He would then position himself against the door with an axe by his side. He said he was guarding them against the roving bandits, who were plentiful and were taking advantage of both refugees and locals.

They reached a village on the outskirts of Wlodzimierz, the mid-point of their journey, where the peasant left them. From here Mrs. Przeracka and aunt Helen would make daily treks to Luck to get news of the current situation. Wlodzimierz was full of refugees from Western Poland who were waiting for permission from the Soviet authorities to cross the river Bug, the division between the Soviet and German occupation zones of Poland. Finally after almost three weeks' wait, permission was received and they went to Uscilug, still on the east (Soviet) side of the river.

The next month in Uscilug was a nightmare. They had to stay in an overcrowded school, on a hay-strewn floor, waiting for a permit to cross which was given to only a limited number of persons daily. The chaotic crossing of the river Bug was done on a makeshift plank bridge, where people pushed and fell into the river in their haste to make it to the other side.

While waiting here, aunt Helen and her group met two young Polish pilots who were in civilian clothes and were also trying to reach Warsaw. The two young men attached themselves to aunt Helen and were particularly helpful with the younger children, Marysia and Andrew, when their turn finally came for the crossing. They held unto them and guided the kids through the perilous bridge crossing. Upon reaching the west bank and the German occupation zone, the segregation of people began; Poles to the right, Germans to the left and Jews forward. The Germans then began to register each group. When they asked aunt for her home address and she answered in her flawless German and said Chobielin, they assumed that they were Germans and put them on the transporting freight train that was going to Warsaw. The 150 mile distance to Warsaw took them two days and they arrived at the bombed out rail station where aunt Helen and Mrs. Przeracka parted. Mrs. Przeracka stayed in Warsaw, where she had some family, and aunt Helen was able to catch a passenger train for Bydgoszcz.

The five of them arrived in Bydgoszcz during the night and left the station looking for a place to spend the night. The streets were totally deserted, and as they turned into a nearby street a man darted out of the doorway and, grabbing aunts elbow, pulled her in.

"Get off the street!" he commanded in a hushed voice. "If you're caught after curfew you will be shot!" he informed the startled group, which quickly darted into the shadows of the doorway.

After aunt explained their predicament the man, who lived in this building, took pity on them and put them up for the night and fed them. The following day they went by train to Naklo where they arrived bedraggled, hungry and very tired. Here, aunt had her sister-in-law, uncle Jan's sister, who had been bombed out of her home and was now living in an attic room of a synagogue. She gave them shelter and already had received news from the POW camp, from uncle Jan and my father.

After resting and recovering, aunt Helen was anxious to get back home where she was ordered to register in accordance with the German occupational rule. So she and the children set out on foot to Chobielin, about 5 miles distant from Naklo. Here, she found a new occupier. He was a young SS man who quartered himself in the manor house and was running the mill operation. He was taken aback by aunt's and the children's shabby appearance and permitted them to stay the night in the house. The next morning he informed them that they might stay in the small cottage adjoining the mill but made it clear that it could not be for long. However, Mr. Franc Poll, grandfather's friend and owner of the neighboring estate, "Jaruzyn", and chauffeur Hildebrandt's employer, who was a German (now the name of the estate changed to Ulmenhof) intervened on their behalf and they were permitted to stay.

As aunt Helen and the children were staying in the cottage and trying to figure out what to do next, the occupants of the manor house changed. The young SS man left and a German family named Turman, with a son and daughter from Bessarabia, were resettled there and remained "owners" of Chobielin until January 1945.

Mr. Turman turned out to be a decent person who, knowing that if he turned aunt Helen out, she would be deported to Germany for labor, employed her as manager of the kitchen in Chobielin. Here, with our housekeeper Victoria, aunt worked as a domestic, bringing home scraps of food in the evening for the children. Janusz, who was sixteen years old, got a job in the office of Chobielin's gamekeeper, and the girls, when spring came, worked in the gardens.

Aunt Helen even managed to get a job as a watchman for uncle Maks (her brother), with which he got a place to live for himself and his family. In addition, aunt secured work for her two cousins from Naklo.

Hence father, when he received the news of aunt Helen's return, presumed that mother and I would soon follow and also return to Chobielin. Therefore, he wrote another letter to mother, addressed to Chobielin:

NOVEMBER 17, 1939
ITZEHOE, GERMANY
My beloved Nusienko,

Yesterday we received a postcard from Helen, from which I surmise that you too, Nusienko, are returning. It is a sad return, but we should thank God that you are alive. I was just about devastated not having any news. My dearest Treasures, I feel so sorry for all of you. Please Beloved, write in detail your whole tragedy. In our apartment (in Grudziadz) live strangers—Mrs. Sziller wrote to me. The street is now renamed "Friedrichstrasse". Please liquidate the apartment.

I am asking only, if you can, please send a set of warm underwear because during the war I lost my complete suitcase. Tuesday I will send a letter in which I will write more. Kissing you tenderly my beloved and a kiss for sweet Terenia as well as regards for father, Helen, Luta and Maria and all of you.

Your Stach

P.S. What is happening with Wacek?

(As previously mentioned, Wacek, who was aunt Maria's husband, had been taken as a prisoner of war by the Soviets and died along with the more than 10,000 other Polish officers whom the Soviets executed at Katyn forest in the spring of 1940.)

A few days after sending the previous postcard to mother, father wrote to aunt Helen:

NOVEMBER 24, 1939
ITZEHOE, GERMANY
Dear Helen,

First of all, I thank you for the postcard that I received yesterday. With all your troubles you found time, for which I am very indebted. Supposedly, the news about Ann's whereabouts and the rest of family seems to be good but the fact that they are not coming back worries me greatly.

All of you lived through a great deal of turmoil and suffered a great deal, but let's ask God that it only ends with that.

Please tell Ania that our housekeeper from Grudziadz wrote to me, telling that our apartment is occupied by some strangers. Who are they? We should probably presume that it is now military quarters. I asked her to put all our furniture in one room, but she replied that she can't do this by herself. So when Ania returns she has to take care of it.

For the promised package I thank you sincerely. Jas and I live in the same room. What is happening with Wacek? Ending, I kiss your hand, as well as sending embraces to all.

Stach

Now father continued to keep up correspondence with aunt Helen, not only for himself, but also for uncle Jas, who was afraid to bring attention to himself since the Germans were interrogating him about his regiment's war activities. He had commanded a company that had defended Bydgoszcz and was involved in the execution of German saboteurs. The two men, father and uncle Jas, had always been good friends, but now their friendship grew into a very close attachment that provided solace throughout the years of imprisonment. Here in Itzehoe, they were not in the same room, because uncle Jas was a major and father a captain, but throughout all the shuffling about of the prisoners they did manage to stay in the same camp.

Father continued writing to aunt Helen since mother's letters from Soviet occupied Poland did not reach him as yet. All father knew was that we had survived the two invasions, German and then Soviet, and that at present we were trapped under the Soviet occupation.

DECEMBER 5, 1939
ITZEHOE, GERMANY
Dear Helen,

I received the package from you, as well as the other things for Jas. For all the things that I have received, Helen, I thank you warmly and sincerely. All these things are combined with a great effort on your part. I am very worried about Ania as well as the rest of family's destiny, from whom I am awaiting news. But so far without results.

About the changes that occurred in Chobielin I know from post-cards that I have received. I also know that in our apartment now live strangers. I would like very much to save our furniture but maybe Ania will be able to do so since I am helpless.

I ask you if Ania left my officer's top coat in Chobielin; if so, could you be so kind and send it to me. I am sending some money, please don't be offended and accept it since I know you don't have much. Anyway, if you don't want to accept it for yourself, please keep it for Ania.

Did you hear anything from Wacek? I can't understand why you separated in Luck. It not for that, all of you would be together at home.

Personally, I feel regrets towards Maks. I wrote to him four post-cards but I have not received an answer, what can one do ff someone does not want to write.

I don't need any clothes, I have everything. When Ania returns, tell her to write immediately in Polish; it is allowed. Tell her to write about all their adventures.

Once more I thank you sincerely for remembering me, as well thanks to Bernard for the sweater.

I kiss your hand and hugs for all.
Stach

Maks was mother's brother with whom we spent our first night in Labiszyn after leaving Chobielin on September 1st, and who returned there with his wife, son and infant daughter only to die at the hands of the Germans. With regard to father's reference to money; that was money that the Germans gave the officer POW's as their monthly allowance, known as LAGER MARKS. Father as a captain received 30 Lager Marks a month.

Bernard was another brother of mother's, who managed to get into the part of Poland that the Germans referred General Government. Here it was a little easier to survive than in the other parts of Poland that were designated as a slave state providing labor for the service of Germany.

> *DECEMBER 22, 1939*
> *ITZEHOE, GERMANY*
> *Dear Helen,*
> *I received a postcard from you dated December 16, as well as slippers, for which I thank you from the bottom of my heart. I ask you to make use of the money that I have sent you. I ask you that since it will make me very happy that I can help you in such a small way. These will be sad Holidays for all. If only I had some news from Ania, my heart would be lighter. For you Helen, I wish a better New Year, one that would bring good changes. Regards to Barbara*
> *I kiss your hand.*
> *Stach*

CHRISTMAS 1939
ITZEHOE, GERMANY

Christmas here, though sad, was full of hope; everyone was trying to maintain high spirits and optimism that this situation was only temporary—spring will come and with it changes for the better!

The German camp commander, a cavalry colonel named Von Fuchs, was a civil individual who had been brought out of retirement to run the POW camp. He permitted the prisoners to gather and put up Christmas trees that they in turn decorated with great ingenuity. Now the otherwise bare vestibules of the barracks attained a festive look with the placement of the decorated trees, the symbols of Christmas.

Furthermore, the commandant allowed the POWs to construct a makeshift altar which was placed in one of the riding galleries, and a Midnight Mass was to be held. In addition, the dusk to dawn curfew was lifted and the prisoners were allowed to leave their barracks to attend the Christmas Mass celebration.

So on a cold and snow less Christmas night in a former riding stable, the men gathered to give thanks for surviving the battles and at the same time prayed for the safety of their families. They sang ancient Polish Christmas carols of peace and hope that resounded through the camp, remembering Christmases of the past and hoping that the next holiday would find them back in their free homeland with their families and friends.

Father's prayers were with the rest of his comrades, but as soon as the holiday was over, he resumed his search for his family. All his efforts were concentrated in his attempt to contact mother, but it is evident from his letters that he was running out of leads to pursue.

DECEMBER 28, 1939
ITZEHOE, GERMANY
Dear Helen,

I have received permission to look for Ania's address at the refugee office in Romania. Since today I also received your card, dated December 19, in which you inform me that you probably have her address, I won't write to Romania where she is not, but instead to you to and ask you please send me her address.

We are allowed to write to Russia [the east part of Poland where we were had been annexed by Stalin to the Soviet Union.] and the letters from that side do reach our camp. We have received today your packages, for which I thank you sincerely but at the same time I beg you not to send me anything because it is unnecessary since I have everything. If I need anything I will ask you. I kiss your hand.

Stach

[Post script from uncle Jas]

Father refers to Romania; it was a route of escape for many Poles; also, the Red Cross was there helping to locate the families separated by the war.

Part Two

1940

Chapter 8

Lwow, Przemysl

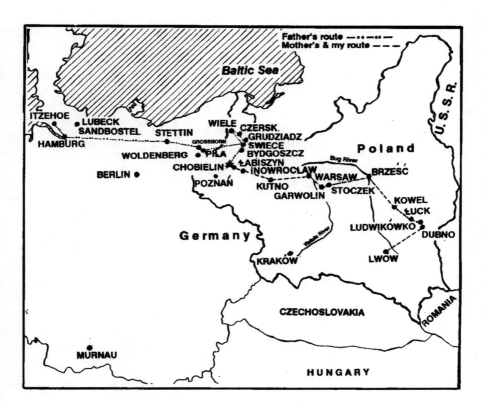

FEBRUARY 1940
LWOW, SOVIET OCCUPIED POLAND

There still had been no word to us from aunt Helen, although many letters and telegrams were sent to let her know our whereabouts. Then, at the beginning of the month of February came long-awaited news from Chobielin. Mother answered immediately, as follows:

FEBRUARY 13,1940
LWOW,
SOVIET OCCUPIED POLAND
My dearest Helen,
I don't know how to thank you for your letter, which brought us great joy that is hard to describe.

The letter arrived Sunday and Luta brought it to father, where I was staying with Terenia for the last two days. Usually it's Maria who stays with father. He lives quite far from us, near the railroad station, and we are way out of town— at least we have lovely walks.

Right now father feels a little better. He has been confined to bed for the last two months and he spent five weeks in the hospital with pneumonia. On the day before Christmas I took father to Dr. Rendkiewicz' clinic; he is father's friend from Morszyn. Father had good medical care but the food was poor. We visited him daily. I think he will now recover faster after receiving your letter. We were very concerned about you and the rest of the family. Helen, I never thought that you were back in our beloved Chobielin, and so is Maks. I hope Maks is helping you, as Bernard is in his own place [he lived around Warsaw]. Barbara and her children have it well, I wish her the best.

We have no news of Wacek, not even a postcard, and Maria is worried about him. Dear, write me and tell me where are our husbands.

We are living here on the outskirts of town at the home of Domaszkiewicz, very good people. There are eight of us sleeping in one room, it's a large room but cold. Fuel is very expensive and so is food. One kilo of bacon is 60 rubles and flour is also pricey. I sold lots of my things. Now I am starting to pull out some of your things, because you can only get food by bartering. With us we have all the belongings that we salvaged from Ludwikowko.

My dear Helen, I am ending because Luta wants to write a few words. Please send my letter on to Stach. Kisses for all from

Ania and Maria

P. S. My Viktoria, [our housekeeper] what is she doing? Did she get my letter? Did Zosia return the coat? Walkiewicz seems to be wandering for a long time with your suitcase; ours was stolen.

Helen, we all revived after receiving news from you.

It is not too bad for us here. We manage as well as we can. Don't worry about us. I will write more to you tomorrow.

Many, many, embraces from

Luta and the rest.

With the above letter mother included the following letter to my father, since this seemed to be the only way she could contact him at that time.

FEBRUARY 13,1940

My dearest Stach,

I finally know that you are alive! I was endlessly waiting to hear some news of your regiment, sometimes the news were bad. I have lived in such uncertainness for five months and now my dearest, I am ecstatic that you are alive; that there is some hope and purpose to my life.

I don't know your address since I did not receive your first post-card from Helen. It was on Sunday, February 11 that we received the joyous letter from Helen.

Father is not feeling well, he is confined to bed for the last two months. He was in hospital for five weeks with pneumonia. I think he will get better now after receiving the letter from Helen. It was a great surprise for all of us to get news from Helen from Chobielin.

Our little Teresa was so happy to hear that her daddy is alive and that he will write to us. Stach, it is hard to believe that once again I will be able to wait for letters from you. Write often; I think that your letters will reach us better than our mail from here.

Dearest, don't worry about us, we are managing well since we were able to salvage many of our belongings; we sell them now, though everything is very expensive. There are very few of your things left. Your fur vest came in handy for me, as well as your ski jacket. With great regret I had to sell your riding boots and with that I bought myself warm boots. So, in spite of the severe cold, my feet were warm. For Teresa I made a fur lined coat from Helen's old seal jacket—she even has fur lined sleeves. For the outside shell I sacrificed my navy fall suit. I also managed to get some shoes for her. So now our Teresa is dressed warm.

We live quite far from town and we have lovely walks to the city if there is not too much snow. We live with good people, engineers Domaszkiewicz, whose house is located adjacent to the grounds of a brick factory. Eight of us sleep in one room. It is a large room but rather drafty. It is cold, since fuel is as expensive as food. But we are able to survive.

We are eagerly waiting for spring after this severe winter, we long for the warmth of the sun. Stach, I am ending and impatiently waiting for a letter from you— write often to me. We are very happy to hear that you are together with Jas. Write me all about yourself.

I kiss you tenderly
Your Niusia
Dearest Daddy,
I miss you very much. Are you well? I love you very much.
Your Terenia
Our dearest Stach and Jas,

It is difficult to describe our joy when we heard that you were well. I embrace you.

Luta

The postscripts that were written by me in this letter as well as most other ones were done with the "help" of my mother, since I did not know how to write at this point. I would hold the pen and mother would hold my hand and write with it.

Aunt Helen was able to forward this letter to father, since the letter has the stamp of "Oflag Xa 15 gepruft", meaning that it passed the censor of the camp. This was the officers' prisoner of war camp in Itzehoe near Hamburg. But the incoming mail to Lwow was very inconsistent and sparse, so mother kept on writing without receiving any response from father.

FEBRUARY 15, 1940

LWOW,

SOVIET OCCUPIED POLAND

My dearest Stach,

I am writing a second letter to you and sending it through Helen because I don't have your address. I am happy that I am able to write a few words to you and at the same time hope that your letters will reach me.

I am curious to hear what occurred to you during the last months, if you could write about it. Since our arrival here we are waiting for the opening of the border. Once they closed the border on the evening before our scheduled departure. Now, they are saying that the border will be opened again and they will permit a certain number of people through. I hope that we will be fortunate and be able to go in the desired direction. Our Terenia is well; I take her to town often because it is a beautiful walk for her since it is too cold to be in the house.

We do have problems with father. If he would only will himself to get well. He does feel better now, but is weak.

Maria is worried now about Wacek because she does not know where he is.

Stach, please write to me that happened to your friends. Are they all alive? I only heard that Rusio was killed in action. They said the same thing about you, that you drowned with your whole squadron—they just told me that now. Thank God that I was not told that news before, since l was concerned about you dearest anyway.

A few days ago I also wrote a letter to Krakow asking about you. I presume you wrote to them [In Krakow lived my father's family; his father, brother and a married sister].

Terenia is enclosing her masterpiece because the kids draw all day.

Forgive me for writing with a pencil but we are short of ink—everything around us has disappeared like in a dream.

How are you looking my dear, did you lose much weight? Because here we look wonderful, just like after the Morszyn Spa. Luta finally achieved her normal weight, she lost 10 kilo.

From all of us fondest embraces for you and Jas.

Ending, I kiss you fondly

Your Niusia

Within a few days mother finally received some of father's long delayed postcards with his return address. Now she was able to write to him directly.

FEBRUARY 27,1940

LWOW,

SOVIET OCCUPIED POLAND

My dearest Stach,

Already I have sent six letters to you and I presume that you received them. For the last two days have been at father's, but tomorrow I will go to my own place. We are kidding ourselves that they will let us return home, but it really doesn't look like it. Tomorrow I will write a letter. How are you both feeling; are you well? Dad is feeling a little bit better but is still in bed. He is sending his regards. I am ending and kissing you.

Niusia

A few days later followed mother's next promised letter, also addressed
to the camp Oflag XA.

MARCH 2, 1940
LWOW,
SOVIET OCCUPIED POLAND
My dearest Stach,

*I am already writing to you my seventh letter in addition to the
postcard and telegram. I don't know if they reach you, since I heard
that you don't receive mail often. Therefore, I decided to write
shorter letters but as often as I can. Ten days ago I received your postcards and I am waiting for further news from you.*

*We are well, but very worried since new orders came out that all
refugees are to leave Lwow in the next fourteen days. We are to choose
from several places that will be given to us. This is a ray of hope for
our return home. They say that a German commission came to register us for the departure. The Commission is supposed to choose only
specific people, but I presume we will not have any problems. If there
should be a change of address or we return home, I will let you know
immediately by telegraph.*

*Dear, why do you write so little; I wait for your card everyday,
they probably take a long time to reach us. How are doing and how
is Jas? I found a small photo of Hela and I am sending it for Jas; I
think that he will be pleased. Terenia's photos are supposed to be
ready today so I will send them in my next letter. She is enthusiastically collecting stamps; it is amazing that such a little person has
such specific interest and knowledge. I assure you that she has a better knowledge of stamps than I!*

*We are happy with the coming of spring. The sun warms us won-
derfully, it is just like in the mountains; we even have a tan!*

*We miss you terribly and wonder when we will be able to be
together again, but for now at least am content that I can write to
you, even though not very openly. That is better than nothing. I have*

some of your photographs, but I was hesitant to look at them until I found out about your whereabouts. Looking at them I reminisce about our past, dearest. These are now terrible circumstances for all of us, but despite of it we have to believe in divine protection.

Stach, I long so much to be able to go to Helen, maybe there we would find some peace. Though I do realize that it is not so sweet there either, but at least we would be in our own place. Right now all prices have dropped very much, but there are no buyers. We are selling the rest of the oriental carpets.

My sweetest dear I kiss you tenderly,

Your Ania and Terenia

P.S. Warmest regards to you and Jas from everyone here.

Mother's letters continued to go out, in the hope that one of them would reach father and she might receive a response.

MARCH 3, 1940

LWOW,

SOVIET OCCUPIED POLAND

My dearest Stach,

I am now writing an eighth letter to you, besides the postcard and a telegram, because I am not sure if you are receiving any of these letters. This week I will also send a letter through the Geneva Red Cross.

Dearest, today is three weeks that I received Helen's letter telling me that you are alive, my beloved. Because of it my life took on a different meaning; now I can live with thoughts of hope for the future. As I mentioned before, father was laid up in the hospital for six weeks with pneumonia; right now he feels a little better. We live in a beautifully located place on the outskirts of Lwow. It's a half an hour of a lovely walk to town. The climate is healthy, almost mountain-like but the lodgings are a bit drafty.

Yesterday, when returning from town I met the mailman and he handed me postcards from you. I received all of your four cards.

There was also a telegram, but it was returned since they claim they could not find me.

You can't imagine how happy I am with every bit of news that I receive from you. They lift my spirits and give me a hopeful outlook for the future.

Right now the authorities are after all the refugees to register and they are using scaring tactics in order that we leave Lwow. Supposedly we have new places assigned. In case of our change of address, I would telegraph immediately. They are saying that a German Commission is supposed to register us for the evacuation; we are looking forward to that. In November, we were all set to leave but they closed the border.

I also write to Helen but I don't know if she receives any of my letters. Postcards from you travel a whole month. I am sending you our new photos made especially for you. I think they came out alright, in particular the ones of Terenia.

My dearest, don't worry about us. I have clothing for us. For Terenia I made a coat with fur lining.

We are slowly selling our belongings in order to live but I think the worst is over and the long awaited spring is approaching. Only I am concerned, my dearest, if you have what you need?

Dearest, I am ending since I don't want to write too much. Many times I kiss you my beloved.

Your Ania and Terenia

Please give my warmest regards to Jas.

A few weeks later mother wrote another letter to aunt Helen.

MARCH 22,1940

LWOW,

SOVIET OCCUPIED POLAND

My dearest Helen,

I am already writing a fourth letter to you without any answer, I wanted to send a telegram but they would not accept it. Since your

Namesday is coming soon, I wanted once again to send you my best wishes.

Helen, father asks that you tell Maks to try to get "Rosafof" potatoes for planting. He might be able to get them in Samoklenski. He is to put.... under the beets and potatoes. How many horses and cattle are left? And why did Maks leave Labiszyn? Please write to father about all this. I am for the last two days at father's, together with Terenia, since I relieved Maria for a few days.

The poor girl is worried what will happen to her. [Maria was at this time about eight months pregnant and did not know the whereabouts of her husband.]

We are dreaming about being able to be with you and live there unnoticed. Maybe I could find there some work in an office. Helen, you have no idea how much we long to be with you. From my Stach, I finally received postcards, a week ago, they all came together. Supposedly, there was also a telegram for me, but they could not find me since there are three houses belonging to the number 108 and we live at Domaszewski's who is an engineer. I have sent a telegram to my Stach through the Red Cross in Geneva.

What is my Viktoria doing? Terenia often asks about her. Tell her to write to us; we would be most happy to hear from her.

Are you well? Father is feeling a little bit better now.

Do you receive any letters from Jas? When you write to him, please ask him to tell Stach that I was most happy to receive his postcards. Dear Helen, when I received your letter telling me that Stach is alive and together with Jas, a great weight was lifted from my heart. God will continue to look after them. Finally the long awaited spring is coming. You can't imagine how we yearn for some warmth. We are so fed up with frost You can't imagine how the cold got to us!

Are your kids well? I am ending and kissing you, dearest Helen, as well as Barbara, Maks and your children.

Fondly, Ania

Father sends regards to all of you, as well as Terenia.

About a month later mother wrote to father and continued to be frustrated by the erratic incoming as well as outgoing mail, as is evident from her letter.

APRIL 3,1940
LWOW,
SOVIET OCCUPIED POLAND
My dearest Stach,

I am already writing a fifteenth letter, I have received seven post-cards from you, the last one was written on March lst. I was very concerned about you since I had no news from you for two weeks. I wait every day to hear a few words from you.

We have registered for our return. Supposedly, today there were notices for the refugees announcing that they will be able to return on April 26th, if they have obtained passes. The railroad stations that were listed where the train would stop were all in the protectorate; we have hopes that if we are able to go we might be able to go further once we cross the border. I wish so much to be able to go to Helen. With the coming of spring the terrible longing for home awakens within me; that is, if we still have a home. It would be better to live in a rural area at the present since it would be easier to obtain food. Here, at the moment one can get everything if you have money.

Terenia has grown much, looks well, has a good appetite. Sometimes eats three eggs a day,- she likes them best when they are beaten. As long as I am able I give her everything, even apples. My dearest, I would like to leave here as soon as possible so I could be closer to you. This way would be able to send you some packages since there one can buy some things.

I am ending; be of good thoughts and don't worry about us.
I kiss you tenderly.
Your Ania

Dear Daddy,

Renia [Terenia] misses you very much but don't be sad Daddy. I grew a lot and Mommy had to lengthen all my dresses. Daddy, Terenia went through terrible bombing! I was very scared because I thought that they would fall on my back.

I end and kiss your hands (that is what they do in Lwow) and your face.

Terenia

The weeks that followed were full of anticipation as well as apprehension. The anticipated opening of the border on the 26th of April did not materialize for us. But on April 29th, aunt Maria gave birth to a little boy whom she named Krystofer. Since the communist rules were in place and any religious practices forbidden, little Krystofer could not be officially baptized, so the ceremony was secretly performed in the hospital coatroom. My new little cousin was a joy to everyone and gave me an opportunity to be a "big sister" and have someone around who was younger than myself. Unfortunately, the happy event of Krystofer's birth did not dispel the concern over his father's whereabouts. All the members of our family, though we were scattered, were accounted for with the exception of uncle Wacek. All that was known that his regiment fell into Soviet hands. Inquiries made to the Soviet authorities fell on deaf ears. It was not till after the war that we found out that uncle Wacek was executed by the Russians, along with thousands of Polish officers, in Katyn forest. And it was not until the end of the cold war, fifty years later, that the Official list from the NKVD was published, marking him for execution in April 1940.

MAY 1940
PRZEMYSL,
SOVIET OCCUPIED POLAND

It was the second week in May when news came that the border would be open for a short while so that the people who wished to return to their homes could do so. On the appointed day the family packed up what was left of our belongings and took the train to Przemysl, where the trains for the crossing of the border were to be found. Here in Przemysl was more chaos, since the news brought to that city hundreds of people who were displaced by war and yearned to be reunited with their families. This time the registration was handled by black-garbed SS soldiers with their skull and cross-bones emblems flashing on their hats. As they registered the refugees, they were interested in whether you had any German origins or family connections, that is, if you were a "Volksdeutsch". These refugees were immediately permitted to return.

As for us, after spending two nights and days in a crowded and stench-filled railway station, we were told to return to Lwow and wait for further instructions. Weary, dirty and disappointed, our family took a train back to Lwow and to our old place at the Domaszkiewicz house. But the return trip was not without incident.

Before departing for Przemysl, mother and Maria decided to sew into the lining of a suitcase their remaining jewelry as a precaution against any further confiscation that might occur upon the anticipated border crossing. Since Maria had her hands full with the baby, who was now about two weeks old, and mother had me to look after, the job of carrying the "suit case" was intrusted to uncle Alfons.

Hence, it was not till we were back at the Domaszkiewicz' in Lwow, and sorted out the baggage that they realized that "the suitcase" was missing. It seemed that uncle Alfons just forgot it and left it in Przemysl railroad station. This was another major disappointment, as it meant a loss of a good deal of much-needed barter currency.

JUNE 1940
LWOW, SOVIET OCCUPIED POLAND

We resumed our life as before, but with one difference. Grandfather did not return to his old place but came to stay with us, sharing a room with uncle Alfons and Josef. Hildebrandt, who returned with us from Przemysl, did receive a permit to return home and so left Lwow within a few days.

The first spring of the occupation passed, and with it ended hope that the depressing and crushing situation in which we found ourselves would end that season. As summer started, we were saying "let's just wait till next spring; it's bound to change for the better". But the immediate future was not so certain, and for the most part gloomy and at times just depressing. News of constant and random arrests and deportations were reaching us, which made our existence even more unstable. Each trip to the city for any provisions or necessities was made in the knowledge that we might not return home should we get caught in a street raid. This prompted mother never to go to town by herself, but to take me with her so that in any event we would never be separated. The other, humorous side of her preparation consisted of her carrying with us an extra bag which contained a change of underwear. If what she feared had come to pass, we would have been the only two persons in camp with clean underclothes!

The month of June was upon us. During this month I was perfectly happy in the company of my cousins, and with the warm weather could play outside in the lovely park that surrounded the house. In addition, I found a new playmate, Jacek, who was same age as I, the son of the caretaker. We explored various hiding places on the grounds and played hide-and-seek games in which Romek and Barbara sometimes joined us. Of course, we were also curious, and that got Jacek and me into trouble. Since all the adults, with the exception of mother, smoked, the two of us decided to see how it would taste. I was to get some cigarettes and Jacek said that he had the matches. So, after I took one of aunt Maria's cigarettes, we found a hiding place behind the gazebo where we crouched on the ground and very ceremoniously lit the cigarette. Jacek was the first to puff and then handed me the smoke. As I put it into my mouth, I felt a hand on the back of my collar, pulling me up. Startled, I dropped the cigarette and looked behind me— it was aunt Maria, and we were found out. The result was that Jacek received a whipping from his father, and I was under "house arrest" for a couple of days in addition to continuous lectures pointing out my "sins". Needless to say, this episode in early life prevented me from ever trying to smoke again.

The summer was in full swing and it was getting unseasonably warm. Constant rumors of border openings, which always proved to be false, continued to circulate. But other news, of the arrests, was real. Like game in a hunters' drive, we began to feel the catchers' net tighten around us. The pattern of the arrests became clear; all the people that had been displaced from their homes by war and had registered for permission to return, and who had not been accepted for repatriation by the Germans, were systematically arrested and "resettled", that is, deported to the Soviet Union.

Mother's letter to her sister in that month sheds some light on the situation:

JUNE 17,1940

LWOW,

SOVIET OCCUPIED POLAND

My dear Helen,

For your letters, I sincerely thank you; it is always an important moment for us when we receive them.

I presume that good Hildebrandt has already arrived since he left here over three weeks ago. It seems that he was able to manage that. [Since Hildebrandt was working for Mr. Poll, ethnically German, and had a German name, he went home as a "Volksdeutsch"]

At present the committee [for repatriation] has left and they only chose their own "Volksdeutsch" and ones professing to be German. Many people still deceive themselves that all of us will be able to return, but from today I have no such illusions. As you see dear Helen, all our hopes of return are gone, but if only our husbands would return, we could manage.

As you already know, Maria had a little boy, Krystofer, a darling baby.

If only they would release us so we could return to you. I see that as our only salvation, and then would not care what else is happening as long as we would be together. I am very apprehensive that we might be separated even further, but I believe that God is watching over us.

When I receive letters and postcards from Stach, they are the only moments of joy in my life.

We still have no news of Wacek. I received a postcard from aunt Stasia; she wrote that Maryla Koenningburg lost her leg up to the knee. Evidently she fell under a streetcar. We all were terribly shaken by this news.

All of our kids are well. Dear Helen, if they let us leave here and we are unable to come to you, then Miss Gabrysia will take Maria and me to Strachowic, near Warsaw; her brother is a game keeper there.

We thank Barbara [wife of mother's brother Maks] sincerely for her letter.

Helen dear, I am ending and sending lots of kisses for you and your dear children as well as for Barbara and her children, Maks and Bernard.

Very, very fondly yours
Ania
Dear Helen,
We yearn so very much to return to you but it is so hard to get out from here. My only joy is my baby, who, thank God, is doing well. Helen, don't worry about us; take care of yourself, all is going to be well.

Maria with Krystofer
Hugs for the girls, Janusz, Andrzej, Barbara and Maks with children and for you.

Dear Helen
We ask God that we could finally leave. We so much long for our
home. Hugs for all
Luta with family

JUNE 28,1940
LWOW, SOVIET OCCUPIED POLAND

It was Friday and mother and I were in town that day. Returning home in the afternoon we were contented in the knowledge that we once more "escaped the fates." In the evening, the various members of the family sat on the veranda recalling their individual escapes from and near misses of the street dragnets that had occurred during the last month. The evening was warm; the freshness of an early summer surrounded us. June bugs were humming in the dusk; the aroma of flowers was pleasantly drifting through the air while the quietness settled around, giving a lolling effect of peace. It was hard to believe at this moment that only several months ago this was a burning city!

Darkness came and the gathering begun to break up. With the parting "good nights" went expressions of how fortunate we all were for escaping this past week's arrests and, should we survive tonight's arrests, we would be "safe" for the time being.

Since we all slept in the large living room, my "bed" on the floor was against the wall facing the french windows that opened to the veranda. The preparations for the night were more or less simultaneous for all occupants because once the bedding was spread for the night it was difficult to move around without disturbing others. Mother tucked me in after hearing my prayers of thanks for our deliverance from the last weeks' fate and the daily request for providence's protection of father; then sleep came fast.

The next thing I recall was my mother's hand gently nudging me from sleep—it was almost light. There was commotion in the room and as I looked around most of the people were dressed. I rubbed my eyes and sat up, still trying to pull the covers around me. The french doors were still closed but outside were several armed soldiers standing guard. As I looked more closely at them, now fully awake, they appeared different than any Soviet soldiers that I had seen before. These guards were squatty, with ill-fitting uniforms, and on their heads were pointed hats; their round faces were accentuated by high cheek bones and slanted eyes—I recalled that I had seen such faces on my postage stamps; they were Mongols! I had never seen an Asian before so these men, with their guns and expressionless faces, put fear in me, Mother tried to calm me down while helping me to dress, at the same time explaining that we were being arrested. To soothe me, she was reassuring me that we were all going together and that I would be taking a ride on a truck.

There was a Soviet officer in the room overseeing the chaos, shouting out his rules:

"We are doing this for your own good, you must understand" he said. "You are allowed to take with you as much as you can carry. Everything else will be provided for you."

While every adult was trying to pack the "important" clothing and articles which they perceived might be necessary, I slipped out of the house. My destination was the next door cottage of the gardener's family and their son Jacek, my playmate of the last few months. As I knocked at the door and came in, I found the family huddled around the kitchen table, probably wondering if they were next to be taken away.

"You know, Jacek" I started to brag jubilantly, excited at the prospect of this new adventure, "I will get a ride in the truck! In the back of the truck! So, I came to say goodbye…we are leaving."

At this moment, Jacek's mother could no longer hold back her tears. She burst out sobbing and hugged me, muttering:

"Poor child, my poor child, poor people…."

Though I was puzzled at her reaction, I did not dwell on it. Instead, I parted with Jacek and happily skipped back to the main house where preparations for departure were about completed and we were to be loaded unto the lorry. The guards were now stationed in a line that extended from the front door to the truck. The officer took the last head count and gave orders to load. So into the truck went grandfather, stout with his walking cane and panama hat, helped by pale and frail-looking uncle Alfons. Then came aunt Maria, holding the little bundle that was Krystofer, now two months old. She was assisted by Miss Gabrysia, who was carrying extra bundles. Mother followed, holding my hand while I was clutching my treasured possession-my Shirley Temple doll. Then came the Muslewski family— aunt Luta with her husband Josef, with her arm around his, followed by my cousins Romek and Barbara under the watchful eye of their governess, Miss Flora.

The Domaszkiewiczes and Jacek's parents were helping to put our belongings on the truck. They also managed to hastily pack any available food for our journey. Everyone was gloomy, some were crying, and I could not comprehend the gravity of the event since I was excited that I will be riding in the back of the truck!

Finally all were in the open lorry, together with several soldiers who positioned themselves around the perimeter of the truck walls; the back gate of the truck was hoisted up and shut with a bang, the Soviet officer seated himself next to the driver and gave the order to proceed. The vehicle began to move on the winding road from Zielona Gora to town. We waved to the people left behind until they disappeared from view when the truck turned the bend heading for the railroad station.

A warm summer day was just beginning when we arrived at Personowka train station in Lwow, where there were already hundreds of people who, just like us, had been caught in this night's dragnet and were being unloaded from military lorries. Cordons of soldiers encircled the unloading area, while officers were in charge of allocating deportees into the waiting cattle-cars. Our turn came. We all tried to stay close together, so as not to get separated. As we were unloaded from the truck we were marched by our guards to a nearby railcar.

The wooden cattle car had its gates wide open and in order to ease entry a plank was set up on an incline. Beside the entrance stood another Soviet soldier, armed only with a side arm, overseeing the boarding as well as keeping count of how many people went into the car. Just like cattle we proceeded, dragging our belongings with us. My enthusiasm over the truck ride quickly evaporated in these dismal surroundings, and fear came over me.

"Mommy, mommy…let's run away from here!" I began to cry, tightening my grip on mother's hand as we were climbing the plank into the train-car.

The Soviet soldier tried to console me, saying in Russian that there was nothing to be afraid of, that we were just going to take a train ride. That did not reassure me, as I started to scream and cry even more. Mother had to pick me up and carry me in, since I was not about to enter the forbidding confines of this train voluntarily.

The train-car already contained some people who settled themselves on one of the bottom shelves that were constructed on both ends of the cattle-car. We, mother and I, and aunt Maria with Krystofer, climbed to the front top plank shelf that extended from one side of the car wall to the other, thus having the opportunity to be near the small top window. Our folding camping bed, which was among the articles that we were able to take with us, was set up against the wall. The cot was for grandfather, so he could rest in better comfort than the present situation provided. The rest of the members of our group were trying to accommodate themselves and their meager belongings as best as possible.

The time stretched on, as the heat of the day was rising and more people were being brought into the station and loaded onto the train. The commotion, shouting of people looking for relatives and friends, intermingled with Soviet commands, continued. As the day progressed, in addition to the people arrested, onlookers began to arrive, bringing food and clothing for their friends who were scheduled to be shipped out. They were held back by the cordon of guards, but were able to pass the goods hand over hand to their detained friends.

Dusk fell and the prison train was filled. The headcount of each car was taken by the guards, then the walk-up plank was removed and the large sliding door slammed shut and locked from the outside. Darkness enveloped us in the car: no lights, only the four small windows at each corner of the car filtered in the last rays of the day. Silence engulfed us. Like a funeral march the echo of the slamming of gates continued for the next half hour while we sat in dark silence and waited. Then there were no more "bangs"; just some orders were shouted, and the train slowly began to move. We didn't go very far, only to the next station in Lwow where there was another several hours of standing and waiting; the doors were never opened. Then again there was some motion of the train—more cars were being added that were also packed with people. Finally the train started moving out of the station towards the east.

Chapter 9

Germany-Itzehoe

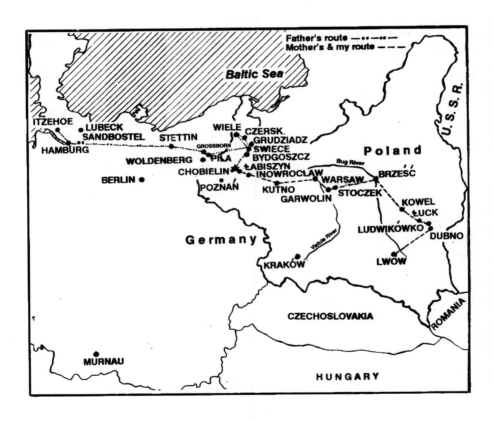

JANUARY 1940
ITZEHOE, GERMANY

The new year started in the camp just as any other day there with the usual daily 8 A.M. check of all prisoners. At that time everyone had to leave the barracks except the company's "quarters man " who happened to have duty on that particular day. While the prisoners went through the daily roll call and head-count, the cleaning crews, which consisted of the Polish enlisted prisoners of war, went about the barracks mopping the floors. This daily routine only varied once a month when the camp administration performed the so called "stamp check".

The "stamp check" was done with a comic precision; the Germans would bring a table outside, behind which three camp officials, reinforced with books that contained names and photographs of each prisoner, would sit and check their captives. Each prisoner was called out one by one, by name and rank, and identified with his photograph from the book against his own photo ID that he wore around his neck. The process took several hours during which, despite inclement weather, all had to be standing outdoors and endure not only their captors' regimentation but also the whims of weather.

Though the check was not a welcome routine to the POWs, it was an effective procedure for the camp officials to spot escapees. There were many escapes, or rather attempted ones, that ended futilely, since if one succeeded in leaving the actual camp, the neighboring German population was on constant watch and cooperated in snaring the fugitives. In the first months of imprisonment the recaptured escapees were returned to the camp and punished by solitary confinement; but as time progressed and escape attempts increased, the Germans issued strict orders:

"Any escaping prisoners when caught, will be sent to a concentration camp." With that threat the attempted escapes were completely eliminated for at least the immediate future.

Life for father continued unchanged and he sustained himself with his correspondence to aunt Helen, who by now, though herself in hiding so as not to be deported to Germany for forced labor, managed to write and send meager packages to father and uncle Jas.

JANUARY 31, 1940
ITZEHOE, GERMANY
Dear Helen,

I received from you a post card dated Jan. 20 on Jan 25. Thank you very much for remembering me. I send two post cards as well as a telegram to Ania, through some friends in Belgium, so I hope she will finally know that I am alive.

I was happy to hear news about possibilities of Ania living at Mr. P. when she will be able to return. But I doubt that the return from Lwow will come before spring; but that is understandable since it is not prudent to travel in such cold weather. I worry about her if she has enough money and warm clothes, as well as heat in the house, because you know Helen how susceptible she is to colds.

If Viktoria could find out if Jackowiak returned, who was with me. If he returned, tell him to write what has happened to them after crossing the Vistula River. [Jackowiak was father's orderly who managed to cross the river with the rest of father's company]

For the bread that I received, I thank you Helen. I have sent you 40 marks which I ask you use for your needs and by so doing you will please me that I can at least help a little to ease your predicament.

Today Jas received a letter from Barbara [Maks's wife]; we read it together. There were some news about our apartment. I was sorry to hear about our furniture; [Germans appropriated it and sent it to Germany] maybe it is funny, but a person attaches themselves to objects.

Helen, do you have any photographs of Ania and Terenia, because I lost all the ones I had. Soon I will be able to send my photo. Thank

*Barbara for the long letter. Be of good thoughts because everything is
in the hands of God, and He is just.*

Stach

*Dear Helen, thank Barbara for a informative letter and all the
news it contained. Tell Bemard that today I received the bread that
he sent me.*

Jas

The reference that my father is making in the letter to Mr. P. is about
Mr. Poll who was grandfather's German friend and neighbor at the
Jaruzyn estate. He was very helpful to aunt Helen and other members of
our family, so father thought that he might help us when we would return.

FEBRUARY 20,1940

ITZEHOE, GERMANY

Dear Helen

*The package with biscuits I have received February 7, for which I
thank you very much. Finally, I send you money in the sum of 40
marks. As far as the money is concerned, I will be sending it and I
ask you to use half of every sum for your needs and keep the other
half for Ania. Do that please Helen, and you will give me great
pleasure.*

*From Ania I have no news. This lack of news worries me greatly,
since the skimpy news that do come from Lwow are unsettling. I am
concerned that Ania or Terenia would not get sick because there is a
typhoid epidemic there. The bitter cold makes the misery of my poor
beloved ones worse. Sometimes it is very hard for me, but then there
are moments that I gratify myself with thoughts of their possible
return. We just have to wait and believe in God.*

*I received the photographs, for which I thank you; I was happy to
see my dear ones. I thank Bemard for the package which I received
on the 15th of February. Also thank Maria for her regards. I am
glad to see that the young ladies grew so much and weigh a lot.
Danka weighs even more than Ania, which is very good. [Maria*

*and Danka are aunt Helen's teenage daughters] Soon I will send my
photo. We think about you a great deal and we deeply believe in justice. We put a great deal of hope into the coming of spring which
awakens hope and new life.*

Ending, hugs for all the children, for Maks regards.

Stach

[Post script from uncle Jas]

Helen

*Jackowiak, when he wrote to Stach, wrote a few words to me.
Thank him and give regards to all the people.* [This is a reference
to the people that worked on the estate]

By the end of March father's efforts to locate mother materialized, since
she was able to contact the Red Cross in Geneva. Thus on March 4, 1940
he received a card:

Laut eines Telegrammes aus Lwow datient 22.2.40

*Wir sind gesund, schreibe oft, antworter Lwow Zielona Gora 1
08 Anna Mikosz*

Comite international de Ia Croix-Rouge.

Agence centrale des prisoners de guerre.

*[We are well. Your writing has been received. Lwow, Zielona
Gora 108, Anna Mikosz]*

Father now had mother's address but direct correspondence did not
materialize till many months later. Nevertheless, mother continued to
write to aunt Helen and she in turn forwarded the news to father.

APRIL 9, 1940

ITZEHOE, GERMANY

Dear Helen,

*I am writing to you after a long while. I had some other writing
obligations, so that there was a long pause. Today, Jas received your letter in which you mentioned that Ania has written; that might be, but
I have not received anything from her. That lack of correspondence
worries me, since a few of my friends here have received information*

that the Moskovites are resettling the Polish population into the depths of Russia. If that fate met them it would be terrible.

I have sent 250 marks to Bernard's address, so you could buy necessary things for Ania and Terenia; you will know what is best to buy.

Jas and I are separated, he is living on the floor above me.

In March I have received seven parcels, and two in April, for which I warmly thank you. Give a kiss from me to Danusia for the postcard that she wrote to me; it made me happy. As soon as will be able I will write to her personally. Let her write whenever she would like.

Did you go to Warsaw? Time for us passes lazily and monotonously, with only small insignificant news. I am sending my likeness so as to remind you how I look.

Ending, regards to Bernard, kisses for Danusia and Marysia, embraces for Janusz and Andrzej.

Stach

[PS from uncle Jas]

Is Karol and Stefan still working? Tell them to write to me about the work on the estate. What is happening to Maks?

Your Jas

Uncle Jas' postscript refers to his two cousins who were now employed by the German overseer Mr. Turman, and to uncle Maks, whom aunt Helen also managed to place and by so doing avoided his being sent to a labor camp or to Germany as a forced laborer.

The passage of time, which father referred to as being slow and monotonous, was interrupted in April when the loud speakers that were scattered throughout the camp began to shout out news of the German march on Denmark and Norway. Since the camp was located only fifty miles south of the Danish border, the invading German panzer divisions rumbled north on the road that wound past the camp. Through the barbed-wire fence father and his comrades watched the continuous, sprawled out lines of motor vehicles going to their next target for conquest. Above, the skies were clouded with airplanes heading in the same direction.

The camp's loud speakers were never allowed to rest, but instead blazed out continually the news of German conquests. The propaganda news fervor lasted about a week and ended as abruptly as it had begun. The news of these victories dampened the hopes of the POWs, since it appeared that the conflict was not ending but rather beginning. In addition to the unwelcome news of German victories, father received news of Polish nationals in Soviet occupied Poland that was beginning to filter into the camp.

> *May 3, 1940*
> *ITZEHOE, GERMANY*
> *Dear Helen,*
>
> *Thank you very much for the delicious pound cake and eggs which we received all in good condition. A few were cracked but nothing destroyed. Dear Helen, all that I received from you is too much; it is unnecessary because I think about your effort and Ania's dilemma. So please don't send me more than one package a month. Do that Helen and I will give you a hug.*
>
> *From the lst of May the border is open; maybe the dear ones will return. I had 5 letters from Ania and a postcard. I kiss you, embrace Danka and all.*
>
> *Stach*

By the end of the month another letter was written that included instructions and new camp regulations that the Germans had implemented for the POW's mail, both incoming and outgoing.

> *May 28, 1940*
> *ITZEHOE, GERMANY*
> *Dear Helen*
>
> *In the previous letter written to you and Danka, I mentioned that there are news of people returning from Russia. [Poland occupied by*

the Soviets] Many of my colleagues received postcards from families who are on that side. I have not received anything from Ania since April 4th but expect some news from her upon her return and that maybe soon.

From the 15th of June you will only be permitted to write back on sections of paper that will be sent to you by us, since no other letters will be delivered to us. Therefore, if I will not have Ania's address by then, she won't be able to write to me. I will be writing to you Helen, and if you would be so kind and send her the return piece of paper in an envelope so Ania will write back. These rules are for all the mail, in case they return to this side after June 15th. Mail rules are changed, one letter and 2 postcards per month and only so many times you can write back since you will only have that amount of official paper. The June 15th date includes also parcels, hence I will send two colored stickers which you have to put on the parcel. Parcels without the sticker will not be delivered. It is allowed for us to receive two parcels a month. Tell that to everybody and to Bernard.

In one of the letters Danka mentioned that some of our things survived in Chobielin; that is good. Ania will be happy to hear that. I doubt if she will be able to come to you. Life in Warsaw is very hard and expensive, e.g. one kilo of butter is 80 zl. Therefore it would be best for them to live in the country. I long terribly for Ania and all of you and I yearn for freedom and here it does not look that the end of war is going to be soon. Have to wait patiently. Anyway, what do we know here, almost nothing because what you read and hear is far from reality. I am sending to you Helen warm greetings, embraces for Danka and the rest.

Stach

Regards from Jas

Father continues to search for mother through the same route as well as other avenues. His frustration is evident in the letter to uncle Bernard, mother's brother who went to live in the part of Poland that the Germans referred as General Government.

JUNE 4,1940
ITZEHOE, GERMANY
Dear Bernard,

I am writing to you again. I would write more often but I have only a limited number of letters, and that is the reason that I can't write often. I have sent you a printed card with instructions how to send postcards and letters, as well as packages, after June 15. Until you receive a letter or postcard from me with the appropriate sticker on which you have to write back, write as usual. The same is for parcels, for which I will send stickers that you have to attach to the package. They will only deliver a package with the appropriate sticker.

When Ania returns I will still ask you to be so good and send me the food as usual, since I won't be able to ask her because she will be living in the Protectorate and the conditions there are difficult. This month you can send everything as usual.

How is work, are the conditions that you have good? It is true that it is hard everywhere, but a person can survive a great deal. We have to wait quietly with faith and believe that justice will triumph.

Many friends here received news that the Bolsheviks deported their families as far as Siberia. But I also have news that others have returned from Russia. [This refers to Soviet occupied Poland]

I am worried about our family and about Ania and Terenia, because it is already two months since I heard from them. I am living through very depressing moments, worrying about their fate. I hear that supposedly the officers were released from Russia; maybe Wacek will be able to return to Wilno. [Wilno was uncle Wacek's hometown]

It seems Maks is not acting very nice, that might cost him a lot.

Days are hopelessly gray and pass slowly and the end does not seem in sight. We often talk about all of you with Jas. Write, embracing you, kisses for Helen.

Your Stach

Regards from Jas

Father's apprehensions and fears mounted as the months passed by and he was still without any concrete news of our whereabouts. Two weeks after writing to uncle Bernard, father dispatched another letter to aunt Helen.

JUNE 22,1940

ITZEHOE, GERMANY

Dear Helen

I can't understand what is happening with our family in Lwow. Why is Ania not writing, and why are they not coming back? Almost all my friends here have news of their families returning, since the deadline for the return has been June 6th. I had no news for almost two months, since April 8th. I cannot describe how much I am worrying because the Moskovites are deporting to Siberia those that have not returned. That fate met many families, because friends are receiving letters from there. They have deported captain Centnaroswski's wife and child, the one that was at Maria's wedding. I have a premonition that this has happened to our family; this would be a tragedy. Poor Ania and Terenia.

Your Stach

There are several more letters that followed in the month ahead. Unknown to father or aunt Helen, we had already met our fate and while father was trying to reach us in Lwow, we were deep in the Soviet wilderness.

JULY 2,1940

ITZEHOE, GERMANY

Dear Helen.

I have received parcels from June 20, and a letter from June 24. I thank you deeply for so much kindness and remembrance.

The pajamas are beautiful, such a luxury! I ask you to thank Bernard in my and Jas's name for the parcels that things, particularly cigars for Jas. I can't write to him because the enclosed card I want to keep for Ania. I have received all letters and parcels. I am awaiting Ania's return. I have some money for her. I will thank God when they return. I embrace all.
Stach

AUGUST 12,1940
ITZEHOE, GERMANY
Dear Helen,
Last time I have sent you 50 marks. This money is exclusively for your use, as well as all the money that I have sent so far, except for 250 that Bernard has sent. That money is for Ania's use. I sympathize with you Helen, life is hard but you can't give up, one must trust, believe and wait. From Ania I have no word since May 20th, except that she has sent to you. Nobody can understand the apprehension and worry that I am living through. My poor loved ones. Please write Helen, you have the stickers.
Dear Helen, embracing Danka and all.
Stach

SEPTEMBER 12,1940
ITZEHOE, GERMANY
Dear Helen,
I don't have any news from Ania, which indescribably worries me since all kinds of contrary news are circulating. There are moments that I see their fate as very grim but there are moments of hope also, but these don't come often. One great sorrow fills my soul and deep down I feel resentment towards Ania that she did not listen to my wish and not left Chobielin and that she did not return with you. Oh, how much more easy it would be for me to survive the imprisonment if she

was here. I think of them all the time without stop; and a lack of letter since May, that is hardship and it is really a hard life. Helen, I live on memories because we really were so happy.

Believe me Helen, that my longing for Ania and Terenia is inde-scribable; they were everything in my life. But you understand that Jas and I are happy about the change in your residence, we think that it will be better there.

The parcels that I received from you were slightly damaged because of the tomatoes. Dear Helen I ask you don't send any of them because they crush and destroy the sugar, bouillon and the rest of the good stuff. And it is a shame to lose all those things. Please, Helen in the next packages could you always send bread because it seems I eat quite a bit of it.

I will now send you a little bit of money regularly for your own use, as I wrote before. For Ania's account send money especially marked.

Ending, Helen; have good thoughts and the sun will shine. There are already rays that bring hope for better tomorrow.

Embraces for Danka and the rest of family, be brave.

Stach

P.S. Did you write to Ania?

The reference in the letter to aunt Helen's change in residency is that since Mr. Turman could not hide her any longer Franz Poll once again came to the rescue, as aunt Helen and the children were in danger of being sent to Germany as forced labor. This time he took them to his estate and put them up in his summer cottage on the grounds, where the children had to work in the fields, but not aunt Helen since her health was in a serious decline.

Then the news that father most dreaded came. Mother was able to send a postcard to father after we reached a Soviet camp that was located in the central Soviet Union. Wanting to inform aunt Helen of our fate, father wrote the following letter:

SEPTEMBER 23,1940
ITZEHOE, GERMANY
Dear Helen,

Long and with longing I have waited for the news from Ania, and finally I receive it. The news that they were deported into the center of Russia fell upon me like lightning. Even today I can't believe that it could be true; that they, my dearest in the world, are condemned to poverty and wandering, without adequate means and among strange people. Dear Helen, my sorrow is indescribable; I have no words to describe the state of my soul. So many people returned, all the wives from the regiment, women with children, by foot or on wagons, all came back in autumn as well as many other families: only our family tried it so careless. I can't forgive Wacek that he dragged you to Garwolin, and Josef that he was so blind and pulled everyone to Lwow with himself. The news from the deported is terrible. Everyone has to work very hard, women in the fields or in the barns, men are employed in cutting down forests. The living and food conditions are frightening. My beloved Ania, so frail, is she going to survive all this, or father? We have to save them, move every stone. The only hope is Zwieszchowski, he has contacts and maybe he can obtain an exit for them to America, where they could sit out the war. That is the best and the most feasible thing because in Russia exists some kind of American committee But we have to hurry before they are completely wasted out.

There was an episode about one of the wives returning from Russia after her mother, who now lives near Poznan, petitioned the German Consul in Moscow and presented papers from local authorities. I can't do anything for them. Helen, our only hope is in Zwieszchowski who can do this. Please send me his address because I want to write to him personally. Ania's letter that was supposed to be in a parcel that Pradum sent, I did not receive.

Hugs for Danka and all.
Stach

Chapter 10

Journey to Soviet Union, Nuziar

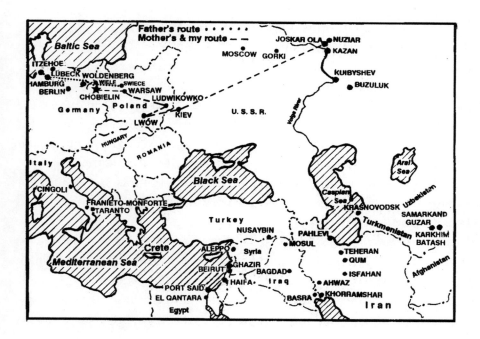

JUNE 1940
JOURNEY INTO THE SOVIET UNION

Looking around the primitive cramped quarters of the rail car, everyone was uncomfortable, hot and tired. In addition to this dismal situation, the two month-old Krystofer kept crying almost continuously despite the efforts of several women who tried to rock him. We were enclosed in these confines with only the food that we were able to bring with us. There was no water; the only fluids were thermoses of tea and coffee that were in our possession. The toilet facility consisted of a hole in the floor of the car; a piece of cloth was hung around it for some semblance of privacy.

The train kept speeding on east throughout the day and it was not till night that we stopped at a rail station somewhere in the Ukraine. The lack of motion awakened most of the people and the ones who were near the windows tried to assess where we were by peering through the openings. It appeared that the train was stopped on the outer fringes of the station. The guards began to pour out of their car and started to slide open the doors of each car while positioning two of themselves at each entrance. With the open doors came the fresh warm night air and its welcome relief. Everyone inhaled deeply and moved towards the open doors where the soldiers were motioning and giving instructions for people to line up for food. Out of the train-cars the deportees gingerly started to emerge and head toward some Russian women who were tending kettles. Mother, aunt Luta, Gabrysia, and Flora scrounged up some pots and headed for the food line. The food was some watery substance that was supposed to be soup and tea. Though it was not appetizing it was a warm meal, the first one in twenty-four hours. In addition, some water was found and mother came upon local peasant women who had some milk for which she bartered with them.

After several hours of stretching our legs and inhaling the outside air, we were rounded up and put back into the train cars. The Soviet soldiers began to shout orders to get back in and the doors were once again slammed shut. The train was on the move again before the light of dawn. The system of traveling during the day and stopping at night in order to "feed" people became a routine. Through the day the train kept pushing north-east for almost two weeks; the station signs were the clue where we were heading: Kiev, Kharkov, Gorki.

Beyond Gorki a few of the railcars were detached and left at a side station while we continued into another equally small, isolated stop that was in the midst of woods and consisted of a wooden hut. Nearby was a river, that we later found out was named Vituaga. Here, we were finally released from the confines of the railcar and ordered to unload and proceed a short distance to the nearby banks of the river where waiting for us were moored rafts. Reluctantly and cautiously we proceeded to follow orders and climb onto them.

As the rafts reached the opposite shore another group of guards was waiting and herding us into waiting trucks. The rafts then kept going back for the next load of prisoners and the process continued until all were loaded into the trucks.

Finally, when all the people had crossed and were in the trucks, the convoy proceeded on a sandy road that led through a heavily forested area. Several times one or another truck would get stuck in the deep sand of the road and the rest of the caravan would stop to give the driver some help. By late evening, though it was still very light, we reached a clearing.

JULY 14, 1940
NUZIAR, MARIJSKA OBLAST, USSR

It was the evening of July 14th when the trucks that carried us drove through what seemed an endless forest until they reached a clearing in the woods that had several large log barracks. It's name was Nuziar, in Marijska Oblast district, whose capital was Yoshkar-Ola. This was one of the numerous camps, referred to it by the Soviets as "settlements, " that were scattered throughout the country. Although it was late evening, it was still light when the convoy came to a stop and the deportees were allocated quarters in the order of their arrival.

Since the steady influx of prisoners was continuing to arrive, Nuziar *posiolek* had no ready accommodations for all of our transport. In order to put the people under some roof, our family group was allocated a crude wood shed that consisted of four walls and a roof, with a couple of wooden tables. Before we were able to settle in, the settlement authorities provided all the people with something that was supposed to be soup and some hot water, known as *kipiatok*, but we had to bring our own utensils.

After consuming the warm food and cleaning ourselves, we began the process of settling into the new quarters.

Here, we arranged ourselves on the floor of the shed, as well as on the tables that served as "beds", with grandfather on his folding cot. Uncle Alfons was very weak and pale, his heart condition worsened by our arduous and exhausting journey. Grandfather, not managing much better, stretched himself on his bed and the rest of us, at the moment content to be out of the confines of the boxcar, spread our meager, dirty bedding on various places on the floor.

It was a hot, humid summer night infested with mosquitoes and numerous other insects that began to attack us with a vengeance. Despite all these discomforts we tried to settle down for the night, which turned out to be not so tranquil since, besides the mosquitoes, the hut, like every other place in the camp, was infested with bed-bugs. These creatures came out in droves and kept us up all night.

After a sleepless night, dirty, bitten up by mosquitoes and bed-bugs, we emerged from the hut and started to survey the surroundings. At the same time, one of the guards came with instructions as to where to report in order to get our food rations and further orders. Several adults from the family followed the soldier to the appointed office where the daily ration coupons were allocated. In addition, the guard informed them, pointing towards the end of the clearing, that there was a public bath. These baths were actually Turkish style baths which were called "bania" and were all over the Soviet Union, I presume in an attempt to get rid of lice which were a fact of life here. Since there was only one "bania", the use was by women on one day and men on the other. Thus alternating the days.

Happy at the prospect of a bath, and since this was women's day, all the females ventured towards the wooden cabin at the edge of the clearing where to our surprise was also a small lake. The placid body of water shimmered in the mid-summer sunlight; its shores were overgrown with an abundance of water lilies.

As we marched into the bathhouse we were able to for the first time in several weeks to wash ourselves. I recall the wonderful feeling of sitting in a wooden tub full of hot water and I did not mind mother scrubbing me extra hard to remove the accumulated dirt. It was a novelty to sit in the steamy room observing, with childish curiosity, all the different shapes of the naked women.

The bathing ritual completed, mother took me to the next section where I put on clean clothes and, after dressing ourselves, we left the hut. Before returning to our quarters, we stopped at the lake's edge where mother washed the dirty clothes. Carrying the wet clothes, mother and I had started back when we spotted one of the camp guards talking to uncle Josef. Fortunately it turned out not to be an interrogation but an order to move our quarters to another wooden structure that was apparently designated as a school/auditorium, where several other families were to be housed temporarily with us.

Since we were the first to arrive, our family took over the elevated part of this one-room structure that was intended to be a stage. Uncle Alfons, still feeling very badly, was set up in a corner and a partition was made for him by hanging a blanket in order to give him some privacy. Grandfather was nearby to him with his now inseparable cot. The rest of us made our beds on various parts of the floor, but we were given some straw to put under our bedding.

AUGUST 1940
NUZIAR, USSR

During the following several days the guards were trying to assert themselves and kept pulling people in for interrogations. One of their targets was uncle Josef, who they thought was a Polish general, and therefore questioned him continuously. In addition, our nights, though uncomfortable because of the bed bugs, were constantly interrupted by guards who would wake us up several times a night to take a head count. There were no barbed wires or gates, but it was still a prison with overseers and guards who controlled everyone's moves. There was strict control by the camp authorities over individuals and everyone over the age of sixteen was forced to work in order to eat. The work was in the forest, cutting wood, and one had to make the "norm" (a certain daily amount designated by the authorities) in order to get food coupons with which you could get bread and soup in the communal kitchen. In our family, only aunt Maria (who had the baby), grandfather and I were exempt from this mandatory labor.

Left to myself, with aunt Maria busy with Krystofer and grandfather staying close to the ailing uncle Alfons, I explored our new surroundings and met numerous children who became playmates, in particular a boy of my age named Otto. Otto and I roamed the bleak grounds of the camp and entertained ourselves with make-believe exploits, since the adults were occupied with the rigors of the new life and had no time for us. One day, after playing near the cabin where Otto's family lived, I was skipping along back to our hut. It was a lovely morning with the sun shining brightly, making the camp look almost friendly. The return route led me past the hut of on official who was overseeing the camp. As I was about to scurry by, a male voice called out to me:

"Where are you running, little one?" I turned around abruptly and there in the doorway stood the military overseer of the camp. He was a young man with a pleasant expression in a typical greenish khaki, ill fitted Russian uniform. His high boots, at least two sizes too big, were his symbol of success since the rest of the population could only afford the felt *valonki*.

"Come here, don't be afraid. I have something for you." Gingerly I turned around and walked toward him, since I knew one had to obey, but never to trust, him. As I walked into his obscure and dingy office, where I knew that if one were summoned here it was trouble, my eyes scanned the sparse surroundings. On the main wall hung an oversized, cheap picture of Stalin, together with some slogans which I could not read. The window was open, letting in the sunshine as well as the multitude of bugs which everyone got used to, and by it stood a crude table which served as his desk, together with two chairs. As he moved towards the desk, I saw a brightly colored foil box on his gray table. He reached for the box, taking the lid off and thrusting the open container in front of my face. I was stunned. I had not seen chocolates in months! "Oh what a wonderful aroma", I thought.

"You see, little one, since you have no Daddy to bring bon-bons to you, I brought them for you…All the way from Moscow! Come on, don't be shy, have one!" he coaxed me.

I was ready to lift my hand and indulge in this unbelievable morsel when my mother's words flashed through my head. "Remember, never take anything from the Russian soldiers. It is a trick to get something from you. Remember...."

"No thank you sir, I…I am not hungry." I almost choked on the lie! I turned around swiftly, trying to get away from the tempting aroma and the sight, before I would lose my resistance.

"Wait a minute, what is your hurry, all I want to do is be nice to you. Sit down here." He motioned to the chair by the wall while he sat on the desk, still holding the open box of chocolates in front of him. I obeyed but kept my eyes glued to the floor—the sight of the chocolates was unbearable.

"You are here with your mother, aren't you?" he started.

"Yes sir" was my response as I began to fidget with the hem of my dress.

"Where is your father?"

"I don't know" (Mother instructed me not to tell them anything about my father being an army officer, but instead to say that he was a postal worker. This way it would be safe.)

"Oh, I am sorry to hear that. What did your father do in Poland?" I heard his pleasant voice and the smell of chocolates permeated my nostrils. I kept thinking "what shall I do?" Oh, I wished mother was here to protect me. Why do I have to say that daddy was a postal worker? This is getting complicated, this man is going to keep on asking questions and maybe take me away from mother—that was what I been told happens to some children.

"He is dead. My father is dead." I blurted out and started crying, not for my father whom I knew was alive someplace, but because I could not stand any longer the torture of refusal of the chocolates!

The soldier thought that I was crying for my father, and finally put the box down on the desk, closing it. Then he patted my head saying:

"Don't cry, little one, we are taking care of you and your mother. Go home...go." I jumped off the chair and gingerly headed toward the door, wiping my eyes with the back of my hand. As soon as I was outside, I broke into a mad dash for our dwelling.

As I returned to our quarters on the stage of the schoolhouse, I found mother and my aunts hovering around uncle Alfons' cubicle. I was told that he was very sick. In the meantime, Miss Flora went to look for a doctor who had been in the rail car with us on our journey there.

Shortly she returned with the doctor, who examined uncle and advised that the camp authorities should be advised so they could take him to a hospital. There was a great amount of reluctance to do so, since no one trusted the Soviets and everyone was apprehensive of any separation. But uncle's condition was serious; he was unconscious. Therefore, the guard reluctantly was approached and asked for help. That brought several Russians to our quarters to assess the situation and, after some time had elapsed, they returned with a truck and stretcher to take uncle Alfons to the hospital. They did not permit anyone from the family to go with him, so we stood around watching the guards carry the pale, thin and unconscious man out into the waiting truck. Everyone stood outside watching the vehicle meander through the camp onto the sandy road that disappeared into the dense forest. The mood in our group was gloomy. Aunt Maria tried to console grandfather that it was the best for uncle Alfons to be in hospital and that he would get proper care.

Within two hours the truck was back at the commandant's hut and one of the guards came over to inform us that uncle Alfons died on the way and that someone should make arrangements to bury him.

Though the news of uncle's death, because of his poor health, should not have been a surprise, it did jolt everyone. Mr. Wozimirski and uncle Josef began to make preparations for next morning's burial since it was too late in the day to complete the task.

My aunts, mother, miss Flora and Gabrysia were consoling each other as well as grandfather in their grief in losing brother, friend and son. The news of uncle's death traveled quickly through the camp, since he was the first casualty. Most of the people in the camp were Polish Jews, with the exception of our group and three or four other families who were Catholic, and there was no clergy to conduct the funeral.

Next morning, early, before the burial, my cousins Barbara, Romek and I went to gather water lilies at the nearby lake, for the upcoming funeral which was due to start within an hour. Our task completed, we gathered with the rest of the family in front of the commandant's hut where all the inhabitants of the camp turned out in order to take uncle Alfons to his final rest.

The cortege consisted of Otto, my playmate, who was Jewish, carrying a crude wooden cross, followed by a small horse drawn cart on which lay the simple pine coffin of uncle Alfons, covered with the water lilies that we gathered for him. Immediately behind the cart was our family group, followed by the rest of the camp's inhabitants of all ages. Slowly the procession started on the same sandy road into the woods that brought us here only a few weeks ago. We did not go far from camp when the procession stopped near a freshly dug grave at the roadside. Here the simple coffin was set in the ground and immediately covered with dirt. The cross that Otto carried was placed at the grave's head and the flowers covered the grave mound. Mr. Wozimirski read some prayers, after which everyone returned slowly to the camp.

SEPTEMBER 1940
NUZIAR, USSR

The work routine of the camp started at 6:00 AM, when most of the people would leave for the lumber camp where they worked. Besides this being strenuous labor, the workers were attacked by the multitude of mosquitoes that made the arduous work even harder. In order to protect herself from insects, mother devised a work costume that consisted of grandfather's pajamas, and her head was wrapped with one of Krystofer's diapers. Aunt Luta was assigned work as a cleaning woman for the two-room school which the children aged 7 to 15 attended, including my friend Otto.

In the first week of September, people in our lodging began to get sick with what appeared to be stomach flu. The first one to come down with it was aunt Luta, and after a couple of days with no relief the authorities took her to the hospital in Yoshkar Ola, where she was diagnosed as having typhoid. By the time the authorities came back with the news, several other people in our quarters were coming down with it and the disease was spreading through the camp. Cousin Romek, miss Gabrysia, aunt Maria and mother were the next victims of typhoid, while the last from our family to get it was Uncle Josef. Since there were so many people stricken, the sick were divided between several hospitals in the vicinity.

One by one, as they got well, the sick returned to the camp, devastated and weakened by the disease. They were but shadows of their former selves, and at times even too weak to walk unaided. Uncle Josef did not return.

Aunt Luta was in the worst shape, completely wasted away. She kept asking about uncle Josef; "when is he returning from the hospital?" Everyone was avoiding telling her the news that he had died a week ago, thinking that tragic blow would be fatal to her in her present condition. But after a small family conference, it was decided that mother was to break the sad news to aunt Luta.

When the camp authorities informed grandfather of uncle Josef's death, they said that he had already been buried at that time. They never gave him any information about the whereabouts of his grave.

OCTOBER 1940
NUZIAR, USSR

Autumn was here, and although mother and Luta were too weak to work, our group was managing with minimal food which was supplemented by selling articles of clothing and gathering berries and mushrooms in the woods. Also, by now additional cabins were completed so we were moved to new living quarters. Though the log cabin was of a crude construction, it was better than the accommodation at the last quarters. The logs themselves were just stacked on top of each other with moss filling the crevices between them. The inside was divided into six "rooms" that were assigned to various families. The dividing wall of the rooms did not reach the ceiling; again one had no privacy but the warm air from the stove would be able to partially heat the rooms. The main room was the entrance, which contained a wood burning stove and served as a communal kitchen and eating area and was the only one which had heat.

Grandfather, Romek, Mr. Wozimirski, miss Flora and miss Gabrysia occupied one room, while aunt Maria with Krystofer, aunt Luta, Basia, mother and I had the other room close to the kitchen. The rest of the rooms were assigned: one to Otto's family (his mother and father, who was a lawyer). The fourth room had the Tepper family, comprised of the parents and their daughter Maryla (my age) and her governess, Miss Maria. Another cubicle went to an elegant older married couple; the husband was also a lawyer. The last room contained four young siblings in their twenties, two brothers and two sisters.

The cubicles contained two tiered planked beds stacked against each wall. The sleeping planks also had straw and as we soon found out, the ever present bed bugs. The only way to eliminate the pests was to pour some gasoline on the planks and light it for a second and quickly extinguish it.

Not the safest process, but it would give a temporary reprieve from the bugs and lice. A few steps beyond the cabin was a small outhouse, which proved to be difficult to reach when the snows come down.

Soon we settled ourselves as best we could into our new quarters. Krystofer was thriving in spite of the poor conditions, and I was content to have my playmates under the same roof. Grandfather, on the other hand, was making his daily treks, weather permitting, to the surrounding woods looking for mushrooms, but this activity resulted in a scratch on one of his toes. Being a diabetic, the cut did not heal and became infected in spite of the precautions we took. The infected toe was getting worse and the infection was spreading to the rest of the foot. Our friend, the doctor from the voyage, advised us to ask the authorities for help, which we did.

They decided that grandfather should go next day to the hospital with the next horse cart that was transporting the sick to and from there. As always, whenever anyone had to be separated, there was a great deal of apprehension. But since Mr. Wozimirski was delegated to drive the almost daily cart, it made grandfather more at ease in leaving us.

Also, because of these trips Mr. Wozimirski was able to report back to us about grandfather's state of health, which was not good. Upon first examination, the local doctor wanted to amputate grandfather's leg since gangrene was spreading. Grandfather refused the operation because he did not see that he would be able to survive it under the prevailing conditions and he saw no aim in further suffering. So, on October 28th he died. Mr. Wozimirski came back with the sad news, and he and Romek were allowed to return to the hospital in order to attend grandfather's burial and locate uncle Josef's grave. Hence the two men were buried in the same cemetery.

This was the third death in the family in the short span of three months; a forbidding outlook for the rest of us; all the adult men were dead. Romek, a teenager, was left as well as Mr. Wozimirski, the adopted family member who took upon himself to help us since mother, aunt Luta and miss Gabrysia were still recuperating from the typhoid.

Mother now renewed trying to let father know where we were, and there was great joy when at the beginning of December she received the first communication from him since leaving Poland. She answered immediately:

DECEMBER 16, 1940
MAPNCKAA A.C.C.R.
TOPOG; UOMKAP-ORA
NORM ZAMNK NO.7
My beloved Stach!

To day I received your postcard written as a fourth one. My happiness had no boundaries. I wrote you one postcard. As you know, besides Alfons, Josef died of typhoid, as well as father on October 28th from blood poisoning. I also had typhoid. We are all well and dreaming about a return. Terenia grew and often talks about you.

I kiss you,
Your Ania and Terenia

Christmas was at hand and although it was not a joyous time, everyone wanted to make it special for the children. We could not have a Christmas play, so instead a variety show with dances and skits was orchestrated where all the children, regardless of religion, who wanted to do so participated. I was in a dance group performing a minuet. The improvised costumes even included a wig made out of cotton.

Romek brought a Christmas tree that he cut in the forest on the way back to camp from his work. Proudly we put it up in the kitchen room and Otto, Maryla and I, with the help of my cousin Basia, made ornaments of bits of paper and any odds and ends we could find. Nothing went to waste and we were extremely proud of our accomplishment. Basia even collected some dough and managed to knead figures for the Nativity set that we put under the tree.

My concern was how Santa would find me here. He found me last year in Lwow. Mother warned me that he will have problems shipping gifts into this remote corner of the world. My spirits were undaunted and I observed everyone, curiously watching for a hint of what will be in store for me.

CHRISTMAS EVE, 1940
NUZIAR, USSR

At that time of year in that part of the world darkness comes early, and we gathered together around the nearly empty table to have our daily soup, which we ate in place of the traditional sumptuous Christmas Eve feast. There was no Christmas wafer to exchange holiday greetings with, so we used part of our rationed bread to do it. The greetings and wishes were to be back home next Christmas and for our health, which was precarious. But for me there was a great surprise waiting under the tree. There was a lovely doll bed with little bedding for my cherished Shirley Temple doll that was my prized possession. Years later when my belief in Santa evaporated, I found out that the bed was made by Mr. Kuchcicki, who was a skilled carpenter and was here in the camp with his wife and four children. The bedding was made by Basia, who continued to create clothes for my dolls.

Chapter 11

Germany-Itzehoe

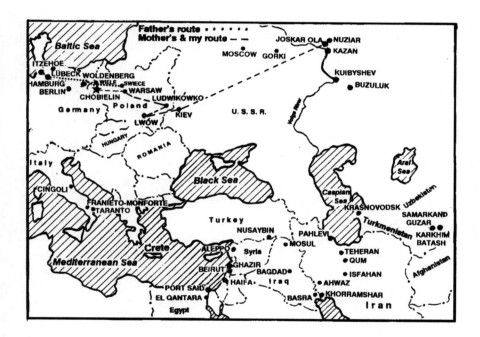

OCTOBER 16, 1940
ITZEHOE, GERMANY

> *Dear Helen,*
> *The letter with the copy of Ania's letter I did not receive, therefore one should presume that it was lost, so if you could write again and tell me what was in the letter. Today Jas received your letter in which you*

*write about your inquiries through Mr. Z—this made me tremen-
dously happy and gave me hope that maybe it will be possible to get
them out from the Bolsheviks. I think that he (Mr. Z) might get permission for their return through a proper office in Berlin. This is only
wishful thinking but nevertheless I am excited, and my intuition tells
me it will work and I will be lucky and our loved ones will return to
where you reported. I am telling you Helen, when Aniusia will be with
you, I will give fervent thanks to God for taking care of them.*

*Of course all this costs money, as you wrote, but that is nothing
compared to the fate of the dearest ones. If you could get a loan then
I could repay at 60 marks. I can't do more since I used up all my
means. Dear Helen, I have no words to express my gratitude for all
you have done for them as well as the kindness you shown to me. For
all that, Helen, you deserve the highest recognition and sincerest
thanks.*

*The last package I have received has arrived all right, except the
meat was slightly damaged but still quite edible. At present I live
filled with hope that they maybe able to return, but if this attempt
fails that will leave only the route of help through America. There is
supposed to be an American Mission in Russian territory to which
one should turn. But I can't do that since I don't know their address.
I am ending dear Helen and for everything I give you sincerest
thanks.*

Stach

Sharing his grief and frustrations with aunt Helen, father does not lose
hope but instead tries to find new ways to cut what he perceives to be only
"red tape". But the correspondence with her dwindles down during the
next few months, since the POWs were allowed to send out only two letters a month and father used his quota to contact people and organizations that could help to get mother and me out of the Soviet Union.

In addition, the overall political situation in Europe did not improve.
The Germans were making further gains—France fell and they started air

raids on London. With these conquests, the Germans became more haughty and boastful; the camp commanding staff, which consisted of retired reservists, began to celebrate the German victories.

One day after such a celebration and a few drinks at the officers club, a German lieutenant decided to make his daily inspection of the POW barracks for which he was responsible and where uncle Jas was living. By chance, father had come to visit Jas and Colonel Janicki, a senior Polish officer with whom he shared the room. As the three men sat in their room sharing a cup of coffee, in strutted Lieutenant Krause, a tall, good looking man in his early sixties who was a professor at Heidelberg University before being called to active duty. Being too old for combat, Lt. Krause was assigned to the staff of the POW camp at Itzehoe. He was a pleasant and talkative man who often enjoyed conversing with the Polish officers who spoke German. As he entered their room he found Col. Janicki, Uncle Jas, and father listening to the loudspeakers putting out the latest German propaganda and news about Britain.

"Well, Colonel.." he addressed the senior officer, Janicki, who spoke German, "I see you heard the news. Things are going well for us! This bombing of England won't last for long...it will all end soon. You know, we have such technology that England won't hold out much longer." The few drinks that he must have had before coming over boosted his confidence as well as loosened his tongue.

"We'll see, we'll see." Nodded Col Janicki, not being in a position to contradict his captor, but Lt. Krause was in a talking mood and had no intentions of leaving. The German sat on the edge of the bunk bed and continued to expound on his nationalistic dreams and his career opportunities:

"You know I speak fluent English, therefore as soon as we occupy England, I will be in charge of a district (he named It) south of London; I am already assigned to it." He paused for a while as a smile of contentment crossed his face, then leisurely got up and as he was leaving the room he continued talking, as if to reassure himself:

"Yes...yes...it will all be over soon. We will be in London for Christmas—you'll see." As he left, the Polish officers looked at each other, startled, and hoped that these words would not come to pass.

As the year 1940 was coming to an end, the war in Europe was not. Father now completed his first full year of captivity and, with the political situation as it was at present, there was not much hope that it would change for the better for him in the near future. The days of his imprisonment were bleak and filled with frustration in that he was helpless in trying to get mother and me out of the Soviet labor camp. But that did not discourage him from trying to reach authorities that might be of help in this situation, which he could do by writing letters.

> *DECEMBER 21, 1940*
> *ITZEHOE, GERMANY*
> *Dear Helen,*
>
> *The package that you sent on December 7, I have received. Thank you very much for everything. I am writing to the United States about our family. I wrote to all kinds of friends in order to get them [the family] out of Russia. Starting from the New Year, I will send you small sums of money for your personal use. I was sick but now I am better. Dear Helen, I wish you and the family a happy and better New Year. In my thoughts I am always with Aniusia and I live on memories and hope.*
>
> *Stach*

Christmas came, a second one in captivity; again everyone reinforced themselves with hope that the next Holiday season would be better and that the New Year would bring changes and a better future.

PART THREE

1941

Chapter 12

USSR-Nuziar

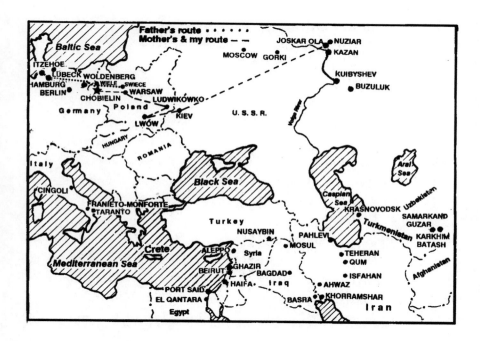

JANUARY 6, 1941
NUZIAR, USSR

> *Beloved Stach,*
> *Today I received your postcard number 4. Also a letter from Helen dated December 12; we were happy to receive it. As you know, Alfons, Josef and Father have died. Winter is in full swing and the*

*temperature goes down to 47C degrees below. We have enough of suf-
ficiently warm clothing. Maria and I are well but we are not working. I am just regaining my strength after typhoid. Don't worry
about me dearest; Terenia has grown quite a bit.*

Kiss you
Your Aniusia and Terenia

Within two weeks came another post card from father and it was
answered immediately with almost identical news:

JANUARY 18, 1941
NUZIAR, USSR
My beloved Stach,

*I have received five of your cards. Write often because this is my
only joy. I also receive letters from Helen. As you know we lost here
Alfons, Josef and Father. We are well. Often I have dreams of us
reuniting. I am not working yet. My stamina is returning after the
typhoid. In spring I will return to work. How do you feel, dearest? I
wrote to Jas.*

I kiss you warmly
Your Ania and Terenia

The Russian winter was now raging, inflicting its bitter cold and many
feet of deep snow. At night the wolves would boldly venture out of the
surrounding forest and come close to the barracks, howling under our
windows. Therefore, it was prudent to be inside before dusk in order not
to be attacked by the hungry beasts who were seeking whatever prey they
could find.

One day in January, as dusk was fast settling over the compound and it
was unmercifully cold, the working inhabitants of the camp were returning to their huts from the day's work in the lumber camp. Against the
gray winter sky the dark forest looked foreboding but as yet silent, since
the wolves had not yet begun their nightly prowling. From between the
trees started to emerge dark shadows; the bent forms of the returning
workers. The winter work days were shorter but much more grueling

because of the severe and biting cold. There were constant cases of dangerous frostbite that ended in amputation of fingers and toes; hence, everyone was constantly preoccupied with watching for primary signs of that dreaded affliction of the Russian winter. Automatically, each person searched his neighbors' face for any sign of a white patch that could result in freezing and further complications as well as infection.

The workers made their trek to the camp, heads bent, shoulders stooped, showing their resignation to the unwarranted fate to which they were sentenced. The snow was cracking under their felt boots; they were returning to their so-called home, which after such a day was truly a haven.

In our cabin, all were back and warming themselves around the only stove at the entrance except cousin Romek, who was lagging behind and was not yet in. Aunt Luta, apprehensive about his whereabouts, was anxiously peering through the frosty window looking for him. As she recognized his approaching form, she sighed with relief and exclaimed: "Romek is coming!"

I ran toward the door to greet him, but as I neared it, I heard him calling out for help and to open the door. Miss Flora, sensing danger, darted for the door, bypassing me, and in an instant had Romek inside. He stood there, covered with snow, with his gloved arms stretched forward, repeating: "I don't feel my hands…I don't feel them."

In an instant, Miss Flora removed Romek's gloves in order to see the hands and assess the frostbite damage. It was bad. All Romek's fingers were white and stiff. Quickly, she and Miss Gabrysia scooped snow from the outside and began rubbing it on his fingers, trying to restore the circulation. The fingers continued to be white and more people joined in the rescue effort. Consternation continued while Romek's shoes were removed in order to check his feet to see if they were affected by the frost. Fortunately, the feet were all right but the hands were in very bad shape.

In the next days Romek's fingers were swollen and festering, and the diagnosis was that there was a good possibility that he might lose some of them. All the home remedies were applied though the next weeks and though it was a painful process, Romek recuperated without losing any of his fingers. But he was unable to work for several months, which deprived the family of food rations, adding further hardship to this dismal situation.

The remaining winter months were difficult not only because of cold the but also the continuing lack of food and having to be in such confined and crowded quarters while being assaulted by lice and bedbugs. Even the bitter cold could not eliminate Russian bugs.

> *MAY 1941*
> *NUZIAR, USSR*
> *Dearest Daddy,*
> *I am writing this card. We are well and I study. We miss you and I pray we would be together and again happy. Don't worry daddy, we love you very much though from afar. Write please what you are doing. I kiss you many times and also uncle Jas.*
> *Your Terenia*

It was my first attempt at writing, with a great deal of "help" from mother. Although I was not going to the Russian school I was being secretly taught Polish by Miss Maryla, governess of my playmate Otto, who tutored both of us.

SUMMER 1941
NUZIAR, USSR

With the coming of spring and warmer weather everyone was forced back to work in the lumber camp with the exception of aunt Maria, who, because she had an infant, remained behind. So I would look after Krystofer while she tried to plant a garden that would help to supplement our meager rations.

Summer arrived with the same sudden impact as had the winter. Our little garden, to our surprise, showed signs of bearing the fruits of our work. This was a welcome sight, since it meant we would have fresh vegetables of our own. Krystofer was now over a year old and was a lively little boy with a mop of curly blond hair. He and I and aunt Maria were together continuously. Sometimes we would walk the half-mile to the lumber camp where mother was working, and bring her food if it was available. One time even were we able to get some sugar cubes that we took to her, since she had never totally returned to health after the typhoid and the sugar gave her more energy.

The work done by mother's group consisted of sawing wood stumps, which were cut down by another group, into two-inch cubes and loading them into wheelbarrows. Then one of them had to push the wheelbarrow up a ramp into the upper level of a barn-like structure from which they were distributed to various locations to be used as fuel for trucks, since there was a shortage of gasoline. The work continued from 6:00 AM to late afternoon, with only a half hour break.

This strenuous work went on and on without any end in sight. People began to lose hope that anyone would indefinitely survive this hard labor and lack of food. The perception was that our days were numbered. In addition, we had no news of the outside world except the Soviet propaganda bulletins that tended to repeat themselves. Contact with father was very infrequent and not dependable, but mother continued to try to let him know where we were. The last correspondence by us from the Soviet Union to father was a postcard written by me:

> *JUNE 6, 1941*
> *NUZIAR, USSR*
> *Beloved Daddy,*
> *I am writing a third card. I am well and I like to study. We miss you very much and we are waiting for the moment when we see each other again. I will hug you daddy so hard, so very hard.*
> *I kiss you.*
> *Terenia*
> *(Post script from mother)*
> *I also kiss you and Jas*
> *Ania*

Toward the end of June an official communiqué announced that the Germans had invaded the Soviet Union and the country was in a state of war. No one knew what this meant for us, and although all kinds of rumors circulated we were still in the dark. The situation in the camp became worse, because people were expected to work even harder for fewer rations in order to help the war effort.

Towards the end of August a group of NKVD personnel arrived in the camp and everyone was rounded up into the school, where it was announced that because of the German invasion of the Soviet Union, the Soviets had signed an agreement providing that the Poles who had been deported and arrested were now free to leave. However, anyone who wanted to leave had to inform the commandant of their destination and the authorities would furnish a "pass". (In the Soviet Union even up to the fall of Communism in 1991 one could not move beyond a 30 mile radius of one's residence without such a pass.) But, they were quick to add, we were welcome to stay and work for the glory and victory of the USSR.

The fantastic news of liberation took everyone by surprise; it was hard to believe that we were free! This news of freedom brought consternation to the camp, as everyone was trying to decide where to go since we were not able to return to Poland. Our small group, with Mr. Wozimirski at the helm, held a conference as to where would be the best place to go. Mr. Wozimirski had previously done some "checking out" since he had some contacts in the nearby town, and had found out that a Polish Army was to be formed in the USSR in Buzuluk, 100 miles southeast of Kuibyshev, which is on the Volga river. Therefore, he decided that would be our destination. In addition, aunt Maria hoped that there she would be able to find her husband who she presumed was a Soviet prisoner of war.

It was now time to plan the logistics of our next journey and to have money for the voyage. Our dwindling possessions were quickly assessed and Miss Gabrysia, Flora and mother ventured with them to the local Russians who were eager to buy and barter. Mr. Wozimirski and Romek went to procure means to transport us to the nearest rail station, which was in Joskar Ola. They were successful in obtaining a hay cart and a horse.

On a gray overcast day in the first week of September 1941, our group of ten, with Mr. Wozimirski in charge, was ready to depart from Nuziar. Into the cart went our bundles and suitcases. Aunt Maria, with Krystofer in her arms, was the first to be situated and I was next to her with mother. Then Aunt Luta and Barbara were allocated places. Mr. Wozimirski took the reins with Miss Gabrysia next to him. Miss Flora and Romek sat at the end of the cart. Our possessions packed, we headed out on the same sandy road that had brought us here over a year ago. As we moved on the road we passed the grave of uncle Alfons, leaving him, uncle Josef, and grandfather, behind on foreign soil.

The cart was overloaded, so the journey was slower than anticipated. Toward evening, we were still on the road when it started to drizzle. Soon the drizzle developed into steady rain, which made the sandy road difficult to traverse. The cart had to be lightened and Romek, Barbara, Miss Flora and Miss Gabrysia walked beside the lumbering cart. I was huddled in a corner with Krystofer, under the cover of a blanket.

It was just before midnight when we approached the outskirts of Joskar Ola; most of the houses were darkened, with their inhabitants asleep. Mr. Wozimirski knocked at several nearby house doors inquiring for lodging, but to no avail. The situation was dismal; we were cold, wet, tired and hungry, with no place to stay. More attempts were made knocking at houses on the side road, which finally resulted in obtaining lodging for all of us.

Content to find a roof over our heads, we settled down for the night. Tomorrow would be a day to work out the logistics of the next step of the journey.

Chapter 13

GERMANY-ITZEHOE, SANDBOSTEL

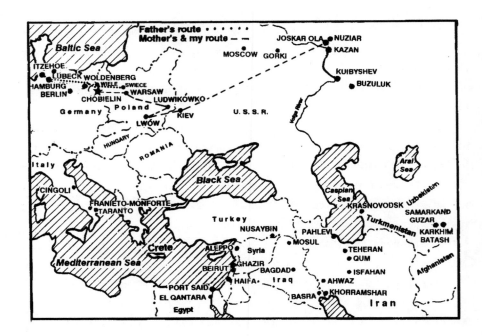

JANUARY 4, 1941
ITZEHOE, GERMANY

>*Dear Helen,*
>*I thank you for the package that I received Christmas Eve. I have
>no news from Ania for the last six months. Nobody can understand
>the turmoil of my soul. I am afraid for their fate. I always return to*

the thought that all that happened to them was the fault of the men (of the family) as well as the idea of leaving Chobielin.

I wrote to a certain lady in America, it is the sixth foreign place where I asked for their help.

I wish you Helen all the best in the New Year, so we could be together in this year.

Stach

And changes did come with the new year, but not as all had hoped for. Within two weeks the Germans announced that the segment of the camp which contained Polish POWs was going to be moved, since the quarters were needed for their ever-expanding forces. The prisoners were to be divided into two groups and sent to different camps.

It was not known where the first group of Polish prisoners was taken, but father and, as luck would have it, uncle Jas, were together in the second group that was marched out of the Itzehoe camp the following day (January 21st) and put on a freight train that headed for Sandbostel. Just before his departure, father received news from aunt Helen, to which he responded upon arrival at the new camp.

JANUARY 27, 1941
SANDBOSTEL, GERMANY
Dear Helen,

I was deeply shaken by the news of father's and Josef's deaths. My grief is indescribable because in father I lost the best man to whom I owe my personal happiness. I grieve deeply with you, dear Helen, and I am sending my sincere sympathies. From the letter, I surmise what my dear ones must have endured. Poor Luta. I hope in God and believe and pray that He looks after our little group of deportees. I had a premonition about this and it has not failed me. Dear Helen, be brave, we have to live for the rest of them.

I kiss your hands.

Stach

Sandbostel, near Bremen, was an international POW camp where there were prisoners from all the allied nations that the Germans had managed to conquer; British sailors, Yugoslavians, Frenchmen and Polish officers. The camp itself was especially built by the Germans as a POW camp and stood on marshes. The camp quarters consisted of paper-thin wooden rectangular barracks that were turn put on stilts so as not to be buried in the foot-deep mud. The only plumbing consisted of a few faucets of cold water scattered through the camp, above the ground, that served not only for drinking, but also washing and bathing all year round! The toilet facilities were even more primitive and without privacy; here and there was an open ditch with a pole across that served as a toilet. When the ditch was filled with excrement it would be covered with dirt and a new one would be dug nearby.

Father's barrack was located at the perimeter of the camp, so that only a barbed wire divided him from the road that led to the town. Beyond the road were more marshes with a grove of trees sprouting out. In spring, when the weather permitted, he was able to sit in the sun and block out, if only for a moment, the macabre living conditions, and observe the wild life of the marshes. The spongy wet ground was covered with reeds, which provided sanctuary for birds that darted in and out of their hiding places. In the evening the frogs would take over and fill the camp air with their throaty croaking.

With the beginning of March, father sent a card to aunt Helen:

MARCH 4, 1941
SANDBOSTEL, GERMANY
Dear Helen,

On occasion of your Namesday, I am sending best wishes that your dreams come true very soon. Also I wish you health and that you be happy. From Ania I have received three cards. She writes that she received your letter and four of my cards. She is not working and slowly is returning to health. They are deeply convinced that there will be help and they will return but it is taking so long. Do you

think that Mr. Z is just fooling? I thank you for the package. Is
Bernard still in Bialosliwie? Regards to Bernard and your children.
    Stach

(Mr. Z was a contact that father and aunt Helen were writing to, who was supposed to be able to get us all out of the Soviet Union. The reference to Bernard is to my mother's brother who was in Bialosliwie for some time and then was able to move to the section of Poland referred to by the Germans as General Government.)

The living conditions, or lack of them, affected father's health which began to deteriorate. His body was now covered with boils and self-doctoring did not bring any relief, though he hoped that the coming of warm weather would be of some help. Unfortunately, his health did not improve, but he was hesitant about going to the infirmary since it was a common practice with the Germans to send the seriously ill prisoners to concentration camps rather than to a hospital.

Finally father's health regressed to a point that the boils were so painful that he was unable to walk and he was also running a high fever. His friend and bunkmate, Captain Dobrowolski, persuaded father to chance it and to try to get help in the infirmary. Leaning on his friend, father made his way through the muddy road to the camp infirmary where a young German doctor who had been wounded in action was in charge of its operation.

"Sir" started Captain Dobrowolski, who spoke fluent German, "my colleague is running a high fever and is in great pain...could you please help him?"

The young doctor examined father and explained that he had no facilities at hand to treat him but he would send him to a POW hospital that was nearby. Father was to report back to the infirmary in the afternoon

Thus, upon returning to his barrack, father sat down and wrote his long overdue letter to aunt Helen:

APRIL 9, 1941
SANDBOSTEL, GERMANY
Dear Helen,

I am sorry for the long silence but I had all sorts of obligations of writing on behalf of Ania's case and to Ania. I am sending stickers [these were the stickers which were issued to the POW to be affixed to their incoming packages. They could not receive a package without one.] *Besides that I will send you 50 marks every month which is for your use, don't be offended that it is such a small amount.*

I have no words from Ania beyond the four postcards that I have received in March.

I have been sick for the last five months; I am pestered by boils. I have suffered patiently but today I am going to hospital where there is good care and I hope good living conditions that will quickly help me to return to good health.

I have not written Ania about my sickness, so I ask you not to mention that to her. As for parcels, I would like to ask you especially for certain items that are important to me; e.g., bread, as well as onions or garlic. The rest, please add whatever you think is appropriate. There is no restriction on the amount of fats that one can receive but if you receive too much it is kept in a magazine and then rationed out on demand.

Jas is well and looks good and in the evenings we often talk about our loved ones. I am wishing you Helen a Happy Holiday (Easter) hoping that the next one will be spent together.

My fondest regards to Danusia, Marysia, Janusz and little Andrzej.

Be of good thoughts and all will be well.
Stach

After finishing the letter father folded it and started to gather his meager personal belongings that he would take with him to the hospital. That being done, he again, with the help of Captain Dobrowolski, walked back to the infirmary. On the way father posted the just-written letter and then reported to the assigned place where another ailing Polish officer joined him. The two sick officers, under the escort of a German armed guard, went to the hospital.

The hospital was located on the grounds of a camp that had previously served as a German military cadet quarters, so it had solidly built barracks with full sanitary conditions. The hospital itself was staffed and run by Yugoslavian prisoners of war, but most of the patients were British sailors captured in different parts of the world. The chief doctor, a corpulent short Yugoslavian major, examined father thoroughly and began to inquire:

"Captain, did you ever have any heart problems?" He spoke Slovak that father could understand.

"No."

"Well you see...I will cure you. You will be well but the cure will be a harsh one." Then he proceeded to explain the procedure.

"I will give injections of milk for two weeks and the sores will increase daily. It wont be very pleasant but you will get well."

With the examination finished, father was taken to a ward where there were six bunk beds occupied by various wounded British sailors recuperating from the wounds that they had sustained in battle. As he was led to an empty top bunk, father's attendant turned to the occupant of the lower bunk:

"Captain Harding!" he addressed the reclining man in pajamas. "This is Captain Mikosz, Polish cavalry, he will be getting injections and would need the lower bunk. Could you please move to the upper bunk?"

Of course!" replied the British officer with a smile, and extended his hand to father, saying "How do you do, Captain?"

Father returned the handshake, but not knowing the English language, the conversation ended with that. The Englishman climbed to the top bunk while father lay down savoring the luxury of what he considered a perfect bed—it had a mattress and sheets!

The two weeks that followed, during which father received the injections, were indeed very unpleasant and full of the cure's side effects, but the boils were eliminated. The only evidences that remained of the affliction were dark blotches on his skin which in due time also dissipated. The stay in the hospital was eventually extended to six weeks, giving father a chance to get on his feet and to make friends with his roommates.

Captain Harding, who was recuperating from battle wounds, began to teach father English. He had some speech problems, since in addition to being wounded he also had lost his dentures, but managed to explain that the Red Cross had taken impressions and he would get his new set shortly.

Father was eager to learn the language so he could communicate with his new friends and learned enough rudimentary English so that by the end of his stay they were all able to understand each other. Besides the language lessons, the British friends generously shared with father the contents of their "care" packages which they received on a regular basis. The packages contained luxuries in the form of chocolates, cookies and dried fruits, none of which father had seen in the past year and a half.

By the end of May, having recovered completely, father was released from the hospital and had to part with his newly acquired friends and the comfortable living conditions. Reluctantly he returned to the camp, where he was enthusiastically greeted by his old friends and in particular by uncle Jas, who embraced him and, looking father over, exclaimed:

"By God, you are looking splendid!"

Indeed he did, and in addition father felt splendid, so even the dismal surroundings of the barracks did not look as bad now; the sun was shining, some of the mud had dried out, and he thought:

"Things will get better...they must get better!"

But unfortunately, things did not get better for them, though a spark of hope was lighted in his and all prisoners' hearts when news came on June 22nd, that Hitler had attacked the Soviet Union. The Polish POWs shared the hope that the two aggressors against Poland would finish themselves off. Further news filtered into the camp telling of a deal that the Soviets had made with the Polish Government in exile which resided in London for the release of the Poles that had been deported to Soviet camps and prisons.

AUGUST 21, 1941
SANDBOSTEL, GERMANY
Dear Helen,

I thank you for your sincere words. I am also happy that the money sent by me could be of some use to you. I have no letters from Ania, which is understandable. But with all that is happening now in Lwow, maybe it is better that they are not there. I hope that now they will be able to get help from the Government (the Polish Government in exile in London) because they have representatives there and everything is on the good road. For us, it is only to wait quietly for the end of the war; the rest is in the hands of God. Everything is well that ends well; It won't be bad for us.

Both Jas and I have sent you some things that we don't need, but we were delayed since it is not easy to do it from here.

I wrote to the Red Cross in Switzerland about our family and I am waiting for the answer. I asked the Red Cross to forward the correspondence, as well as look after them.

For the packages, Helen, I thank you. I value greatly your effort and I don't know how to reciprocate. It is very good that into each package you put some bread.

What is Zwieszchowski's address?

Are you well? The young ladies have probably grown and when we will return we won't recognize them. We so often talk about all of you with Jas and we reminisce about the beautiful times.

I am ending, dear Helen, kissing your hands in gratitude for their help. I embrace Danusia, Marysia and warmest regards to Janusz and Andrzej. Helen, be sure of the fact that happiness will return.

Stach

Chapter 14

USSR-Joskar Ola, Kazan, Kuibyshev; Uzbekistan-Samarkand

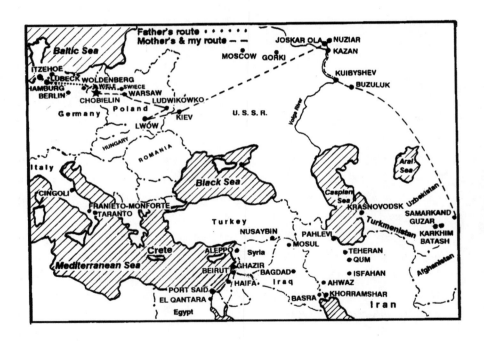

SEPTEMBER 1941
JOSKAR OLA TO KAZAN, USSR

The next morning, after our arrival in Joskar Ola, Mr. Wozimirski and
Romek had to go and return the horses and cart to the people from whom
they were hired. At the same time mother, together with Miss Gabrysia,

ventured out to sell some clothes in order to get provisions for the journey that lay ahead of us. Miss Flora, on the other hand, made contact with some acquaintances, since she had been born in Russia and was familiar with the area.

Regrouping and rest took a couple of days since rail tickets for Kazan were hard to obtain. We ultimately departed on a very crowded train full of Russian and Ukrainian refugees and evacuees from Soviet territory in which the Germans were making speedy advances. The ride was chaotic, with train cars bursting at the seams with people and their assorted baggage in every available bit of space. Our group managed to find a space in a passageway and sat on our bundles, not only because of necessity due to lack of space but also for protection.

The train chugged slowly and laboriously along, but made it to Kazan by nightfall. Kazan, the capital of the former Tatar Autonomous Soviet Republic of the USSR, is on the east bank of the Volga River. It is here where the Volga alters its course from eastward to southward. In the 13th century it was home to the Tartars of the Golden Horde; now it was overcrowded with a motley assortment of refugees from various parts of the Soviet Union.

Again, Mr. Wozimirski was able to find a cart and we were able to go to the river port building where we found more crowds and chaos. We managed to squeeze into the waiting room and settle ourselves on top of our baggage. The situation looked hopeless; the smell of bodies in this overcrowded waiting room was overpowering, in addition to the lice that were visible. Mother and aunt Maria found, by chance, that the harbor had special facilities for small children.

The children's facility was a room clean and spartan, with cribs, managed by large Russian women in white, nurse-like uniforms. Krystofer and I were deposited there for the night, where we got a warm meal and a clean bed to sleep in while the rest of the family huddled on the baggage and among the crowds.

We were in Kazan another few days while Mr. Wozimirski and Miss Flora were trying to get tickets for a boat to Kuibyshev. Here, the authorities were putting obstacles in our way, not only in obtaining the passage on the boat but questioning our passage papers that had been issued at the camp. Then, suddenly, with little notice, the tickets were issued for the next departing boat which was already being loaded. A fast scramble got us onto the boat, where we found room under the roof of a lower deck and situated ourselves once again on our suitcases and bundles.

This was a new adventure for me, since I had never been on a boat; everything fascinated me. The adults, having secured a place where we would spend the next few days, took turns exploring the available facilities. Miss Gabrysia returned with the good news that there was a food counter where we could obtain some meals at a reasonable cost.

For several days the boat continued its journey down river. We passed towns and settlements and the boat occasionally made a stop where a few people disembarked but a multitude was waiting, to no avail, to get on. The most memorable stop was at Ulianovsk since the Russians were pointing out that this was the birthplace of Lenin [original name "Ulyanov"]. With my usual curiosity, I was observing the landscape of the Volga River, which was ever changing as the boat proceeded down stream. Finally we reached our destination, Kuibyshev.

OCTOBER 1941
KUIBYSHEV, USSR

The city of Kuibyshev is about 200 miles down stream from Kazan on the Volga. It was founded in the 16th century as a fortress, Samara, in order to protect the busy Volga trade route. Now it was a busy river-port town full of an assortment of refugees fleeing the battle zone of the western Soviet Union, as well as Polish people that had been released from camps and prisons to reach Polish authorities. The city also was the center for all the embassies, since all had been evacuated from Moscow. In addition, most of the Soviet government had been moved here. Hence, it was a city overcrowded and in turmoil.

We disembarked and again made our living quarters at the port facilities, with the rest of the homeless and transients who huddled in the corners of the building. Again, mother sought out and found the sleeping quarters for the small children, where both Krystofer and I spent the night and got some milk while the rest of the family were in the outside room.

As we disembarked and brought off our bags, it was noticed that two were missing. Miss Flora came to the conclusion that they had been left in Kazan and she decided to go back and try to retrieve them. She was to come back on the next boat but that was the last that we saw of her. The presumption was that since she knew some people in Kazan, she decided to stay there rather than risk the unknown.

In the meantime, Mr. Wozimirski found the Polish embassy and was told that the center for Polish military personnel and for the refugees was in Buzuluk, 100 miles southeast of Kuibyshev. It was not a long distance, but because of war and everyone trying to distance themselves from the battle, train tickets were almost impossible to obtain.

Every morning for the next few days, Mr. Wozimirski and Romek would spend many hours waiting in line at the train station to get seats. In the meantime mother and aunt Luta would go to town to buy some food, which was scarce. On one such day they took me with them, and as we reached some buildings we saw a very long line of people. After inquiring what was being sold, we were told that there was bread. Wanting to ensure that we would be able to get some of it, mother and aunt Luta decided that each would wait in a separate line; I went with mother. Hours passed and the lines moved slowly. Aunt Luta's line went through a courtyard of the building while mother's ran along the sidewalk. To keep myself entertained I started going between mother and aunt Luta until one time when I left mother and came to the courtyard and my aunt was not there. I went looking for her up and down the line but to no avail; I decided to return to the sidewalk where mother's line was, but the line was gone. I shouted for mother and then for aunt, but no one answered.

"Well," I thought to myself, "since I can't find them I had better return to the port. They are probably there. Anyway, it's not too far.." It was getting dark and the early drizzle changed to snow, so I decided that I should return to the waiting room at the river dock.

I remembered that I was on the same street on which we had come there, so I continued to walk down hill toward the river until I reached a busy intersection where a policeman was directing traffic. Now I was confused as to which road to take, since both ways seemed to go to the river. I stopped a passing man and questioned him:

"Excuse me, could you tell me which is the road to the river dock?"

"Mmm, I am not sure."; he said, but he stopped another person to inquire and in a short time there were several people gathered around me.

Seeing the group of people on the corner, the policeman directing traffic came over to see what was the problem.

"The child is lost and wants to get to the docks," explained first man of whom I had first enquired.

The policeman looked at me and the crowd of people gathered around me, and decided that he would take charge. He asked my name and then got hold of my arm and said:

"All right, come with me, I will take you to the docks."

I was panic stricken, because all my mother's warnings and stories flashed before me. "Remember, never go with any Russian soldiers or policemen because they take children to orphanages and you will never see me." I squirmed to free myself from the policeman's grasp and started screaming at the top of my voice:

"I am not going with you! Let go! I don't want to go with you!" tears were pouring down my face and I sat on the sidewalk while he kept holding my hand.

Then a middle aged, plump women, who was standing by me, seeing that I was not letting up the crying, tried to calm me down. She turned to the policeman and said that she was going in the direction of the docks and would take me there. The policeman hesitated for a moment and wanting to disperse the crowd, agreed and released me from his grip.

"All right, everyone move on. Go on. I have to get back to my job." He shooed people on their way and returned to the intersection.

The woman got me off the sidewalk and wiped my face.

"It's all right, little one. Don't be frightened. I will take you to your mother." She took my hand and we walked to the docks, where among the many people I pointed our corner. Aunt Maria was there with Krys, but no sign of mother or aunt Luta. The women relinquished me to aunt Maria, telling her what happened, and left.

Meanwhile, since the care room for children was now open, Maria put Krystofer and me into it and returned to the waiting room. It was quite late and dark when mother and aunt Luta returned, jubilant that each had managed to get some bread and, in addition, mother bought a quilted pants and jacket for me. But they were oblivious to what had happened to me. Each presumed that I was with the other and aunt Maria repeated the incident to them, reassuring them that I was all right and by now sleeping in the children's care room.

After several days of waiting and living in the lice-infected waiting room at the dock with a multitude of people scrounging for food, Mr. Wozimirski returned triumphant, with tickets to Buzuluk. The train was to leave the next morning but we immediately moved to the waiting room at the train station. This was even more crowded, since in addition to all the refugees, there were soldiers being moved to the front to oppose the ever-encroaching German army. There was no room for children here, so Krystofer and I slept on a makeshift bed made of our suitcases and the rest of our group huddled around as best they could.

Next morning, hours before the arrival of the train, we were on the platform trying to position ourselves so we would be able to get on the train. Having tickets did not mean that one would be able to get on, since the trains were overcrowded with people trying to get away.

It was still dark when we piled out onto the platform, and the snow was gently falling. Krystofer was bundled up in blankets and was sleeping. I was warm in my new winter togs and perched myself on top of our luggage and played some word games with Romek and Barbara. Adults would sit for a while and then, one by one, would get up, stamp their feet and wave their arms to keep themselves warm.

Hours passed before the train lumbered into the station. As expected, it was full, so the mad scramble began to reach the nearest door and to get onto it. Pushing, shoving and yelling started even before the train came to a full stop. The main concern of our family was to be able to stay together, since it was very easy to get separated and lost in this melee. Mr. Wozimirski and Miss Gabrysia were "the front" people whom we all followed, while Romek was behind to make sure than none of us were pushed aside.

Everyone holding some suitcase or bundle, aunt Maria with Krys in her arms shoved and pushed our way into the rail car and even managed to get two seats. Aunt Maria was given the one seat and aunt Luta the other, and I was able to sit in her lap while the rest sat around them on their baggage.

The train ride lasted several hours, with several checks by the military, but fortunately without incident we arrived in Buzuluk.

BUZULUK, USSR

Here in this town was the Polish Army HQ in USSR, with several locations serving as receiving centers for the volunteers who were streaming in from the prisons and labor camps in spite of the obstacles that were created by the Soviets and the logistics of travel.

Because no one knew the exact location of the center, Mr. Wozimirski decided that it would be best if we stayed for time being at the station waiting room, while he, together with mother and aunt Maria, would go and report to the Polish authorities. Mother and aunt Maria were military dependents and aunt also wanted to find some news of her husband.

Half a day passed when they all returned with disappointing news. Mr. Wozimirski was accepted immediately, and mother with me and aunt Maria with Krys would qualify to stay, but the rest of the family would have to go south to Samarkand where the repatriation of other civilians was in progress. The sisters did not want to be separated, so they decided that all of us would venture to the south.

Before departing, Mr. Wozimirski managed to get tickets, but that did not mean that there would be a place for all of us on the next train, as well as the documents needed for travel in the USSR. The train was leaving that evening, and we bid a tearful farewell to our guardian who was left standing and waiving on the platform as the train pulled out of the station.

END OF OCTOBER 1941
JOURNEY TO
SAMARKAND, UZBEKISTAN

When our train left Buzuluk, the journey under ordinary circumstances would be at most a couple of days but instead it was almost two weeks. The trains were always filled to and most of the time over, their capacity, crammed full of a multitude of people of different nationalities, refugees from camps and prisons. There were constant document checks and Romek was always singled out, since the military was collecting young males for the armed forces. Fortunately, Mr. Wozimirski had seen to it that Romek had proper papers stating that he was going to the Polish repatriation center.

When the train reached some station and would not go further or broke down, we would have to disembark and look for the next available train to take us further. Hence, with protracted stops we spent many nights or days on platforms, on stone floors of unlit waiting rooms, sprawled on top of our belongings among the multitude of people heading south. Many trains would just pass without stopping while people elbowed their way to the ticket booth. In these stations we would come across Poles who, like us, were going south to the promised centers.

The train often would stop in the middle of nowhere and some people would get off to stretch their legs and use the barren facilities, since the train car toilets were most of the time non-functional and filthy. These stops were usually made to let an army train which was headed north to the German-Soviet front pass by. The Russians would wave the soldiers on and then burst into some patriotic song, encouraging them to save "mother Russia".

As we inched our way south into Kazakhstan the climate began to warm up. The journey took us through Aral, by the Aral Sea, along the bed of the Syr Darya River through the Kazak Steppe, through Turkestan and Tashkent into Uzbekistan.

The snows vanished and we entered a different world. The Uzbeks are the descendants of 14th century nomads that constituted the Golden Horde. Their colorful clothing and Asiatic features, combined with the unique landscape, invoked curiosity. I was fascinated by the half naked, bare footed children selling melons and raisins at the wayside stations; things that I had not seen for the last year.

NOVEMBER 1941
SAMARKAND, UZBEKISTAN

It was already dark when we reached the station at Samarkand. The waiting room by this time of the day was overcrowded and permeated with the odor of the hungry, tired and dirty people occupying the enclosed quarters. Romek and Miss Gabrysia decided to go and see if there was any other place where we could find temporary quarters. They returned in a short while and informed us that the only place for us to spend the night, since it was warm, was in the park square across from the station and, since there were already other Polish refugees, we had safety in numbers.

So, carting our belongings, we crossed the road and found a place under a palm tree where mother settled Krys and me in for the night. Though there were people around us and more were coming continuously, it seemed peaceful lying in the warm night looking at the sky full of glittering stars. Exhausted, I soon fell asleep, waking up at sunrise to an unfamiliar call.

The call was coming from one of the minarets of the nearby mosque, the Muslim call to prayer. As the sun rose it illuminated the blue mosaic domes of ancient mosques erected during the golden era of Tamerlane, who was now buried here. The city existed long before that and was sought as a prize by Alexander the Great, and Genghis Khan. Now, the once magnificent structures were not in good condition but still awakened the mystery of the ancient East.

Since there was no dwelling place to be found, we continued to live in the park for the next few days while trying to find the Polish relocation center, but to no avail. A decision was made that we should go further to Guzar, but the NKVD came to our park and, disregarding our travel documents, loaded everyone who was in the park square into trucks and took us to one of the nearby Kolhozes (co-operative farms).

NOVEMBER 1942
KOLHOZ "STALIN", near SAMARKAND, UZBEKISTAN

We were herded into the back of an already full truck that was waiting nearby. The occupants of the vehicle silently inched forward to make room for our group. Most of the rounded-up people who were in the truck were, like us, Poles, who were trying to reach the Polish centers and were caught.

The truck meandered through the dusty and crowded city into a country road that passed through fields of cotton. Here and there were groups of shabby people walking between the rows of cotton bushes and picking the ripe, fluffy, white product. A mile or so further on, the truck turned into a side road and came to a stop in front of several square, box-like mud huts. The soldiers that had positioned themselves at the end of the truck hopped down and shouted orders for all of us to come out.

Since we were the first to be off the truck the officer in charge assigned us the nearest hut, along with a young couple, in order to complete the mandatory capacity of ten to a dwelling, which in this case was a small one-room hut with one door and one window. There was no floor, just dirt. The walls were made of sun-baked mud. We entered with our now meager bundles and each found a space against the walls, leaving a foot-wide path in the middle. Outside the hut was a large kettle nestled in a primitive mud stand that was to be our cooking oven. A little beyond the hut was a mud outhouse. There was no electricity or even a lamp, no running water, and the adults were told that in the morning they would have to start working, picking cotton, in order to get their rations. This was a collective farm (Kolhoz) and the name of it was "Stalin".

Mother, Miss Gabrysia, Basia and Romek, together with the young couple in our hut, set out at daybreak to the assigned place where they were to start work. Aunt Maria, with Krys in her arms and I walked to the nearby Uzbek huts looking to get some milk or other provisions in exchange for some articles of clothing which she had brought with us. We were successful and triumphantly returned to our "home". Aunt Maria and Luta managed to build a fire under the outside kettle and with the vegetables that we brought concocted a soup which was ready when the rest returned from the fields.

We were not fortunate with food as time went by, since the rations issued to the workers were sparse: one slice of bread per person per week. The rest would be the result of constant scrounging for scraps in the already harvested fields of grain, or vegetables which would go into the communal pot. The picked-up kernels of wheat were ground and mixed with water, then shaped into a patty and baked on the inside walls of the pot which also served as an oven. It was a tasteless, coarse tasting piece of food that was hard to swallow, but one got used to it.

The Uzbek people themselves were very traditional Muslims and were poor. I soon found native friends but it was hard to communicate with them since they spoke no Russian and I only picked up a few words in Uzbek. Nevertheless, I soon adapted to their hospitality and friendliness as well as their customs, which fascinated me.

Toward the end of the month I became sick, which turned out to be the measles that was going around among the Uzbek children. Mother nursed me to health with the help of our couple in the hut, who had turned out to be a doctor and his wife from Poland. Measles is highly contagious under any circumstances and here in the crowded quarters was impossible to avoid, thus Krys came down with them next.

Krys was now a twenty month old boy with golden curly hair and the darling of the Uzbek natives, who whenever they would pass by would play with him or give him rides on their donkeys. Now, he was sick and there were more children in the vicinity who were down with measles, so the Russian health workers came around and took him to the hospital in Samarkand. Aunt Maria went with him. Within a few days complications developed; Krys came down with pneumonia and died.

With the news of Krys's death, Miss Gabrysia obtained permission to go and be with Aunt Maria. The two women buried the little boy in a local cemetery, in a suitcase which served as a coffin since there were none available.

Maria, with Miss Gabrysia, returned to the Kolhoz and tried to hold up under the tragic circumstance of losing her only child, whom she had managed to keep alive through many previous ordeals only to lose him when there was hope of coming freedom. She was now in her early twenties and at this time was not aware that her husband, Wacek, was also dead. As I have stated he was one of the thousands of Polish officers who were victims of the Katyn massacre in 1940, shot by the Russians.

Not too long after death of Krys, there was another funeral, that of a young Uzbek girl. The young woman belonged to an orthodox Muslim sect that did not allow any medical help, and so she died. The funeral in an Uzbek community was a social event with professional mourners who wailed through the night and accompanied the shroud-wrapped body to the cemetery. After the burial a banquet followed and, hungry, all of us participated.

DECEMBER 1941
KOLHOZ "STALIN", UZBEKISTAN

The rainy part of the season started and the work in the cotton field was sporadic due to the weather. This particular day the rains were not letting up and we were confined our hut for most of the day. By evening, the flimsy mud hut began to leak here and there. Various utensils were put out to catch the water and the beddings were moved out of the way wherever possible. Whoever had an umbrella huddled under it for protection.

Darkness fell, and the rains still had not let up. Mother looked around our wet surroundings and decided that she would try to find a different place for the night. Aunt Luta and Maria agreed, but came to the conclusion that we all should do it separately since it would be easier to find sleeping quarters. Mother, taking me by one hand and an umbrella in the other, set off into the dark pouring rain in the direction of some Uzbek huts.

We passed two smaller huts, knowing that they would be crowded because of their size. The next was a substantially larger house and the light was escaping through its closed shutters. We came to the door and knocked; no answer. We knocked again, louder, and the door opened with a squeak; a barefooted Uzbek who quizzically looked at us. Mother, with gestures and some Uzbek words, made him understand that we needed a lodging for the night. He opened the door wider, gesturing for us to come into the one-room house. He extended the tribal hospitality by gesturing to us to join the members of the household who were in the midst of consuming a meal. They sat on the rug cross-legged around a large bowl of steaming yogurt soup. As we joined them they passed a communal wooden spoon around to partake of the liquid as others, and us, would dip our hand into the bowl in order to fish out the noodles. After the soup there was a pot of "cha"-tea. Again it was poured into a small wooden bowl and when one person finished their portion, the empty bowl was passed on to the next individual.

The meal finished, preparation for the night started by unrolling the rugs and quilts which were stacked against the walls. They provided one for mother and I and soon all the occupants of the hut lay next to each other and settled down for the night.

On the following morning, before departing, mother gave the head man a gift of her treasured manicure scissors, since it was all she had. They were greatly prized by him.

During this month we were able to gather information from other Poles who were being detained here that the Polish Army Command had been moved to Yanghi Yul in Kirgiz. Letters and telegrams were sent to Mr. Wozimirski in the hope that since he was in the army the letters would be forwarded to him. But news of the German invasion of the Soviet Union also reached us and the already sparse supply of food and goods was to dwindle down even further.

Soon it was to be Christmas. As always I was anxiously anticipating Christmas Eve, though I knew that there were not going to be any gifts. For the first time we had no Christmas tree, though Basia was making a small nativity set out of clay and we set it up in the corner of our hut.

CHRISTMAS, 1941
UZBEKISTAN

There was no Christmas Eve dinner or anything close to the traditional food, since there were barely any scraps to be put into the communal pot for the daily soup. But despite the grim and starving surroundings we tried to make this evening a festive one. So when everyone returned from the fields we sat outside and exchanged traditional Christmas greetings sharing a coarse unleavened bread instead of the usual wafer. The soup was ladled out, and for dessert we a had handful of raisins which added a festive touch. A Christmas wish was repeated by each of us that on the next Holyday we would be back in our homeland.

After the soup was consumed, instead of what usually would have been a look under the Tree for gifts, mom instead gave me two little dolls about four inches tall. I had seen such dolls in native markets and admired them. I was the happiest kid! Aunt Maria got some ribbon for my hair while aunt Luta had a slice of white bread for me. I had not seen or eaten such a delicacy in a long time. Needless to say , the bread was consumed by me immediately.

But wanting to share and show off my gifts, I went to find my Uzbek playmate who lived down the road from us in another hut. She was my age and had long braided dark hair. She was always dressed in the native garb of pantaloons and a multicolored blouse. Besides playing with her, I always liked to go to her hut where there were always several people.

To me, their house was an exotic place where everyone sat on the carpets and ate out of the same bowl, placed on the floor in front of them. I also caught on quickly that their eastern hospitality would extend to me if I happened to be there when the meal was served. The meal was simple fare, since they were poor, but it was always more than what we were able to have.

So on this evening, again I managed to come at the opportune time, to share in their meal and show my friend my treasures.

Chapter 15

Germany-Sandbostel, Lubeck

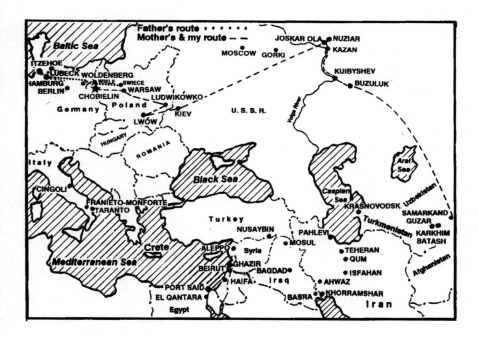

SUMMER 1941
SANDBOSTEL, GERMANY

It was a warm late summer day and father sat on his makeshift bench behind the barrack writing letters, while at the same time trying to soak up some sun. He was about to leave and post the letter when two German military trucks passed by on the road, adjacent to the camp fence. The trucks, instead of continuing on the road, slowed down and turned into a dirt road that crossed the marshy field towards a cluster of trees. His curiosity piqued, father remained sitting and decided to observe.

The trucks came to a stop when they reached the trees and out of the first vehicle piled out, one by one, German soldiers who brought with them French POWs. Then the soldiers opened the back plank of the second truck and ordered the prisoners to roll out balls of barbed wire, with which they started to encompass the perimeter of the trees that now served as posts for the wire. Roll after roll was strung until the fence reached approximately seven to eight in feet height.

"What on earth are they doing?"; father pondered, as he watched.

Father could not think of any reason why the Germans would enclose a clump of trees, which covered an acre of land and in a place where there was nothing else. He knew that the fields were scattered with these small woods in order to provide sanctuary for wildlife, but why the barbed wire?

As the French prisoners completed the enclosure, they cut a narrow gate on one side and secured it. The guards shouted orders for the POWs to get into trucks and they departed. Still puzzled by this odd structure, but since it did not appear that anything more was going to happen, father left his lookout place.

A week passed after this incident and the weather there near the North Sea began to change, cold winds chilling the air. It was beginning to drizzle and the fog had rolled in from the sea when father noticed a column of marching men approaching on the road, who were escorted by armed guards.

The marchers looked weary and haggard, and were dragging their feet. Some of the men could only walk with the support of others. The column wound by the camp, attracting the attention of other POWs who, like father, were curious to see who these prisoners were. Upon examining the remnants of their insignia, as well as recognizing some of their uniforms, father realized that they were Soviet prisoners.

The German guards led the Soviet prisoners off the main road toward the trees and into the barbed wire enclosure which had been constructed only a week ago. As the weary captives, one by one, entered the open-air former wildlife sanctuary, the gate was shut behind them and guards with machine guns positioned themselves outside the enclosure. Father and others in his camp, observing the open air compound, thought that this must be only temporary quarters for the Soviet POWs, who he estimated must have numbered around 800 strong.

Watching these Soviet captives brought back to Germany, everyone in father's camp began to worry that the Germans were victorious on the Russian front.

It must be only a temporary situation...there is no shelter or anything else there." Father thought to himself as he looked toward the enclosure.

As the days passed nothing could be seen from the distance of father's camp but occasional shouting and screaming would reach their ears. Then, after a week, a German truck appeared with what looked like a load of bread which the guards began to toss over the fence to the Russian prisoners, now emerging from the cover of the trees. The starving Russians started to scramble and fight, screaming and yelling, over the tossed loaves of moldy bread.

This procedure, which the Germans called "feeding", repeated itself once a week; every week, the number of prisoners that appeared for feeding was smaller. Then the rains came and the cold started to get worse, but the Russians were still kept in the open-air wooded compound without any housing facilities.

While watching helplessly the slow elimination of the Russian prisoners, father dispatched a letter to aunt Helen.

OCTOBER 24, 1941
SANDBOSTEL, GERMANY
Dear Helen,
I have received your package for which I thank you. If you could please send me a little bit of barley or dry peas. I have sent a little less money because I had to have some shoes made for myself.

Don't worry Helen, it has to get better for them now in Russia, as long as they stay well. In four days it will be our wedding anniversary.[Their 8th] I miss Ania and Terenia very much; I need them so much.

We are well; we ask God that this war would finally end. How all this will turn out, it is better not to think.

I embrace you.

Stach

It was the middle of November when finally the Germans came to transfer whatever was left of the Soviet prisoners. As father and some of his friends watched, the gate of the compound was opened and the guards went in shouting orders to assemble. Staggering and stumbling, five bearded and ragged individuals emerged from among the trees. Their backs bent and moving their feet with difficulty, the men shuffled out the gate and into the waiting truck that took them away. The following day, the French POWs were brought back and started to clear out the bodies and remains of who ever was left of the Soviet prisoners that could be buried.

Soon after the Russian incident, the camp officials announced that the contingent of Polish officers would be shipped out of Sandbostel the following day to a camp in Lubeck. Hence, the next evening father and the rest of the Polish POWs, who numbered around two thousand, were marched to the nearby railroad station and packed into freight cars headed north; destination Lubeck.

NOVEMBER 1941
JOURNEY TO LUBECK, GERMANY

The train was under blackout orders, since British bombers already were continually penetrating German territory in order to destroy anything needed for their enemy's war machine. The passage through Bremen went without problem, but as the train was passing Hamburg the wailing of air-raid sirens halted it on one of city's numerous tracks. The German guards and the train crew dispersed seeking cover, leaving the locked-up prisoners in the train. The sirens had no chance to stop when the roar of bomber engines was heard from above, followed by the whining sound of falling bombs and thunderous explosions. The targets that had been hit blew to bits, shaking the surrounding ground.

The station and the prisoner train standing in it managed by some unfathomable luck to be spared any direct hit, but the dark and crewless train with its helpless human cargo rocked to and fro on its track. In one of the cars the occupants decided to take advantage of the lack of guards and turmoil of the air raid and attempt to escape.

The prisoners managed to pry out bars from a window; then the smallest of the POWs was hoisted up to it and he squeezed through and jumped to the ground. With the air raid still in progress, the man lifted the wooden beam that served as a large latch on the wide doors of the freight car. The doors rolled back and, one by one, some of its occupants began to jump out and disappear into the darkness of the night.

When the bombing finally ceased and the all-clear sirens were heard, the guards and crew returned to the train. The guards, glad that the ordeal was over, did not notice that one of the car doors had been opened. The night was lit by the glow of the burning city as the train slowly started to lumber out of the station. From the open car of the moving train the rest of the men began jumping out, one by one. By the time the train reached Lubeck forty Polish POWs had escaped!

When the initial head-count of the prisoners was made at the Lubeck train station, the initial consternation of the German authorities grew to comical proportions, which brought hidden joy to the rest of the prisoners. The Germans, not quite believing that they were missing so large a number, lined up all POWs on the station platform, interrogating, searching and threatening them with disciplinary action while counting and recounting them; to their frustration, they always came up forty heads short.

Father, together with his fellow officers, was held standing on the platform for six hours as they watched a short, rotund, old Prussian Colonel wearing a saber fastened to his belt, run around shouting and threatening that if the prisoners would not cooperate, the Gestapo would come and would take care of the situation. The colonel was the commander of the Lubeck camp, Freiherr Von Wahmaister. Not having received any response or success from the tired, standing group, the German commander's rage focused on the senior Polish POW officer, Colonel Janicki.

"Colonel Janicki!" Von Wahmaister hissed through his clenched teeth, his small mustache twitching, "you are responsible for your men! There will be severe repercussions if you and your men do not cooperate!"

"Colonel, I did not escape.." replied the Polish officer in a low , nonchalant voice, "and I don't guard them. I suggest you talk to your guards who are supposed to guard us."

The Germans, after hours of delay and ultimately realizing that there was nothing to be gained by more of the same, marched the POWs to the camp, which was located on the outskirts of the city and adjacent to the port of Lubeck. The buildings of the camp had previously been used by the Hitler Jugend and therefore were better facilities than in Sandbostel, but it was a semi-disciplinary camp that again contained international POWs.

The contingent of prisoners from Sandbostel were assigned housing in the north side of camp, which was closest to the sea. But before the POWs could settle in, they were told that as punishment for the escape of the officers from the train in Hamburg, all of them were confined to their barracks for a period of a month: only once a day were they allowed to step out for a fifteen minute interval. To further harass and intimidate the prisoners the guards, who were positioned on watch-towers that encircled the camp, would spray the ground with volley a of bullets at any small pretext.

Here, the food was barely adequate, and as further disciplinary action by the camp commander the Polish POWs were not allowed to receive any packages from abroad, such as Red Cross packages. Fortunately, letters and packages from aunt Helen were not under that ban and they continued to come, but father responded less frequently, as is evident from his letters.

DECEMBER 6, 1941
LUBECK, GERMANY
Dear Helen,

I am sorry for the lull in my writing but I wrote abroad in order that I might get some news from Ania. I am waiting in vain but I have some second-hand news that living conditions are good (in Soviet Union) and the authorities (Polish) are in charge.

Only today I have send you the money. If possible Helen, I would like you to send me some flour or barley because I have an opportunity to cook.

I am wishing you dear Helen that you spent your Holiday happily with a thought of hope and faith in better times that will come.

Stach

From father's letter it was evident that they knew about the amnesty for Poles in the Soviet Union but were not aware of the obstacles that the Soviet authorities were creating. He was not aware, since no correspondence was possible between USSR and Germany, that we were incarcerated in an Uzbek "Kolhoz". But he continued to write to aunt Helen.

DECEMBER 23, 1941
LUBECK, GERMANY
Dear Helen,

Day before yesterday I have received your package for which I thank you very much. We did not send any money because there was an interruption. The money was mailed on December 21. Jas has not received any news from you for a long while, not even a letter or a postcard;

I don't have any news from Ania. On December 16th a year has passed since she wrote the last card besides that I had a few cards from Terenia.

Dear Helen, I wish you a happy Holiday and don't worry, the New year is going to be better.

Stach

That day, the 23rd of December, several cars with SS men arrived in the camp and ordered all prisoners, regardless of their physical condition, be they sick or well, to line up outdoors and form a double file. While the POWs stood shivering in bitter cold for over four hours, the SS rummaged through the meager belongings of the imprisoned, confiscating items such as underwear and any blankets in excess of one; this included shoes or any items that SS deemed that the German soldiers could use. The raid on the prisoners did not stop at that.

After having pillaged the contents of the barracks, the SS turned on each POW individually; each man had to unbutton his overcoat and if he was fortunate enough to be wearing a sweater, scarf or warm coat lining, it was immediately taken away from him. Neither father or uncle Jas had anything taken from them, since neither possessed items that the Germans were looking for.

On the following day another inspection and head count of the prisoners was made, but this time assisting the German camp commander was a young officer introduced as Captain Schultz. As the Captain passed rows of POWs, scanning their faces, he hesitated when his gaze fell upon father; father returned the gaze while searching his memory, because the face of this man looked familiar.

"I have seen him someplace...Schultz, Schultz...but where?"

The German captain passed on but father continued to sort out his memories while standing in the bleak and cold winter day, trying to recall why this man looked so familiar. Suddenly the puzzle started to fall in place.

"Oh yes, Schultz...summer of '35, that's him!"

It was sometime during 1935 when father was on his annual military maneuvers in Pomorze where, as was the custom then, the officers were usually quartered in various neighboring estates. Father was assigned to an estate of a very hospitable ethnic German who lived in Poland and was a captain in the reserves; the name of the estate was Plewo. At that time the German host happened to have a guest, his young nephew named Schultz, who had come from Germany to Plewo for a holiday.

Since the nephew did not speak Polish and father's German was not fluent, there was not much conversation between them. But one day young Schultz approached father, bringing with him the administrator of the estate, who served as an interpreter:

"Lieutenant Mikosz," the administrator addressed father, "the young man wants me to ask you if he could go horseback riding with you; is it possible?"

"Of course! Let me get one of the lancers to saddle a horse for him." Turning from them, father gave instructions to a soldier standing nearby to ready a horse. In a few minutes, father and young Schultz went riding through his uncle's estate, enjoying the afternoon although a language barrier still existed. Upon their return from the ride, the young man thanked father warmly.

And now...Captain Schultz was father's captor. It seemed that he also recognized him, but was not in a position to acknowledge the long-ago acquaintance.

A few days had passed since father saw Captain Schultz, when he received a package from uncle Bernard with various items, among them a woolen blanket. Since it was not allowed POWs to have more than one blanket, this one was confiscated. Not wanting this precious possession to get away from him, father requested through an interpreter to register a formal complaint with the camp authorities. This was a normal procedure but rarely did any good. Father in due course was brought in front of the officer on duty, who at that time was captain Schultz, in order to air his grievance.

Captain Schultz received father very courteously, and father again perceived that he recognized him but did not wish to acknowledge the fact. Having heard father out, he thanked him and promised to look into the matter and see what he could do.

Two days then passed when, to father's great surprise, a camp guard appeared in his barrack bearing a large box that contained the confiscated blanket.

"Captain Mikosz, Captain Schultz told me to give this package to you," said the guard, handing the box to father.

DECEMBER 31, 1941
LUBECK, GERMANY
Dear Helen,

I received the package before the Holidays, it took long to reach me but finally it arrived. Today I received your card from December 12th. You are writing that you are planning to send bread by regular mail; that is allowed since other friends receive it that way. Last time I sent you a sticker for a parcel because it might be to hard for you Helen otherwise. Don't be angry but Jas has sent everything. Jas has not received any correspondence from you for a long time. The card that I got from you made him very happy. If you send sugar, please wrap it well because it will spoil the bread. This happens to things that absorb humidity. I don't have any news from Ania and I don't expect any since correspondence from Russia is forbidden. Physically I feel well but I can't wait till this war comes to an end. Tomorrow is a New Year- it seems possible that this year this terrible turmoil will end, that we will return home because everything in this world comes to an end eventually. We talk a great deal about all of you, reminiscing about former moments and we live in hope. Only you Helen don't give up hope because after a storm comes the bright sun of happiness which will also shine for all of us. In the New Year, dear Helen, Danka, Janusz, Marysia and Andrzej, I wish you that joy and health will not leave you because better times are near.

Stach

Part Four

1942

Chapter 16

Uzbekistan-Kolhoz "Stalin", Guzar, KHARMKIM BATASH; TURKMENISTAN-KRASNOVODSK

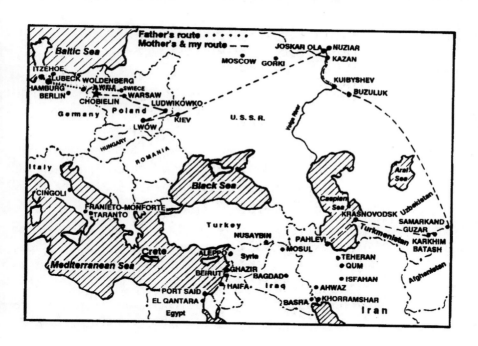

JANUARY 1942
KOLHOZ "STALIN", UZBEKISTAN

The perfect winter weather finally arrived. The rainy season ended and it was a time of clear blue skies and warm days with cool nights, making the miserable conditions of our everyday existence more palatable. The cotton fields shimmered in the sunlight and were ready for harvesting.

Our lives were intermingled with those of the Uzbeks who shared our hard existence and newfound friendships with us. Just as I had my Uzbek friend and playmate, Romek and Basia developed their own individual friendships, which provoked an amusing incident.

Romek was then 15 years old and became friends with a gregarious twenty-year-old Uzbek, Ali, who was also very fond of Krystofer and, while the child was alive, often would give him rides on his horse. Ali admired Romek's well-worn high school uniform, in particular his navy blue blazer, even though it was by now worn out, being basically the only outer garment that Romek possessed. Ali continuously tried, without any result, to have Romek part with the blazer, since Ali was getting married the following week. The matter of having the blazer became an obsession, since he wanted to impress his wedding guests. Two days before the wedding, Romek, after our work in the fields ended, was out with Ali and some of his clansmen, who started the celebrations early by drinking vodka. Fortified by the alcohol, Ali and his buddies decided that it was time the coveted blazer be obtained by force. So, while we were sitting in front of the hut, we spotted Romek darting through the fields and heading in our direction at great speed.

"Quick…I have to hide." he gasped, and headed into the hut.

Before anyone could ask what was the reason for this frantic dash, Ali came galloping on his horse, eyes glazed and very much in a huff, yelling something incomprehensible except for the word "Romek" that he repeated several times.

Everyone was acting dumb and Miss Gabrysia convinced Ali that we didn't know where Romek was. Accepting the explanation with some hesitation, Ali gave his horse a nudge with his heels and sped off in search of his prey. Meanwhile, Romek lay covered with blankets in the hut, very much shaken up. After he calmed down he explained what had occurred when he, Ali, and some friends went to celebrate. The Uzbeks became brave with the help of alcohol and since Romek did not want to part with his jacket voluntarily, they were going to strip him; that was when Romek darted home. Since they had been drinking long before Romek came, he was able to out run the tipsy Uzbeks. Needless to say, on the next day, after Ali and his friends slept off their drinking, everything was forgotten and the village wedding went on with Ali in his traditional colorful Uzbek garb.

January was coming to an end and, as on most days, everyone from our hut left at daybreak to work in the cotton fields. Now, with the afternoon sun warming the air, they were returning one by one after hours of back-breaking work. Mother and aunt Maria were the first to come back and brought with them scraps of vegetables that they were able to scrounge on their way back in order to make a meal.

The two of them were cleaning the vegetable discards and talking while throwing them into the nearby cauldron that was standing by the hut. These talks usually turned into a sibling altercation ignored by the rest of the family. I was nearby playing with my doll when I noticed someone coming across the fields towards us. I turned to mother, nudging her and pointing to the oncoming figure.

"Look, mother, who is that?" She looked up and, shielding her eyes with her hand, began to scrutinize the approaching figure.

"Maria, look, it looks like a soldier...but not a Russian." Mother motioned to aunt Maria.

Now both of them stood there, squinting, while trying to make out who this person was. As the man came nearer, he waved his hand and mother and aunt Maria exclaimed;

"It's one of our soldiers, he's Polish!"

The uniformed man came closer and said: "I am looking for Mrs. Maria Stankiewicz and Mrs. Anna Mikosz. Do you know in which hut they are living?"

There was a stunned silence that lasted a few seconds; aunt Maria hesitantly acknowledged that she and mother were the persons that the individual was looking for. The man then introduced himself as a sergeant who Captain Wozimirski had sent to get us all out of there. The sergeant was quick to explain that he had the necessary papers for the Soviet authorities that would permit us to travel to Guzar, since one could not move from one district to another without permission from the Soviet authorities.

Soon the rest of the family returned from the fields; they could hardly believe the good news and were curious to know how the sergeant was able to find us. The sergeant then related his story; Captain Wozimirski gave him the address of the kolhoz but because the complex was so spread out, he opted to go first to the kolhoz infirmary. Here he found Mrs. Kwiatkowska, who worked there and who knew us. She pointed out the way to our living quarters.

It was a happy evening, not only because we were able to leave the next day, but the sergeant had been provisioned by Captain Wozimirski with food that we had not seen in years; he brought real bread, sugar and even some coffee. The joyful evening was full of anticipation of the new tomorrow. We talked late into the night, questioning the sergeant about the status of the repatriation and mobilization of the Polish army. Aunt Maria was particularly anxious about the news, if any, that might have come from the prisoner of war camp of Kozielsk, since that was where her husband had been taken, but unfortunately the question of Kozielsk was still a mystery and the officers from that camp were unaccounted for.

While hasty goodbyes were exchanged with friends in the kolhoz who were unable to leave, I went to see my Uzbek playmate to say that we were leaving; but she did not comprehend, since here no one left unless they died.

On the following day we were up with the first rays of dawn, packed our bundles and scrambled into a previously hired horse cart heading for the Samarkand train station.

Our group consisted of aunt Luta with her teenage children Romek and Barbara, aunt Maria, Miss Gabrysia, mother and me, and was headed by the sergeant. It was very early in the morning and the cart rumbled up the empty, dusty, bumpy road, leaving behind us months of misery and Krystofer's grave. Aunt Maria was quiet. She just held her arm around me and tears rolled down her cheeks. She knew that she was leaving behind whatever link she would have with Krystofer, her baby. Where her husband was she did not know.

We arrived at the train station. The sergeant went to get the tickets for our passage to Guzar and he found that the prospect did not look too promising. The trains were full or even over their capacity, since the news of amnesty had spread rapidly to hundreds of Polish camps throughout vast expanses of the Soviet Union and thousands of people were heading towards Guzar and other recruiting centers, just like us. Several trains passed and we were still unable to get onto any of them. Finally, towards the evening a train carrying Polish military personnel stopped in Samarkand. It also was full to its capacity but the sergeant, being a quick thinking individual and not to be deterred by such a minor problem, began to wave his official papers, explaining that we were military dependents entitled to transportation and by so doing got us a place on the train.

We were happy to be on board and on the way, away from the Kolhoz. We were assigned the only available space on the train; a space on the floor of the field kitchen-car. Exhausted, we scrambled onto the car and located ourselves in corners, so as not to hamper anyone, and spread out our pallets for sleeping. In addition, we were fed with what I thought was most wonderful food—a real soup with meat and vegetables. The evening came, activity in the car subsided, and exhausted, we fell asleep.. When I awoke we were in Guzar station.

FEBRUARY 1942
GUZAR, UZBEKISTAN

The station was buzzing with activity. Polish military personnel were everywhere, intermingled with the colorful robes of Uzbek men and women. Guzar was the location of the Army Depot for the forming of the Polish Armed Forces. In addition to Guzar center, there were a dozen other localities in Kirgiztan, Kazakhstan, Tadzikistan and Uzbekistan, where different Polish Army divisions were formed. The sergeant gathered our group together and took us to the Polish repatriation center where we had to register. Here, aunt Maria found Captain Nowicki, who was a good friend of her husband Wacek, and again her first questions were about uncle Wacek's whereabouts.

"He has not reported yet. But don't worry, he will turn up soon. You know how difficult it is to move around Russia. There are still thousands of officers that are unaccounted for. Be patient, every day men are coming." said Captain Nowicki, trying to reassure her.

He then took personal charge of us and found housing in the center of town, which housed Polish non-military people. These Spartan accommodations consisted of a large warehouse structure. Everyone was put on the bare floor, but at least we were free and under the protection of the Polish authorities. Miss Gabrysia and Romek were more resourceful and managed to find some crude wooden tables that we could sleep on instead of on the dirt floor.

Mother and aunt Maria, through the intervention of captain Nowicki, were garbed in Polish army uniforms and got jobs at the officers' mess as waitresses. The job did not last more than ten days, since mother and aunt Maria were so inept that they were unable to collect the necessary money from officers for the meals. The whole "working" episode ended with them not only not getting paid but in addition owing money to the mess.

Though Guzar was a haven for all who came there from prisons and camps, it also became a death trap for thousands. With the influx of such a multitude of people who, after two years of hardship, under severe climatic conditions, accompanied by starvation and lack of proper medical attention, had impaired health, we were faced with another problem. The city did not have an adequate sanitation system; as a result, the water supply became contaminated, which in turn caused epidemics of dysentery, typhus and typhoid.

The Uzbeks themselves were always very well inclined towards the Poles and regarded the Soviets as oppressors, since some of the Khanates did not lose their independence till the mid 1930s. This was a very deprived section of the USSR, and particularly now when they had to "contribute" to the western front where the Germans were making rapid advances. In addition, the Soviet authorities appropriated for themselves great portions of supplies and food which had been sent for Polish relief by the western allies.

After our initial contact with the Uzbeks, and when they realized that we were not Russian, friendly relations between the two nationalities developed. The main reason for the Uzbeks viewing Poles as friends was based on a medieval legend that was not known to us but was soon to be explained, after some curious Polish individuals inquired about it and the story began to unfold. To understand the legend one must go back into Polish history of the 12th century. In the southern city of Krakow, from the top of the spire of St. Mary's church a trumpet fanfare was played every hour (the tradition continues to this day). When the city was invaded by the tartars of the Golden Horde, the sentry's trumpeted warning (the "Hejnal") was abruptly interrupted by an arrow shot through the trumpeter's throat by one of Genghis Khan's cavalryman. The Poles were fascinated to learn that through the intervening centuries the story had evidently been told here in the steppes. Because of this legend, the Uzbeks, who are very superstitious, asked the Polish authorities to have their trumpeter play the "Hejnal" here, which was done; for their prophecy said that they, the Uzbeks, would not be free until a Polish trumpeter played the "Hejnal" on Uzbek soil. So, whatever one thinks of legends, in the 1990's the Uzbeks once again regained their independence—do you think that the fulfillment in 1942 of the 12th century legend had anything to do with it?

With a typhoid epidemic ravaging the town, it was only a matter of days when the disease reached our family group. Aunt Luta was first to come down with typhoid, followed then by Basia, and then I became ill. Mother, being alarmed, took me to a Soviet hospital where they had a children's ward and after a doctor examined me he diagnosed me with having typhoid, but the hospital authorities said that there was no room and refused to admit me. Frantic and concerned, having no place to which to turn, mother then took me to the Polish military hospital, technically only for military personnel, which was housed in an old dilapidated mosque complex that had been given to the Polish military to be used as a hospital. This facility was lacking almost all basic essentials, and now, with the epidemic raging, was overcrowded with the sick and the dying. There were not enough beds, so a majority of the sick lay in rows on the floors next to each other. In spite of the primitive and overcrowded conditions, I was admitted.

My first memories of this place were obliterated by high fever, but when finally I regained awareness, I found myself in a small windowless room that had an opening for a door, but no door. The doorway was a source of light for the room, and it faced a square courtyard that was encircled with other similar rooms. My place on the floor was next to the doorway, giving me an opportunity to observe the goings on in the courtyard; by so doing I kept myself amused while I returned to health.

Within a day of two after I passed the critical stage of my sickness, the nurses brought mother and placed her bedding next to mine. Evidently, she came down with typhoid soon after I did but was placed in another ward. By now she had passed her critical phase but was so weak that she was unable to lift her head. I, on the other hand, was recuperating fast, mostly due to the tender care of the staff who were trying to please and help me in every way. They would scrounge extra food for me and give me chunks of sugar, a great delicacy that the nurses and the hospital chaplain would somehow find and indulge me with. I of course would look forward to these visits and crunch my acquisition with delight.

I was getting better, but not well enough to be released. In addition, mother was still not mended, so the days began to drag for me. To pass this monotonous time I would sit on my floor-pallet and observe the goings-on in the courtyard, which swirled with activity; a constant flow of incoming sick and the attending staff that continued day and night.

One morning I awakened early and noticed that, besides the staff and the ambulatory sick, there were people lying on the bare stones of the courtyard. With time more people were placed on the ground, so I began to count; I reached the number twenty-five and stopped, because through the arched entrance of the court came a horse drawn cart. Polish soldiers jumped out of it and proceeded to place these people into the cart. I found it odd that they were stacking them one on top of each other. At that moment I realized these were not live persons but corpses; people who had died during the night. As I continued to observe the proceeding with great curiosity, the cart was filled up with bodies and then rolled out of the gate, followed by a priest and a few soldiers who formed the mass funeral cortege. Unfortunately this scene was repeated several times daily, since the typhoid epidemic was not subsiding but rather was taking more victims.

Mother and I were well enough to be released, and here Captain Nowicki came to the rescue once again. He arranged that mother and I would go to the nearby settlement of Kharkim Batash, where the Polish authorities had organized an orphanage for children whose parents had died either in camps or here, or in some cases got separated from them. The facilities were much better, as well as healthier, than in Guzar, and in addition aunt Luta, Basia, Romek and aunt Maria were here.

MARCH 1942
KARKHIM BATASH, UZBEKISTAN

The following is an excerpt of the report of the organization of the orphanage. The official document is in the General Sikorski Historical Institute in London.

March 6, 1942

Report concerning the work of organizing centers for Polish families and children in the Guzar area.

In the region of Guzar and Dekanabat there are, in Kolhozes, about 6,000 Polish families-living in the worst possible conditions and poverty. This situation compelled the military authorities to take certain steps to help our unfortunate compatriots. The most urgent

*problem was that of abandoned children, old people and those inca-
pable of work. For this reason an orphanage is to be established.*

The orphanage.

*In the kolhoz of Kharkim-Batash, 7km from Guzar, situated in
beautiful, picturesque and healthy surroundings, with a large open
space, we found buildings, at present ruined, but adaptable as an
orphanage capable of accommodating up to 300 children.*

*Therefore a complete repair program has been set in hand, which
has with considerable expense and difficulty been partly completed,
so that there is now accommodation for 200 children plus buildings
for administration, kitchens and personnel.*

*Further building is in progress. Disinfestation, baths and health
care are assured at the nearby army company. The children will sleep
on mats and mattresses and some will use camp beds. There is a total
absence of bed linen, clothing and underwear etc. I enclose a list of
items needed. In order to finish the repair of the accommodation for
the orphanage and to supply other needs it is absolutely necessary to
receive the sum of 20,000 roubles, requested here to be allocated. We
project an extension of the orphanage to accommodate up to 500
children.*

On an early morning came aunt Maria, accompanied by a soldier whom
Captain Nowicki sent to help her get mother and me from the hospital and
transfer us to the new settlement. They came with a small horse-drawn cart
that the Captain was able to hire from an Uzbek farmer. Mother, though
over the typhoid, was so devastated that she could not even stand up by
herself; she was carried by two orderlies and laid down on the floor of the
cart. Aunt Maria and I sat beside her. The soldier sat in front, next to the
Uzbek who prodded the worn-out horse on to our destination.

After a couple of hours on a bumpy road, we reached Kharkim-Batash
and waiting aunt Luta, together with mother's friend, Mrs. Berdowska.
Mrs. Berdowska's husband was a captain like my father, and both of them
had served in the same regiment in Grudziadz before the war. She,

together with her two children, Barbara and Krys, were deported to the Soviet Union from Lwow and were sent to a camp in the north. They managed to reach the Polish repatriation center earlier than we did, and Mrs. Berdowska was now on the staff of the orphanage and arranged that we were to share the same hut. In addition, Mrs. Berdowska managed to acquire a bed for mother, a luxury that mother appreciated greatly. Though the bed was a crude one, consisting of only a few bare planks and a large bag of hay for a mattress, it was a treat after sleeping on the floor for the last year.

It turned out that Mrs. Berdowska was not only a good friend to us but also a very enterprising woman. Mother, who still was the process of re-learning to walk, was unable to make the walking distance to the out-house, so Mrs. Berdowska acquired a chamber pot. The day after our arrival, she walked into our room with beaming smile on her face, and tri-umphantly produced a chamber pot that she had "appropriated" from an Uzbek who had hung the pot out to dry on his house's fence post.

Barbara Berdowska was my age and I now had a friend to share time with, since my cousin Basia went back to temporary classes and Romek joined a cadet school that was organized in the town of Kerminie in Uzbekistan. On the other hand, Miss Gabrysia was here and was added to the staff of the orphanage, since the influx of children continued to grow.

Though the number of persons was increasing in Kharkim Batash, the Soviet authorities were not increasing the food supply but rather were cut-ting it down. Rumors circulated about the obstacles that Stalin's regime was creating in order to send the newly released people back to the collec-tive farms. In actuality, Stalin proposed to disband all men in excess of the 26,000 that were in the army and send them back to the kolhoz. This solution was not accepted by the Polish authorities; instead, they proposed to evacuate the surplus soldiers to Iran, where they would be supplied by the British and not be dependent on the Soviets. After more bartering, Stalin agreed to the proposal and, not wanting any more delays, the Polish authorities started to immediately evacuate military personnel, and as many civilians as possible, to Iran. The people who were the weakest were the first ones to leave, in order that they might regain their health and get better medical attention.

On March 23rd Mrs. Berdowska came to our hut, very much excited, and announced "Pack your belongings, because day after tomorrow we are leaving; the whole orphanage and all the personnel."

The first question was "where?", but since no one was sure where, we only knew that we were to leave the Soviet Union. That was enough to fill us with excitement and the anticipation of a better tomorrow. So on the 25th of March 1942 we were taken to a train station where cars were waiting for us; this time passenger cars that chugged through Turkmenistan and its vast steppes of Karakumy, which at one time had served as pasturage for goats, sheep and camels. The train headed for Ashkabad and then continued to the port city of Krasnovodsk on the Caspian Sea.

MARCH 30, 1942
KRASNOVODSK, TURKMENISTAN

After being shuttled from the train station to the port, where a large fishing boat was waiting for the evacuees, there were more " paper" formalities imposed by the Soviet. We were all subdued and silently praying that we might get on the boat that could take us to freedom; the boat, ironically, was named "Stalin". Half a day passed before the embarkation started. One by one, the tired, rag-clad and half starved people, trying to hold each other up, proceeded up the makeshift wooden plank after giving their name to the NKVD official who checked his list for the name. Sometimes the Soviet official would tell the person to step aside, and then there would be an exchange with the Polish representative who would try to explain the problem. Finally our turn came. I clung to mother's hand as she answered the NKVD soldier. He scanned the list, made a check next to a name, and said:

"Davay" (Go)

My grip of mother's hand eased as we continued to walk up the plank and I did not look back until I reached the deck. Following us were aunt Luta with Barbara, aunt Maria and Miss Gabrysia. Soon after them came Mrs. Berdowska with her children.

The boat was filling fast and the Polish soldiers who were on board were helping women and children to find places to sit through the upcoming journey. The orphanage from Kharkim Batash was placed on the deck and we with it. So, our bundles stashed against the wall, we sat and watched as the boat was packed with as many people as possible. Finally the plank was up and, as the boat was to leave the shore, a Soviet Army Band that was waiting on shore started to play the Polish National Anthem "Poland is not lost". Though it was an unexpected and ironic moment, it produced a joyful reaction. Out of the tired and hungry people and children arose a spontaneous singing of the Polish anthem.

The children, particularly the smaller ones, did not really comprehend what was going on; they were tired and bewildered and for them it was just another journey. The adults, on the other hand, as they watched the distant shores of the Soviet Union disappear on the horizon, cried because of joy, because every one of us had left so many of their families buried there. As for our family, eleven of us had been taken to the Soviet camps and only six survived to leave this land. Behind we left the graves of Grandfather, uncle Alfons, uncle Josef, uncle Wacek and Krystofer. All the men died, with the exception of Romek who was only now just seventeen. We were among the fortunate ones and still did not fully believe that we were leaving the land in which so much suffering had been inflicted upon us.

Though it was a very hot day, as soon as the sun set the temperature dropped and it became cold. Mother unpacked her battered quilt that she had managed to hold on to despite bartering all other goods which had been in our possession, and she tucked me under it. I was hungry and very uncomfortable, since many people began to get sea sick, but despite these conditions no one complained. Before night fell, a meal that consisted of salted fish, dried biscuits and hot tea was given to us;

not a particularly good choice for a meal on a small swaying ship. The sea remained calm throughout our voyage as we spent two nights and a day on "Stalin", sleeping on the open deck and during the day sunning and being fed the salted fish. I was awakened the second night by activity on the opposite side of the deck but could not see anything; I heard several splashes and then silence. When I asked my cousin if she saw what was going on, she answered that these were burials at sea of people that had died during the day.

We did not know where we were actually going. Rumors started to circulate that we were going to another Soviet port to be taken to other prisons. No matter how much the rumors were denied by the authorities, the denials were not believed. It was not until the third day, when land was sighted and a boat came closer to shore hoisting a Polish flag, that some of the anxiety was quenched. As I peered over the railing I saw a motorboat heading towards our ship. Looking at the oncoming craft, we saw that it carried two flags. One was red, green and white; we were not familiar with that one, but below was the white and red flag of Poland. Sighting of the familiar flag brought on cheering and waving from the deck of "Stalin". The motorboat pulled along our ship and I a saw couple of Polish military personnel scramble aboard by means of a rope ladder that was dropped for them. As they stepped on deck, they were surrounded by people asking "Where are we?"

Smiling, a Polish officer announced in a loud voice:

"You are safe. You are in Iran!"

Chapter 17

Germany-Lubeck

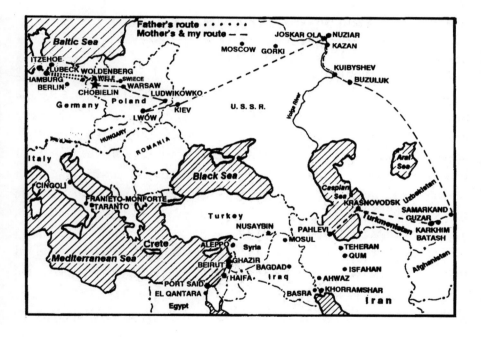

JANUARY 1942
LUBECK, GERMANY

The bleak Holidays passed and a severe winter set in, making the barely livable conditions even worse. The war was not going well for the Germans; their Russian offensive was becoming expensive in terms of losses of men and equipment as demanded by a winter campaign. At present, the Germans were stopped at Moscow with little hope of being able to retreat and return home. Having enough problems with their own army, the Germans considered the POWs an added and unnecessary burden; hence, it became evident to their prisoners that the captors were getting ready to eliminate them. Food, which was never plentiful, now drastically decreased in quantity and could not be supplemented by packages. The order came out that the POWs were not permitted to receive any parcels from families or from abroad.

Regardless of German plans for the camp, however, the number of international prisoners, particularly those of high rank, was increasing and they were observed by the rest of the POWs with some curiosity. These "VIP" prisoners were kept apart from the rest of camp by means of a low barbed wire fence that ran along the back of the barrack in which father was housed. Among these "celebrities" were four Yugoslav generals, a cousin of King George VI of England and a short, dark haired lieutenant in a Soviet uniform. Father thought that it was odd to have a lieutenant among these high-ranking officers but after some inquiries the news spread at the camp: the lieutenant was Stalin's son! He was his son Jocob, who was a child of his first marriage.

The correspondence with aunt Helen continued and father received news that mother's brother Maks, who during the German invasion stayed behind in Poland with his wife and two infant children, had died. Uncle Maks was several times arrested by the Germans and severely interrogated and tortured, so when finally released, he was a broken man.

FEBRUARY 17, 1942
LUBECK, GERMANY
Dear Helen,

Please accept my deepest sympathies because of Maks's death. I feel so sorry for you Helen since you have to bear so many burdens. Personally, I was very moved by these news.

Letter of February 8th and package of February 7th, I have received yesterday. I thank you for it very warmly.

On the occasion of your Namesday, I send you, dear Helen, warmest greetings [so that] your wishes, come true, and for health and strength of will as faith in [future] happiness.

Stach

In addition, father was continuously trying to find our whereabouts through whatever channels he could use. In the next letter to aunt Helen he shares the information that he was able to obtain, since he was in a better position to get such news than she was.

MARCH 17, 1942

LUBECK, GERMANY

Dear Helen,

Today I have received your card dated March 8th. For everything I thank you very much. The money for the two months I will send you in April.

About Ania's fate. I have heard second hand through Ankara (Turkey, Red-Cross) that they are taken care of and that all families are grouped in Tashkent (Uzbekistan). I am waiting for direct news. If you should get a card from my colleague about our family, please let me know. I wish you happy Holidays (Easter).

Stach

I embrace warmly Danuta

The information that father received was not quite correct since we were never in Tashkent, though it was one of the repatriation centers. But unknown to father, mother and I were about to leave the Soviet Union. Making contact was becoming increasingly more difficult, since battlefields were coming closer.

Father's stay in the camp at Lubeck was shortened due to continuous bombing of the city by the British Royal Air Force that came almost every night. Lubeck, the prosperous and busy city of the old Hanseatic League, was now a port that provided shelter for German submarines, as well as being a center for the production of synthetic fuel. Hence, it was a prime objective for Allied destruction in order to hinder the German war effort.

It was late March when the air-raid sirens of Lubeck shattered the stillness of an early night, waking the inhabitants of the city and camp, warning them of oncoming danger. The wailing of the sirens had barely started when they were drowned out by the distant roar of airplane engines that soon overwhelmed the city, in what seemed as one unending, gigantic drone. The search lights illuminated the darkened winter skies, trying to catch bombers in their bright nets. The planes approached their targets; they began to shower the area with bombs that fell without interruption, although the German anti-aircraft batteries were constantly spitting their venom toward the sky.

As father, with the rest of his barrack mates, huddled for shelter under their bunk beds, and tables, they had mixed emotions; seeing the enemy being destroyed before their eyes and apprehension about their own safety. There were no shelters for the POWs and, in addition, they were locked in their barracks for the night.

Then the inevitable happened. Three bombs earmarked for the port missed their target and fell on the camp, one demolishing the infirmary and killing forty POW officers, doctors and all German personnel. A second bomb fell on the camp command building, killing the German commandant and all his staff. The third hit demolished one of the guard towers that had an anti-aircraft gun. The barrack adjacent to father's was set on fire by the flying debris which also wounded several prisoners, including one officer in father's quarters. Father's barrack was sprayed with German machine-gun fire that killed one officer and wounded another. After several hours of continuous bombing, the whistling of the falling bombs ceased as the last of the planes passed over Lubeck. The all clear alarm was sounded, but the skies were bright from the glow of the burning city. From the direction of the port came loud booms, and gusts of flame shot into the sky as tankers and fuel depots which had been hit exploded. The night air was permeated with smoke from the burning city and exploding chemicals.

When dawn came one could see that the British did their assigned task well; the city and port of Lubeck were no longer functioning. As far as the eye could see, the city was just smoldering rubble and the seven tall church steeples that once graced its skyline were leveled. The German civilian population, the ones who had managed to escape the city, were now hovering in ravines and ditches which were adjacent to the POW camp. They came there for safety, since they were aware that the allies were trying to spare these camps from any possible destruction.

Parts of the camp were also on fire, and two of the guard towers had been demolished. The camp was left without water, food and electricity and was completely disorganized. The chaotic situation in the camp persisted for four days without any relief, since all efforts were concentrated on the German population. On the fifth day after the bombing, the camp officials, seeing that they would not be able to maintain prisoners in these conditions any longer, divided the POWs into four groups and decided to disband the camp by relocating the prisoners to other functioning POW camps in Germany.

One group of Polish POWs was sent west to a camp in Desel while father's group, which consisted of approximately one thousand officers, were told that they were going east to Pomerania (present Poland). The name of the camp to which they were being sent was not given at this time. As luck would have it, uncle Jan was assigned to the same group as father, so they were together again. Both of them felt better, since they would be closer to home and particularly my uncle to his family.

Once again they were marched to the railroad station which, although it also had sustained hits in the bombing raid, was already partly operative. Here, the prisoners, after having been loaded into freight cars, started an uneventful journey eastward that lasted almost twelve hours. The short distance was slow moving, since the POW train had to give way to the German military trains that were heading for the Soviet front and which had priority.

As the train pushed further eastward, the German countryside appeared untouched by war. The farm fields lay waiting for spring while the cities bustled with everyday activities, appearing oblivious of the worldwide turmoil.

Finally the train reached Woldenberg (present Poland; the name changed to Dobigniewo) only twenty miles west from the prewar Polish border. This was to be the prisoners' final destination. It was to be one of four POW camps for Polish officers in Germany and was to use buildings that had once served to house German military units.

Chapter 18

Iran-Pahlevi, Tehran, Isfahan

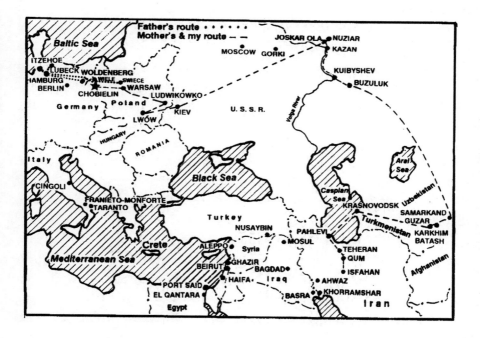

APRIL 1, 1942
PAHLEVI, IRAN

From the deck of the boat I could see the white sandy beach of Pahlevi which sparkled in the intense Iranian sun. Strewn along the beach were many large army tents. Beyond the sandy strip loomed palms heavy with dates and an abundant variety of trees and shrubs laden with multicolored flowers. After the years of bleak camps and wandering, this looked unreal.

The Polish officials who came aboard began the process of disembarkation immediately. We were transported in barges to the beach, where another group sorted us out and gave us food and hot tea. The sick were immediately taken to infirmaries and the rest of us sat on the warm sand, enjoying the fresh sea air and waiting for our turn to be processed. Since there were over a thousand people in our transport the process took some time, but no one complained; we were just happy to be out of the Soviet Union.

After several hours on the sand, our turn came. We went to one of the tents that was serving as a disinfectant facility where we left our dirty, lice infected clothes and other bundles and proceeded to the showers. I did not need to have my hair shaved, as most did, since I had it shaved off when I came down with typhoid a couple of months before. Having only an inch long growth of hair, it was thoroughly washed. Then a nurse looked over everyone coming out to see whether they needed any immediate attention, and we were given clean clothes that had been donated by various charitable organizations. Our other possessions and bundles, if they were able to be fumigated, were returned to the owners; otherwise they were destroyed.

The next two wonderful days and nights we spent housed in tents on the beach, bathing in the sea while waiting for transportation to our next destination. In the meantime, though, there was not to be any contact with the local people, as a precautionary measure against us infecting them with whatever we brought from the Soviet Union. It did not work, because the Iranian vendors came in droves with fruits, colorful wares and things that we had not seen for the last two years. Since we had no local currency, the vendors were willing to barter. Mother still had with her a well-worn seal fur coat which had served her well throughout our journey, and now saw a need and opportunity to part with it. She found a vendor who gave her cash for it, and in turn we were able to buy and gorge ourselves on the fruit and sweet delights of which this land was full. Furthermore, mother came across a small outdoor coffee house and there were able to indulge in coffee with pastries that we had not seen for the last two years. (I was at this time seven years old, but I liked coffee and was always permitted to drink it.)

Early in the morning of the third day of our stay on the beach, the orphanage and we with it, together with some other civilians, were loaded into Dodge trucks and under Polish/British supervision started on the next leg of our journey, heading for Teheran. I scrambled into the corner of the lorry, with mother, aunt Maria, aunt Luta, Barbara and Miss Gabrysia following us. Each of us found a place on the floor and used our bundles to sit on. More children and adults filled the vehicle to capacity and the tailgate was closed. The drivers of the trucks were mostly Iranians since there was shortage of drivers, which soon resulted in very daring driving.

The picturesque as well as hair-raising route took us in the direction of Kazwin, then headed south through the Elbrus Mountains, where the narrow roads twisted dangerously, and as the column sped we hung on, hoping that soon we would reach our destination. Sometimes the trucks were stopped and the local drivers reprimanded to take it easy; this was a moment when we could leave the vehicles and stretch our legs while observing our ruggedly scenic surroundings. In the valleys were scattered villages whose inhabitants would pass us on the narrow road, guiding their heavy leaden donkeys or camels home. The mountains themselves were giant boulders, with small patches of greenery where scattered goats and sheep grazed under the watchful eyes of colorfully clad natives. To pass time, and to take my mind off the frightening driving, Basia suggested that we should pick the wild flowers which grew abundantly by the roadside and, in particular, the red poppies from which we would weave flower crowns while the truck zoomed on. Distracted, time passed faster and, before I realized it, the day was coming to an end and we were leaving behind the rugged mountain road as the terrain had become flat and monotonous. The road became smoother as the truck convoy came closer to the city of Teheran, capital of Iran.

APRIL 4, 1942
TEHERAN, IRAN

The plateau where Teheran is today was always inhabited, but it was not until the 16th century, when Shah Tahmasp I built walls, gates and defensive towers, that it achieved the status of a town. Some of these walls survived into the 19th century. It was not until the 1930's that Shah Reza laid out the modern grid plan for the city which is followed to this day. Now the large thoroughfares intersected at right angles; the city had uncovered drainage canals in the streets, which were lined with trees.

Our truck convoy reached the transit camp that was already occupied by the previous transport. Camp #1 was on the outskirts of Teheran and was a curious conglomeration of buildings, tents, makeshift latrines and dusty roads. The buildings had previously been used by Iranian military personnel and now were transformed into living quarters for the refugees and Polish military. Large tents were set up to accommodate kitchens for the half-starved inhabitants of this encampment and the overflow of people for whom there was no space in the main buildings. Since the buildings did not have sufficient toilet facilities, latrines and showers were set up in each corner of the camp and, in addition, there were several tents that served as a dispensary and provisional hospital that soon became the busiest place in camp.

Our entire orphanage group was housed in the brick barracks on the ground floor. There were no beds, but we were provided with mattresses, so again we made the best of our situation and settled on the floor. The surroundings looked clean and bright and after we were fed I fell asleep, exhausted by the long and tedious journey.

The food that the camp kitchens provided was regular army chow, which would have been excellent to sustain a person of average health, but, as we soon found out, for people that suffered from malnutrition and had not had a heavy meal in the last two years, was a disaster. The irony was that having survived years of starvation we were not able to handle the heavy food. People began to develop severe digestive troubles. After several days, mother took the matter into her own hands and announced to me that she had a plan as to how she and I would overcome this situation.

"Today" she announced, "we are going to town! Let's clean ourselves and go to a restaurant for lunch where we can eat what would agree with us."

I got excited at the idea of what I perceived to be an adventure for me; imagine, we will leave camp and explore the city! I put on my other frock that was a gift from the Red Cross, washed my face and waited for mother as she readied herself. After carefully scrutinizing herself and me, mother was satisfied that we were presentable, gave me a big smile of approval and said:

"Let's go!"

Out of the barracks we went, past the kitchens, where everyone was lining up for lunch, past the hospital, toward the gate. As we approached the gate I began to have the sinking feeling that a guard would shout "halt!" and we could not go any further. At that moment I grabbed mother's hand, but she just gave me a reassuring squeeze and nudged me on. Now we were at the post of the sentry, who was unarmed and greeted us with indifference as we continued on to our destination.

The sun was already high in the perfectly blue, cloudless sky, and it was wonderful to be able to move without fear. Reinforced with feeling of a new found freedom and a sense of adventure, we did not notice the noon-day heat or the dust of the road. We passed walled houses with flowery trees overhanging their walls. Here and there were scattered small stores, with their shades pulled down for the noon hours of rest and their proprietors stretched out on multicolored carpets under canopies. As we continued our excursion the shops began to change—they were becoming larger and there were more of them. Now and then we would come upon a coffee shop full of men sipping their brews, smoking water pipes and looking at us with astonishment that we would venture out into the mid-day sun—neither mad dogs nor Englishmen.

Finally we reached what we assumed was the center of town. Here the buildings were several stories high, and scattered among them were some parks full of fragrant vegetation. With the influx of British, American and Russian military personnel, the city experienced a building boom that seemed to go on round the clock. Teheran during the war became a vital spot for the allies, particularly for the Soviets, since a vast amount of supplies for their front had to go through Iran. The Soviet embassy in the city was the largest compound, with a gigantic picture of Stalin hanging on the outside front wall. Uniformed Soviet soldiers were everywhere, which made us all very uneasy and me very much afraid of them, to the extent that I would cross the street if I spotted them coming towards us.

Mother was looking around, and as she spotted a jewelry store across the street her face lighted up. We crossed the street and as we entered the store the doorman, who also served as a guard, hesitated for a moment whether to let us in. We were a sorry looking sight, not at all candidates for the luxurious merchandise. Here was a woman, gaunt, with a shaven head in an ill-fitting dress, and dusty shoes. I, on the other hand, looked like a starved street urchin with my head shaven. Mother, holding my hand and ignoring the doorman, glided past him and headed straight for a person who appeared to be the proprietor, and before the astonished man could speak, she greeted him in French and at the same time took off her finger her sapphire engagement ring that she had carefully hidden throughout our captivity and announced that she would like to sell it. The man responded to her greeting in a very pleasant voice:

"Bon jour, Madame." Taking his magnifying glass to his eye, he raised the ring for closer inspection.

After a thorough scrutiny, he carefully put the ring on a velvet tray, rolled his eyes as if thinking profoundly and announced some sum that really did not make any sense to mother; however, since she was not familiar with the local currency or the value of the ring, she knew that she needed the money and really had no choice. With a nod of her head she agreed. The dark suited man then moved toward the back of the store, unlocked a drawer under the counter and proceeded to peel off a large stack of bills. Without looking at the ring, mother scooped the money into her purse with a polite: "Merci, messieur." and took my hand as we marched out of the cool jewelry store into the heat of the day. Her   next decision was to find a restaurant—that was not difficult, since down the street was a Hungarian place for which we headed.

For the next two months mother and I walked each day two miles in the hot mid-day sun to town and enjoyed the wonderful food in "our" restaurant where, for the first time since leaving Poland, we ate off china plates and a cloth covered table. We would then walk around the town, exploring shops and the fascinating bazaar that looked to me like something out of Arabian fairytales. Sometimes mother would be joined by aunt Maria and they would go to a cafe while I would window shop at the toy store next to it. Since I knew that I was unable to have the toys, I just gazed at the colorful dolls and stuffed animals that were on display. I must have had a sorrowful look about me because an Iranian man stopped and gestured to me to pick out what I wanted and with some slight hesitation, I pointed to a bear which he in turn bought for me. Triumphantly holding my big, fluffy, white bear in my hands, I returned to mother who immediately reprimanded me for taking gifts from strangers. Well, I soon learned that I could get the toys I coveted if I stood in front of the store window gazing at them with my forlorn face. I repeated the procedure and it worked several times more. In that way I acquired two dolls and a tea set, until finally mother kept a closer look on me and I was forbidden to leave the cafe.

Now classes for religious instruction were organized in the camp and I started attending them, but there were no books or much paper or even classrooms. Children would gather outside either under the shade of a tree or by the building's wall, and an adult would try to teach them. For the first time since we left Poland I attended religious instructions, which were in preparation for my upcoming First Communion, since in a few months I was going to be eight years old.

MAY 24, 1942

After weeks of preparation, I, together with over a hundred other children, received our First Communion at a makeshift altar that was erected outdoors. None of us had the traditional white fluffy dresses with veils, since most of the children were orphans and the rest, like me, could not afford such a luxury. Instead, all of the communicants received little white and blue checkered dresses with white collars from the Polish Red Cross and from a donation from the Shah of Iran. On our little shaven heads we had white ribbon bands intertwined with greenery. Mother bought me white socks and shoes to complete my outfit. The ceremonies ended and to celebrate, our little family group, aunt Maria, Aunt Luta and Basia went to town to our favorite cafe, where another surprise awaited me. Aunt Maria gave me a lovely silver filigree bracelet which became my treasured possession, but unfortunately I promptly lost it.

As the month was nearing its end, aunt Maria announced that she, together with Miss Gabrysia, had joined the Women's Corps of the Polish Armed Forces and that they were going to Palestine for training. Eventually aunt Maria became a nurse and was stationed in a military hospital in El Kantara, Egypt until the end of the war, while Miss Gabrysia remained in Palestine. After the war ended, Miss Gabrysia was the only one of us that returned to Poland. As for mother and I, we were to go with the orphanage to Isfahan, where schools were being organized for the children. Aunt Luta stayed a few months longer in Teheran, waiting for Romek to come out of the Soviet Union, and then joined us in Isfahan.

Transports of civilians and military people continued to arrive at camp #1 and with them many different health problems. Before we were to depart for our new destination, an epidemic of scarlet fever broke out in the camp and I came down with a high temperature. I was immediately placed in the hospital tent under quarantine and we were not able to go on the assigned transport. Fortunately, after a few days in quarantine it turned out that I only had a mild case of flu and was soon released. Now the two of us, mother and I, joined the next transport of orphans going to Isfahan and hoped that aunt Luta and Basia would join us soon.

Before departing, mother went to the office of the Red Cross that we had in our camp and through it sent a note to father:

> *COMITE INTERNATIONAL*
> *DE LA CROIX-ROUGE*
> *Palais du Conseli General*
> *Geneve (Swiss)*
> *ENQUIRER*
> *Name: Mikosz*
> *Christian name: Anna*
> *Street: (this is blocked out by the censor)*
> *Locality: Teheran*
> *Message(25 words, family news of strictly personal character)*
> *Dear Stach. We are well. We are well taken care of. Let us know*
> your state. Miss you very much. Kiss you, Jan, Helen. Ania.
> *(Below is a sentence from me)*
> *Warmly I kiss my beloved daddy and I miss him. Terenia*
> *Date: June 8, 1942*

The message is stamped with several stamps of the censors; since father was not in the camp that this message was addressed to, he did not receive it till March 6, 1943, almost a year later.

JUNE 1942
ISFAHAN, IRAN

The convoy of several trucks packed with children and other civilian personnel headed for Isfahan via the city of Qum, where we spent a night and then continued for another 200 miles to the ancient capital of Persia.

The city of Isfahan began as an oasis located at the foot of the Zagros Mountains and sustained by the waters of the Zayendeh River. It was a natural stop for the caravans that crossed the desert and continued to the north. The name derives from ASPADANA, which means assembly.

Because of its central location, the oasis became an assembly point not only for caravans but also for armies. The city became a capital in the 11th century under the Seljuks and continued to exist as such through the rules of Mongols and Timurians. It reached its zenith during the Safavid dynasty under Shah Abbas the Great (ruled 1587-1629), who came here with his court. Now, in 1942, there still existed the great square of Meidan i Shah, around which are mosques and palaces dating to that era. The main avenue, Chahar Bagh, which had been laid out by the Shah Abbas, was still the city's main thoroughfare, with a polyglot traffic of vehicles, camel caravans, donkeys and people.

As our convoy neared the city, the sun was starting to set, and illuminated the blue tile domes and minarets of Isfahan in a golden glow. The mosques looked even more impressive as they towered over the other buildings, few of which were more than one story high. The air here was balmy and the scent of flowers and blooming almond trees filled the evening.

The truck convoy finally came to a stop at a large two-story house on Chahar Bagh Avenue, and after we unloaded we were led through the gate and greeted by the personnel of what was referred to as building Number 20. Awaiting us was a warm meal and beds in communal rooms. Here in this establishment, all refugees who came to Isfahan had to spend their first two weeks in quarantine before the children could be located in various schools that had been set up for them.

The settling of Polish children in Isfahan started in April 1942 with three boarding schools for some 150 students. By the time we arrived in June there were several hundred more children, and the schools together with their supporting facilities grew to occupy 21 buildings scattered throughout the city. Within the next two years over 2000 refugee children stayed here for some time before being resettled to different parts of the world. All these institutions were operated and maintained by the Polish Government, with the exception of two convent schools that took 100 children each and which were maintained by the Vatican. In addition, Isfahan had a large Armenian Christian population which had been here since the time of Shah Abbas. Throughout our years in the city, the Polish community received support and cooperation from them.

Before the quarantine was finished, mother, through Mrs. Berdowska's intervention, got a job in the Polish Legation at the dental office, as a dental assistant. With a job, she got a two-room apartment to be shared with a new friend, Mrs. Zaydel, who had a four-year-old son, Wiesiek. Like us, Mrs. Zaydel had come through Soviet camps, but together with her husband, who now was in the Polish Armed Forces in Palestine. Mrs. Zaydel also had a job at the Legation, as head bookkeeper. The rooms that they leased together were in a house across from the Legation on Chahar Bagh Avenue and next to school #5, where I was placed after my quarantine.

My School was a two-story building built in typical Middle Eastern style; only the top story windows faced the avenue, while the rest of the house opened into a walled-in garden. The second floor rooms opened into a columned corridor that ran the length of the building. The upstairs rooms were set up as dormitories, and downstairs were classrooms. This particular school had about fifty children from age six to eleven, all girls with the exception of a few boys who attended as day students and who had mothers who worked across the street at the Legation. I lived at the school and mother would only take me home over the weekend. It was a very lonely time for me, since it was the first time I was separated from her and I was homesick.

The routine of the school day started with an early wake-up, followed by prayers, wash up, exercise and breakfast. Classes started after the first meal, lasted till noon, and many times were held under the shade of the trees in the garden. Then came lunch and a couple of hours of mandatory siesta where we had to lie with our eyes closed. After the "nap" came snacks, playtime, supper, evening prayers and bedtime. The staff, which was numerous, was very attentive to our health, feeding us often and weighing us to make sure that the years of deprivation had not left permanent damage. If anyone did not eat sufficiently, or what the staff considered being enough, we were given an appetite stimulus that was some kind of sharp tasting liquid.

The school's academic years were shortened in order to make up for the two years lost, so when I arrived at the school the classes were already several months into the year and I received added tutoring in order to enable me to catch up and be able to finish the year in December.

Meanwhile, mother continued her efforts to contact father and let him know that we were out of the Soviet Union, but it was impossible to do it directly since war was now raging throughout Europe. She therefore was advised to try through the Red Cross in Ankara, Turkey. She finally succeeded, and in July she received correspondence from father, who was searching for us, again via the Red Cross. Now, knowing his new address, she responded through Ankara through a man named Jan Szeligowski.

> *JULY 1942*
> *ISFAHAN, IRAN*
> *Dear Sir,*
> *I am greatly indebted to you for sending the post card from my husband who, as I read, is searching for us. I am enclosing a few words that I ask you kindly to send to my husband at the following address:*
> *Captain Stanislaw Mikosz*
> *Gefanger 97 XA, Baracke 17A*
> *Oflag IIC, Woldenberg, Allemangne*
> *Dear Stach,*
> *It is difficult to describe my joy when once again I saw your writing. We are well. Terenia is a good student and right now looks wonderful. I work at the dentist office. What is happening with you, Jas, Helen and my brothers?*
> *Ending I kiss you warmly*
> *Your Ania and Terenia*
> *P.S. Dear, if you could pass few words from the dentist Emanual Kukier to his wife Peppi, who lives in the Village Pokary, county Nadwerno, woj. Staninislawow-He is well and asks for few words from her.*

Dr. Kukier was the dentist for whom mother worked. He was a reservist who was called up into the armed forces in 1939 and captured by the Soviets, while his wife and family were under the German occupation. Like everyone else, he was trying to contact his family, but the outcome was not too promising since they were Jews and if she was still alive, she was in hiding.

At the beginning of September aunt Luta and Basia came to Isfahan. Since aunt was ill with malaria and other complications that were the result of two bouts with typhoid, she was placed in a sanitarium in the Jolfa section of the city, which was predominately inhabited by Armenians. Basia was in a girls high school nearby.   No sooner had they arrived when a long awaited letter from Romek was forwarded to her through Teheran. She was delighted to hear that he had at last left the Soviet Union and was on free soil.

AUGUST 17, 1942
PAHLEVI, IRAN
Dearest mother,

It is almost a week since the big change occurred when we left the borders (of the Soviet Union). We feel as if we were at a resort- we lack nothing. We even received pay of 6 thumans and 4 krans with which you can buy anything I would want. I presume that you also mother are well off and I am happy thinking that soon we will see each other. Oh, what joy it will be!

The town where we are is named "Pahlevi" and it is on a sea coast so we can swim as much as we want. We are at present in a temporary camp and soon we are to receive new summer uniforms. Then we are supposed to embark on the next voyage which might be to Teheran. Are you well, mother dearest. Where is Barbara, is she in cadet school.

Regards to all friends.
I embrace you dearest mother,
Your loving son
Romek

Romek never did connect with aunt Luta in Teheran, but he did manage to see aunt Maria there since she was taking nursing courses before going to Egypt. Romek continued his journey with his fellow cadets to Palestine, where he completed cadet school and then joined the Polish Air Force in Great Britain, where he stayed until the end of the war.

Mother still wanted to contact father and let him know where we were. At present the letters had to go through Turkey, in hope that one of them might reach father:

SEPTEMBER 1942 (sent from Ankara to Germany on December 13, 1942; father received it January 6, 1943)

ISFAHAN, IRAN

Dear Sir,

I am turning to you again with a great request to send few words to my husband to the following address:

Captain Stanislaw Mikosz

Gengen 97 XA, Baracke 17A

Oflag IIC, Woldenberg, Allemangne

Thank you very much for your kindness and I send my regards, Anna Mikosz.

Dearest Stach,

I am writing already a fifth letter and I hope you received something. I am happy that I had a postcard from you in which you are looking for us. Dearest, don't worry, we are well and now after the long wandering we are well off. I work and earn a little money. Luta and Maria are not here with us, but not too far away. I moved for Terenia's well being. Here is paradise for the children. Terenia has put on weight and is doing well in school. I gained weight and now I weigh 57K (about 125 lbs). What is happening with Helen and all the rest. I am waiting dearest for a card from you, only don't worry about us. I am always with you in my thoughts.

I kiss you warmly

Your Ania and Terenia

The heat of the summer had ended and I was in the full swing of school and the extra activities that were added in order to enrich our development. Though academic progress was the prime objective, we did not lack for diversity; such things as choir practices, play rehearsals and excursions to the ever-fascinating fable-like world that was just outside our school gate. These little trips would take us to mosques, in particular the Madare-e-Shah Koranic School, which was almost next door to our own school. This magnificent building was founded by the mother of the last of the Safavid Shahs, Shah Sultan Hossein, around 1704. Everything in this building, from the entranceway to the slim minarets and glowing cupola, was in every imaginable shade of blue ceramic mosaic. The floors of the various rooms were marble slabs covered with rich oriental carpets, while the walls and the niches were decorated with motifs of stylized flowers. The large inside courtyard had a marble pool surrounded by trees, which not only provided shade but also tranquility. We had to leave our shoes at the entrance while we explored what appeared to us to be an enchanted world, which up to this time I only knew as a fairytale. Since the Madare-e-Shah was nearby, I came to explore it several times on my own or with a friend, when we had a day off from school.

Christmas was approaching, and all the preparations for the holiday that came with it. In school we were rehearsing Christmas carols and learning Polish folk dances. This was to be our first Christmas in freedom, though not yet back in Poland. But before the Holidays, our shortened school year was ending on December 23d and I was to finish first grade, which I did on schedule although I started late; I was now 8 1/2 years old.

A Polish Christmas celebration is always a very solemn family affair that starts after sunset on Christmas Eve after a day of fasting. It consists of very traditional dishes and sharing of the symbolic wafer with friends and family, and then the children are given their presents. Because most children were orphaned or had a parent away in the armed forces, this *Wigilia* (Christmas Eve supper) was in school, and if any of the mothers were in the city they came to join us and be with the rest of the children.

We decorated our Christmas tree and with great anticipation waited for the little gifts that the staff provided for us, sang carols and were allowed to stay up a little late. We were considered too young to go to midnight Mass, so off to bed we went.

Next morning mother came to take me home for a couple of days and after attending the festive holiday mass, we went to Jolfa to spend the rest of the day with aunt Luta and Basia. Mother had a special gift for me, two small baby dolls that she knew I had admired in the toy store window. The ceramic dolls were about six inches tall; one of them was white while the other was black. Basia gave me different sets of clothes for the dolls, which she made herself. In addition I received a small note book in which one had their friends write verses or draw pictures. One memorable entry, written by an older friend from grade five, expressed our uncertain future:

When you will leave Isfahan walls behind
And venture into the world afar
Don't forget a friend from time gone by.

The following evening, which was the second day of Christmas, since aunt Luta was not well, mother, Basia and I attended a *Jaselka*, a Christmas play at one of the Polish schools.

As our first year and holidays in freedom came to an end, the wishes of everyone were that the next ones would be back home with everyone being able to return safely. Though mother knew where father was, she was apprehensive about his safety and continued to make contact with him as regularly as possible.

Chapter 19

Germany-Woldenberg

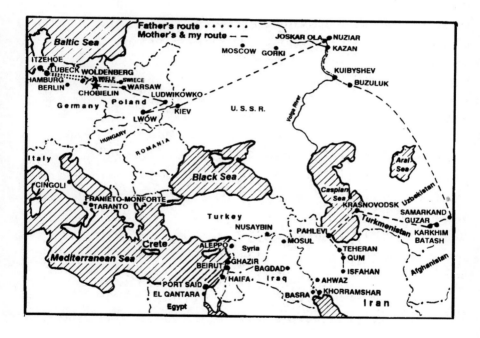

APRIL 1942
WOLDENBERG, GERMANY

The Woldenberg camp known as Oflag XA was a well organized and established facility which consisted of 32 separate red brick, block structures scattered within a large fenced-in perimeter, it housed around 5000 POWs. New arrivals were allocated quarters in various sections of the camp in accordance to their rank and branch of service. Father was placed with cavalry officers, where to his joy and, he found some of his old military friends. Uncle Jas was assigned to different quarters since he was a field grade officer, a Major.

For father Oflag XA was a relatively welcome change after having spent almost two years in conditions that did not meet even basic needs. Though the camp still was far from what one could think of as adequate living quarters, it did have indoor toilets and wash basins at each end of the barrack for the use of 150 prisoners. In addition, for the first time in his captivity, the camp had showers; the time for the use of them was allocated—once a month! Also, the prisoners would use these facilities to wash out some of their meager clothing. The sleeping quarters consisted of shelf-like bunks three tiers high, attached to the walls and infested with bed bugs; the occupants slept in rows adjacent to each other.

With the influx of this last large group of POWs from Lubeck, the Germans were running out of space to accommodate them. When father was assigned to barrack 17A there was no space for him on the communal bunk beds, so three individual bunks were brought in and placed against an empty wall. Here father and two friends that had come with him from Lubeck, Captain Dulski and Captain Szlososki, found their place and in time partitioned off their small corner, thus giving themselves some semblance of privacy.

Having settled himself in his new quarters and received the required forms for letter writing, he sent his first card from here to aunt Helen.

APRIL 25, 1942
WOLDENBERG, GERMANY
Dear Helen,
I have received everything you have sent, and I deeply thank you. Jas and I have changed camps and we feel well. I am not sending you the red stickers for packages because it has been forbidden. At present we are inhaling the nearness of homeland as you see from the address. I long very much for freedom, for Ania and Terenia and all

of you Helen dear. Kisses for Danuta, I was admiring the photo-
graphs.
   Stach.

Father began to look around the camp and to his astonishment found that it was well organized by the officer POWs who had been here for the last two years, providing a variety of activities that helped to pass time with some purpose in the otherwise monotonous life of the camp. Since among the officers who were reservists were many teachers and university professors, they organized various programs and lectures on varied subjects that ranged from literature to foreign language classes. POWs who played musical instruments formed an orchestra that gave regular concerts which were well attended, not only by the prisoners but also by the German staff. The entire atmosphere of the camp was the least restricted imprisonment that father had encountered so far, and in addition included communication with the outside world. Being in such close proximity, only 20 miles, to prewar Poland, it was easier to receive letters from friends and family there. Also, here in Woldenberg, the much sought after packages from the Red Cross began to flow in on a regular basis, easing the hardships of the regulations eliminating individual packages from family or friends.

By this time father had lost the little contact that he previously had with mother and me, but kept on searching in every possible way he could while still maintaining his correspondence with aunt Helen.

JUNE 3, 1942
WOLDENBERG, GERMANY
Dear Helen,
   I have not written to you for a long time since I have used up all my allotted writing cards in searching for contact with Ania and the poor souls that are in Russia. That has used up all my letters. There is some news that their [meaning Polish people in the Soviet Union] conditions have greatly improved but that direct correspondence is very difficult and not reliable. Jas wrote to Mr. Bialy who is in

Constantinople. You might receive news from my friend, captain Masia, who wrote to Turkey on my behalf and from whom I was separated [Capt. Masia was in a group that was sent from Lubeck to a different camp], who will write to you when he receives some news. Please forward the news to me.

Dear Helen the world is so beautiful, even the one that I see through the camp barb fence. It is so misleading because it looks like the surroundings of Chobielin; my spirit longs for that different life. Maybe soon this glorious day will come. I long very much for Ania and Terenia and all of you.

You made me very happy by sending your last photograph. Your photographs remind me of my dearest persons and the never forgotten moments that were so full of happiness. Jas and I often talk about you and relive the family happenings and so the time passes but the hope does not leave us.

I embrace you dear Helen as well as Danuta and Marysia whom I thank very much for the greetings.

Be of good thoughts.

Stach

The next letter was written the following month; father's searching has not brought any results and it express his helplessness.

JULY 28, 1942

WOLDENBERG, GERMANY

Dear Helen,

I am again writing to you even though I have nothing interesting to write. The days are flowing by, the months are passing and soon will start a fourth year (in captivity) and one cannot see the end of it. What can one do, except wait patiently and not be despondent since we have an obligation to survive the war. I still have nothing from Ania. But I did get an answer to my letter from Turkey, unfortunately they are informing me that they [mother and I] are not on the list but that they (Red Cross) are forwarding my letter to Russia.

I wrote again, maybe this time I will find out more. I know dear Helen that it is very hard for you, but we must hold on and hope that the war will end and that our dear ones will come back and joy of life with them. Do you think that it is easy for me to live? But I have faith and hope.

Thank you very much for the little medal. Jas explained everything to me. Dear Helen I have serious reservations about the packages that I receive from you since I know that you have great difficulties to obtain the goods, is this beyond your means? I am thinking to stop sending the stickers to you. Please don't take this the wrong way, but I am thinking about your situation.

Bernard [mother's brother] is still in Zamosc. Jas will write to you about Janusz [their son and my cousin] that he should not do something foolish and impetuous since there are no jokes during the war.

I end dear Helen, and thank you for thoughtfulness and kindness, be of good thoughts.

Stach

Hugs for Danuta, Janusz, Marysia and Andrzej

Cousin Janusz was eighteen and his mother aunt Helen was trying to restrain him from getting involved in partisan groups; if he got caught, that would mean the end for the rest of them. Existence for all of them took a turn from bad to worse when during the previous month Mr. Poll, their benefactor, died suddenly. His two spinster sisters, who were the owners of the Samoklenski estate, renamed Pollsfeld, where the local church was located, took over the Jaruszyn-Ulmenhof. They removed aunt Helen and her children from here and put them up in one room of the parish house which included use of part of the kitchen. All five of them were now forced to work as farm hands. They stayed here until January 21, 1945, when they witnessed the flight of the Germans and in turn, invasion by the Soviets.

Father did not want to add to aunt's burdens by her worrying about him and he restates this in a letter that followed two weeks later and shares the news that started to filter into the camp about the formation of Polish Armed Forces in the Soviet Union. These news were encouraging, but as yet not confirmed.

AUGUST 14, 1942
WOLDENBERG, GERMANY
Dear Helen,

I have received your letter and I hope that it would be true about Mr. Wozimirski. This month I have sent letters to Portugal and Turkey. I am searching for them everywhere. There is no country that I have not written to.

I am sorry that you have misunderstood me as to not sending the package coupons. I don't ask you for anything, I am happy with any kindness that you show me and I only want to ease your burden.

Stach

The mentioned Mr. Wozimirski is the person that had been with us in the Soviet Union and took care of us until we left; since he was military, father found that his name was on the Red Cross list as one that survived.

Now settled into the routine of camp life, father acquired new friends in addition to renewing friendships with his old military comrades. He met a reserve officer, Lieutenant Budek, who had been a professor of law before the war and their acquaintance grew into a long friendship. Professor Budek was an extremely intelligent individual who spoke, in addition to his native Polish, three other languages fluently: German, Spanish and English. He had connections throughout the world, since at one time he served as a Polish mercantile attaché in Argentina. Throughout Lt. Budek's imprisonment he was well remembered by his friends and received packages from all over the world which he always shared with father. Professor Budek was also giving English language classes which father started to attend in earnest in order to master the language.

Christmas was approaching, and with it came hope that the war would come to an end since the Germans were not faring well on either front. The prisoners were allowed to make their holiday preparations, which would put some cheer into the bleak camp atmosphere by setting Christmas trees in hallways and decorating them with makeshift colored paper decorations.

Father was very optimistic even though he had not heard from mother in almost a year; his hopes did not dwindle. He was so sure that he would be with us soon that he had a Christmas gift made for me, just in case we would be reunited. For a few cigarettes, father had Lt. Bednarski, another talented reservist, make a wood relief plaque of my patron saint, St. Teresa, as a Christmas gift for me. The small, 5"x4" plaque, executed with great care and imagination, shows the face of a sad looking saint and on the reverse is an inscription which reads (in Polish):

> *TO MY BELOVED TERENIA*
> *FATHER*
> *WOLDENBERG, DECEMBER 1942*

Below the inscription is a small signature of the artist *J.Bednarski*, who was not as fortunate as father, because during the march out of the camp in the winter of 1945, he disappeared. As of the date this is written (1998), I still have the plaque.

Part Five

1943

Chapter 20

Iran-Isfahan

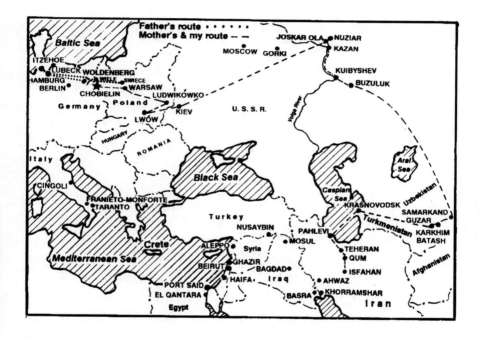

JANUARY 1943
ISFAHAN, IRAN

The few days of the year-end holidays over, I returned to school with great anticipation; I would be starting the second grade and a new class; French. School life by now had become more normalized, and extra activities and celebrations of national as well as religious holidays occupied our time. The local customs and rituals still fascinated us but were a part of everyday activities that we had grown accustomed to; the sunrise calls of the muezzins from the minarets no longer startled us into wakefulness. But I never ceased being fascinated by watching the camel caravans lumbering up and down Chahar Bagh Avenue. Though the avenue had changed its appearance since its days of 17th century splendor, it was still the city's main thoroughfare, lined with shady trees, where people in a varied array of garb, ranging from everyday western dress to colorful flowing caftans and women wrapped in black *chadors*, strolled and shopped. The shops varied from modern to the traditional eastern artisan's cubbyholes with walls laden with fascinating and colorful wares. I never ceased to admire in wonder the artisans who sat cross-legged on the ground and for hours pounded out intricate designs on copper or silver ware. There were shops that specialized in the miniature painting that had been brought to its peak during the Safavid times and now was decorating ivory jewelry and paper mache boxes as well as sheets of paper. The only aspect that marred this exotic appearance of bustling life was the great number of beggars, ranging from small children to old people, many lame or with some disease, who were always extending their needy hands for *bakshish*.

Mother resumed her work at the dental office, as well as her writing to the Red Cross in order to let father know what was happening with us. Direct correspondence with him was impossible since she did not have the required letter blanks from him; she continued to address her letters to the Red Cross contact:

Jan Szeligowski
Ankara, Turkei
Cankay Postasi Kawaklidere 383
JANUARY 6, 1943
ISFAHAN, IRAN
Dear Sir,
I fervently ask you to forward a few words to my husband who is
a German prisoner of war.
Captain Stanislaw Mikosz

Gefangen 97 XA, Barracke 17A
Oflag IIC, Woldenberg, Allemagne
I thank you kindly. A. Mikosz

Dearest Stach,
I have no news from you except one card written on July 21,
1942 in which you are searching for us through Ankara. Dearest are
you well? Where is Jas? What is happening with Helen? Don't worry
about us. I am together with Luta and we will work together. For
the last half of the year I have been working as a dental assistant and
I make a little money. Soon I will send you photographs of Terenia.
On January 1st, Terenia started second grade. It is a whole world
better for us now. Maria is further away from us. Ending, I kiss you
dearest very much
    Your Ania and Terenia
    Embraces for Jas and Helen

The reference to aunt Maria, now in Palestine was vague, because we were not allowed by censors to mention names of places for security reasons.

The influx of Polish children to Isfahan still continued; they were placed into various schools according to their age. One of them, named Danusia, came to #5 in March. Danusia was a fragile, skinny, blond, ten year old girl; we were drawn to each other and quickly became friends. She was an orphan whose parents and siblings had died in Soviet camps and she had no one to look after her; any relatives she had were in Poland. She had problems regaining her health even though the staff pampered her and gave her extra attention. After several bouts in the school infirmary, she was sent to the sanitarium in Jolfa where aunt Luta was resident and the two became inseparable. Aunt Luta gave Danusia the maternal attention and love that she longed for and needed. On weekends, when mother and I would go to the sanitarium to see aunt Luta, I would visit and play with Danusia and give her news from school.

Despite all the help and attention she received, Danusia was getting weaker and after a few months the news came to school that she had died. Though all of us children had lived with death and dying for the past several years, this death was an unexpected jolt for me in the loss of a friend of about the same age.

Danusia was buried at the only Christian cemetery, which belonged to the Armenian community. This was my second visit to this place, since all of us had attended All Souls Day ceremonies here in November, but now it was personal. The cemetery was situated outside Jolfa in a desolate desert plain which then was outside the city. The cemetery was without the usual tombstones; instead, it was a field of dirt mounds that had flat stones pilled on top of them; the stones were a precaution against hyenas, which roamed here and would dig up the graves. Crosses on the graves were few, but instead the grave-heads had vertical stones with Armenian inscriptions. There were two sections to the cemetery, the old and the current. The previous time that I was there, I had visited the old section where there were several graves of Poles, among them that of General Isydor Borowski who served in the Persian army of Shah Mehmet and was killed in the battle for the city of Herat in 1898. Our procession wended its way along the dusty yellow sand path leading to the newer part of the cemetery and to the freshly dug grave where Danusia found her last resting place, so far from home and family. It was very hard to leave her small coffin in that barren place, although the adults were consoling us and telling us that Danusia was in heaven and reunited with her parents.

Our Sunday visits to Jolfa with aunt Luta continued, but it was never the same without Danusia. Aunt Luta, though she did not attend the funeral because of her poor health, was very depressed and missed the girl to whom she referred as "her Danusia".

In the meantime, mother finally received letters from father, still through Ankara but with the necessary blank so she could answer him directly.

APRIL 2, 1943
ISFAHAN, IRAN
My Dearest,
I received today 3 of your letters as well as a photograph. It is hard to describe my joy and happiness. I wished so for your photo and my wish came through. I am sending my photo which was taken a month ago. We feel great but we miss you. I work for a dentist and make a bit of money. I am now dressed suitably. Terenia is chubby and studies well. Luta and Barbara are here also. Romek went fur-ther away and is studying. Maria changed her profession and is now alone since her Krystofer died in November of 1941, as well as Wacek. I am here together with Mrs. Domiszewska and Berdowska.

My dearest, I beg you don't worry [about us], we live with hope that one-day we will be back together and we will be happy as before. I am happy to hear that the rest of the family [in Poland] is well. I kiss all of them warmly.

Dearest Stach, the sun once again shines for me when I read your letters and look at you [his photograph]. It is indescribable joy for me.

Ending I kiss you warmly, hugs for Jas
Ania and Terenia

As in all correspondence, these letters went through the Polish/Allied censors and then through the German one before father could receive them. We were all instructed not to mention place names, so in the letter above mother does not say where Romek is, or aunt Maria, or even the fact that she was training to be a nurse. Mrs. Domiszewska and Mrs. Berdowska were wives of father's military friends, who, like father, were German prisoners of war.

The next two post cards follow the letter and since father had our address, or what he perceived to be our place of residence, are marked as sender. Since all letters that we received in Isfahan came through Teheran, again a security precaution, it read:

Anna Mikosz
Teheran, Iran-(Persia)
Hotel Ferdousy (Here were located the administrative offices of
the Poles in Iran)
MAY 1943
ISFAHAN, IRAN
My dearest,
I am receiving every thing that you send me. I send you our pho-
tographs. Write more about yourself. We are contented and are con-
tinuing to work. Terenia is about to pass to the third grade. She
misses you very much. Send kisses to Helen, Jas and the rest. We live
with hope that soon we will see each other if only we will be able to
maintain health. I kiss you warmly.
Your Ania and Terenia

The correspondence continued with a first postcard from me:
MAY 2, 1943
ISFAHAN, IRAN
Dearest Daddy,
Please send me your photograph since I want to have you [photo].
Soon I will pass to the third grade. I miss you Daddy very much. I
kiss you, uncle Jas, aunt Helen, and all the cousins. Your loving
daughter
Terenia

Mother writes on the same date and as in some previous letters asks
father to contact people in Poland, since it was impossible for anyone
abroad to do so. The POW's received their mail via the Red Cross and
they could and did have contact with German-occupied Poland.
MAY 2, 1943
ISFAHAN, IRAN
My Dearest,
I received 5 postcards and 2 letters from you. Terenia also wrote
you. Our friend asks you to write to Mrs. Wozimirska, Warszawa,

Ul. Szczawnicka 8 that Mr. Wawrzyn from Bydgoszcz is well and asks for your address, he will send you a package. He is together with Szczesniak, they are on holiday. I am ending and kiss you, Jas, Helen warmly.

    Your Ania and Terenia.

The cryptic message that mother sends is a reference to our friend Mr. Wozimirski who was with us in the Soviet Union while his wife was in Poland. They were originally from Bydgoszcz but she was now in Warsaw. Mr. Wozimirski's first name was Wawrzyn, hence the message was "your husband is well". He was in the Polish army in North Africa, but mother could not say that in the letter.

My second school year ended at the end of April and we had a few days' break before resuming classes. During our short breaks we would go on outside trips so as to familiarize us with the history and life of Isfahan. There was first a short class telling us where we were to go and the history that went with that place and, our lunches packed, we were ready for adventure. One time we went west of the city to the Monare Jonban, which means the Shaking minarets.

It is the place where in the 14th century a holy hermit named Amu Abdullah Soqla was buried and later, during the time of the Safavids, the blue tile-covered minarets were built. The attraction and the peculiarity of these slim towers is that if you push hard on the top of one of the minarets, it will start to sway and then the opposite one will also begin to move. Of course there was an individual on the premises who climbed to the top of the 50ft. minaret and with expertise proceeded to demonstrate this phenomenon to our awe-stricken group. From here we hiked to the nearby hill and climbed the steep path to see an ancient Zoroastrian fire altar and enjoy a panoramic view of Isfahan.

The short vacation over, I started third grade and some changes in our curriculum occurred; the decision was made that we would no longer to take French as our second language, but English instead. I was disappointed at first, since I liked the French language and our teacher. In spite of this, it was again a new challenge and an adventure into a totally unknown language. Ironically, our first English instructor was a young Iranian who was our first male teacher.

In addition, on May 22, I was issued an ID document which was in lieu of a passport; it contained notations of various benefits that I received, including the money I received as an military dependent and which was paid bimonthly. The book had a space for keeping track of all the clothing that I received, with all other children, from the Red Cross and the United States. In addition, the ID contained some rules and guidelines for refugees which, abbreviated, read in part as follows:

VI. Guidelines for refugees who are émigrés.

READ CAREFULLY AND REMEMBER THAT:

1. You find yourself in Iran thanks to the goodness and welfare of the Polish Government. Remember all the difficulties that the Government has overcome in order to take care of us. Because of war the transportation of food, supply and finances is hindered. You have to remember that together with us there are millions of people suffering because of war, and that the situation of our coun-trymen under cruel German occupation is a hundred times worse than ours.

2. We are guests on Iranian soil. We are compelled to behave accordingly so as not to tarnish the good name of Poland.

Correspondence with father was becoming more regular and mother dispatched a card and a long letter:

JUNE 1943

ISFAHAN, IRAN

My Dearest,

I do receive your letter which makes me happy. Terenia passed into 3rd grade; has good marks. I am concerned about you [meaning father and uncle Jas], I try to have parcels sent to you, did you at least receive one? It very good for us here but we don't know if we will be here for long. Yesterday, I have received news from Tarnasiewicz who is concerned that I don't reply to his letters and cables. He inquiries about my and Terenia's health. I immediately sent a telegram to him through the Red Cross. I am happy that there is someone who is concerned about us and that we resumed contact. Then I wrote a letter (to him) and gave him your address.

Dearest, don't worry about us, just take care of yourself. Luta is ill and in the hospital, they don't know what is wrong with her. Maria, right now, is close to Romek. She misses us and would like to be with us. I would like to be there, since it's supposed to be very beautiful in that vicinity. The heat wears us out (here). Write Dearest what you need and maybe I will able to send that through Tarnasiewicz. My dearest Stach, have faith and wait. I end and kiss you many times.

Embraces for Jas.

Your Ania and Terenia

Col. Tarnasiewicz, whom mother mentions in the letter, was commander of father's former regiment in Grudziadz in 1939, and he attended aunt Maria's wedding that summer in Chobielin. He had managed to escape to England via Romania and was now in the Polish Army in Great Britain, where he served until 1947. Since his wife and two children were in Poland and he could not get them out after the war, he returned there. He subsequently was harassed by the communist authorities and died a few years later. As for aunt Maria, she, at the time the letter was written, was in Palestine for a short time. As for mother's mention of not knowing whether we would stay here in Isfahan, that was due to the influx of an unexpected number of people into Isfahan. As a result, the Polish authorities started to disperse people to various locations including Uganda, India, Mexico and New Zealand.

Furthermore, once father was located, his military friends who were serving in England, like Col. Tarnasiewicz, were sending parcels through the Red Cross. All these friends never forgot the POWs and continued to help them since the packages were a source of life for the prisoners, whose food rations were decreasing and could no longer sustain them.

Chapter 21

Germany-Woldenberg

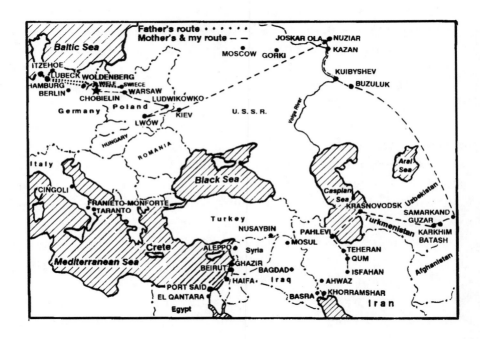

JANUARY 1943
WOLDENBERG, GERMANY

Father's optimism about our whereabouts was justified this month when he received a letter from mother through the Red Cross in Turkey, announcing that we were out of the Soviet Union and free and well. Wanting to share this good news, father wrote to aunt Helen.

FEBRUARY 1943
WOLDENBERG, GERMANY
Dear Helen,
On the day of your Namesday I am sending you my sincerest wishes of good health and that soon you may be reunited with Jas.

I have received six letters from Ania, as well as two from Terenia and her photograph from the First Communion. My happiness is tremendous. Terenia looks lovely and Ania is working at a dentist office. She writes that we should not worry about them now, because they are well taken care of.

I will write in more detail in the next letter.
Stach

My photograph was the first picture that father had of me since he was taken prisoner in 1939. When he saw me last, well over three years previously, I had braids and now in the photo I had shaven head, but it did not matter to him. The promised letter to aunt Helen did not come until two months later, since father was attempting to send the letter blanks to mother. Nevertheless, the explanatory letter was ultimately sent off.

APRIL 7, 1943
WOLDENBERG, GERMANY
Dear Helen,
I did not write to you for some time since almost all my correspondence I am directing towards Ania because not all the letters reach their destination.

You already know that in January I have received six letters from Ania, as well as two postcards from Terenia, as well as her First Communion photograph from Teheran.

They live in hope and are happy. She writes that all the sisters are together though they have different living quarters. Ania, for Terenia's good, moved to town; works at a dentist office and Terenia goes to school. Maria's little son has died. They all had all sorts of sickness, the last was typhoid, but now Ania writes, they have paradise compared to Russia. Reniusia [another diminutive for Teresa] has beautifully grown; I would not recognize her, she is quite a young lady. She is a good student and writes beautifully. It is not surprising since she is soon going to be 9 years old. She sends special hugs to you, Danuta, Marysia and the boys. You would be happy if you saw the photograph. Ania did not send her photo because she writes she has short hair which was cut when she had typhoid. She mentions that she received two of my letters, last one from November 20, 1942.

Dear Helen don't be sad, they are well, this time of separation will pass and soon happiness might return to our life. Again there will be completeness [of life] as we dream of. Keep your head high, sadness will not help.

Stach.

Thus, with the coming of spring and the good news of finding his family safe, father's hopes for a better future were rejuvenated. But at the same time the Germans announced that they had unearthed mass graves of Polish officers in Katyn forest (near Smolensk in the USSR) when the Soviets retreated. The Germans used this evidence for their own propaganda and invited to inspect it committees that were comprised of Red Cross officials and representatives of Polish POWs, among them two designated from Woldenberg. The senior Polish POWs asked father if he would go, since he was one of the few officers that still had a uniform in good shape. Father of course agreed, hoping that he might in that way find some news about his brother-in-law Wacek, although it was presumed that he was not alive. Unfortunately, on the day before the assigned departure date for Katyn, father came down with flu and a very high fever and was not able to go. He lent his uniform to an officer friend who took his place, and asked him to see what he could find out about uncle Wacek.

After ten days the two POWs returned and reported the horrors of the sight and the names of officers whose papers were found. But it was not until after the war that relevant Soviet documents were found. Uncle

Wacek's name appears on an official document which, translated, reads as follows:

NKVD USSR Nr. 022/2

TOP SECRET ONLY PERSONALLY

9 April 1940, Moscow

To: COMMANDANT OF KOZIELSK CAMP OF PRISONERS OF WAR

SENIOR LIEUTENANT OF STATE SECURITY

comrade KOROLEWA

city of Kozielk, county of Smolensk

After receiving this, immediately direct to Smolensk, for the disposition of the chief NKVD of camp Smolensk, the prisoners of war who are in camp Kozielsk...

There are 100 names listed, with the individual's birth date and prisoner number. The last name reads:

100. Stankiewicz, Waclaw ur.[born] *1904.r*[year] *282*

TOTAL ONE HUNDRED PEOPLE

CHIEF OF NKVD, USSR

AFFAIRS OF PRISONERS OF WAR

CAPTAIN OF STATE SECURITY

(SOPRUNIENKO)

Although the war news that reached father's camp was not favorable for the Germans, the end of the war did not yet appear to be near. Therefore, the constant struggle for survival continued among the POWs. The food always was at the bare minimum, and consisted of a bowl of watered down soup that was doled out once a day. But since the camp officials allowed the prisoners to grow their own vegetables, and even provided some seeds for that purpose, the POWs were able to have some extra food.

Accordingly, father and captain Dulski staked out a small plot behind the barrack and planted in their patch of dirt radishes, carrots and green onions. Tending the garden became a chief occupation of their day and impatiently they looked forward to the results of their endeavor. After several weeks, the garden begun to sprout and bear its meager fruits but, as always, the people that did not bother to plant now wanted to "share" in the results. Father and captain Dulski noticed that their vegetables began to disappear and, not wanting to let all their efforts to go unrewarded, they decided to take turns watching the garden.

So, throughout the summer the little patch of ground was under the watchful surveillance of its two gardeners, who one would think were growing gold nuggets and not vegetables! Here, sitting in the sun and guarding his garden, father continued to keep up with his correspondence and shared his joys with aunt Helen:

JUNE 3, 1943
WOLDENBERG, GERMANY
Dear Helen,

I am writing after a long pause since all my correspondence is directed to Ania. A month ago I received a postcard from her and on May 31st a letter on a return blank that I have sent her; written by her on April 4th.

Furthermore, I received new photographs of Ania taken in March and a new, second photograph of Terenia. I am over overjoyed, Helen, I am very happy because they look so well and are also well dressed.

Ania is weighing more than before the war (58kg). Terenia studies well and is already in second grade. Ania writes that she works in a dentist's office and is together with Luta and Barbara. Romek went away to study. Maria changed her profession because she is now alone...so she writes. I don't understand that too well and what this means in regards to Maria, but I hope that Ania will explain everything, since she writes that she received my three letters and a photograph that I have sent her. She asks not to worry about them since after leaving Russia they have it very well.

I am sending sincere regards to you and the children and Teresa asks to give you all big hugs. See, Helen, God is merciful, our dear ones will return; we should not be sad since we can't help the dead ones and life has to go on.

I kiss your hands and ask you to have a smile on your face because happiness will return.

Stach

P.S. Dear Danuta, I thank you for your greetings and I am moved by your remembrance.

I hug you,

Stach

Since mother could not write clearly that aunt Maria was now in military service, she wrote what she thought was a secret code. Well, maybe she thought it was but even father could not grasp what it was all about. He was content and happy to get any news of us and that we were out of the war.

Two months passed before father again wrote to aunt Helen, updating her about us and the rest of the family who were in the Middle East.

AUGUST 3, 1943

WOLDENBERG, GERMANY

Dear Helen,

In the last month I had four letters from Ania. I also got their photographs. They look very well. Ania is working and Terenia is in a boarding school and Ania takes her home every Sunday. Terenia is passing to 3rd grade.

Maria and Gabrysia are living together in Teheran and they often write to Ania. They are sending regards to you and Terenia to her cousins. They have it well there.

Stach

Within days of writing to aunt, father received a card from mother's brother Bernard, who had managed to move to and live in the central section of Poland that the Germans referred to as *General Government*. Here the living conditions were slightly better than in the parts of Poland which the Germans had annexed to their own country.

> *AUGUST 6, 1943*
> *BIALA PODLASKA, POLAND*
> *Dear Stach,*
> *I was happy to hear the news about our closest [family] from T [Teheran]. I am trying to go to see Helen during my vacation and I think that I will be able to receive a pass. Two weeks ago I have sent you the last package.*
> *Regards to the both of you*
> *Bernard*

As in most letters, the names of places are omitted since everything was censored. Uncle's mention of a pass is in reference to permits which individuals had to obtain if they traveled beyond the registered district where they were residing. Uncle Bernard managed to get a travel permit to see his sister, but as the war on the German eastern front escalated, his trip became impossible.

Chapter 22

Iran-Isfahan

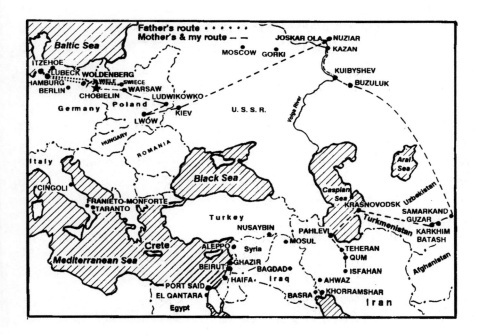

JULY 1943
ISFAHAN, IRAN

The intensive heat of summer curtailed most activities from noon till five o'clock, including our classes and any excursions outside the school. But our curriculum always included current war activities, by means of communiqués or film newsreels that were always shown preceding feature movies, which I attended with great enthusiasm.

The city had two movie theaters in the summer, which were on Chahar Bagh Avenue and were outdoors. Our theater consisted of a large walled-in courtyard with the screen mounted on the end wall. In front of the screen were rows of seats designated for general admission. Behind these seats, separated by a railing and slightly raised, were a few rows of uphol-stered seats that were categorized as "first class"; this area was used by the Europeans and the well-to-do Iranians. Since the cost of admission to this area was much higher than for the general audience, there was no min-gling of the classes.

I would pester mother to take me, or let me go with who ever else was going to the movies. Because the theater was outdoors it would not show the film till after dark, which meant late, and that restricted my atten-dance to the weekends when there was no school. Although at that time my English was rudimentary, I still recall movies that I saw there for the first time. Most memorable were *The Mikado, Thief of Bagdad, Mrs. Miniver* and *Frankenstein.*

> *JULY 10, 1943*
> *ISFAHAN, IRAN*
> *My Dearest,*
>
> *I received your letter and I am happy that you got our photos and letter. I also sent out our photo where we are together and Terenia is wearing the **Krakowski** costume. I am happy that all your corre-spondence reaches me.*
>
> *Dearest, a week ago we experienced a traumatic event, we lost a leader and a very worthwhile person, but we don't despair, we have faith.*
>
> *You ask me many questions which I answered you. Maria is a nurse and works, like I wrote before, with Gabrysia. Romek is study-ing. Just like Josef wished for. Luta is often sick with malaria. Barbara is in high school here. Terenia is going to pass into the 3rd*

grade. The heat here is wearing us out and sometimes I think that I will never get used to it. I am still working, today is a year since I started the job. I surprise myself that I am able to work after so many sicknesses and in this heat. Dearest, I dream about having peace and being able to rest. Beloved, don't worry about us.

I kiss you,
Your Ania

The message about a lost leader refers to the death of General Sikorski, who was Prime Minister of the Polish Government-in-Exile in London and the Commander in Chief of the Polish Armed Forces. He died in an airplane crash over the straits of Gibraltar on July 4th, 1943. This was a tremendous shock and loss to Poles, particularly to us, because as a result of his negotiations the agreement was reached with the Soviets which released us from the Soviet Union. Our community was in deep mourning for our fallen leader. There was a requiem Mass said for the general at the Armenian cathedral which was attended by representatives of many different communities, as well as several memorial services held in various schools.

Meanwhile, I coaxed my mother to write to father, who was becoming to me a very distant figure; since most of my friends had no parents, I accepted the situation as a matter of fact. I was very content in my school and fascinated with the exotic world that surrounded me. The only thing that I missed was living with mother.

AUGUST 3, 1943
ISFAHAN, IRAN
Dear Daddy,
I was very happy to receive your postcard. I am waiting impatiently for your photo Daddy. I am already in the 3rd grade. Is Daddy well? I miss you very much. Are Danuta and Marysia well? I kiss you tenderly. Write to me. I kiss my beloved Daddy
Your Terenia

The summer heat was easing, and since our community was still expanding some changes came about. Toward the end of August mother moved to a new place, a housing area set up for the personnel of the Polish Legation and their dependents and known as #21. Number 21 was situated a short distance from the Legation on a side street off Chahar Bagh avenue, just beyond the Irantur, then the only luxury hotel in the city. Her new designated quarters were in a two story "L" shaped building adjacent to the bank of a small river and surrounded by a high, gated wall. Within the wall around the house was a colorful garden with a variety of scented flowers and shrubs. Mother's room was on the second floor, and like all the other rooms on the higher floor it opened on each end onto a porticoed balcony that ran the length of the building and which faced the stream on one side, while the other side overlooked the garden. Though the room was quite small, it was large enough so I could come and live with her. Mother would drop me off at school and then cross the street to her office at the Legation, and then after work she would pick me up for the return trip. On the short walk home we would sometimes stop at various kiosks to buy fresh fruit and a treat of halva or other "sweet delights" that the Iranians loved and were well known for producing.

At the #21 compound there were more than a half- dozen other children beside myself who lived with their parent or parents, and soon we had bonded into a group that provided many joyful times for all of us. There was no lack of birthday and Namesday celebrations and various group games that we would think up. But the activity which was most daring and fun was looking for crabs in the river.

The river on the bank of which the building was perched, really was more like a large stream since during the summer it contained no more than three feet of water at its highest point. The banks of the stream were overgrown with weeds which would catch some of the debris discarded up stream, making the water not too clean. None of these hygienic disturbances made any impression on us when we decided to go hunting for crabs. We would don our bathing suits and happily sink our feet in the muddy stream bottom, looking for the elusive creatures.

When a catch was made, the captive became a pet in some container until the appropriate parent would tell us to liberate it and return the crab to its own habitat.

Then there was the Sunday ritual to which I always looked forward. After attending Mass, either at Jolfa or at the Chapel of the Gray Nuns, mother and I would have lunch with some of her friends and then head home for the customary afternoon rest, after which we would go to the Irantur Hotel for coffee. This was not "just coffee", since the hotel that hosted it was then the only western hotel in the city and the meeting place for expatriates on Sunday afternoons. I loved the luxurious surroundings of the lobby, where I would sink into a thickly upholstered velour arm-chair while savoring the sweet taste of pastries and the aromatic coffee. Mother's friend Jania would join the group bringing her son Marek, who was the same age as I. The two of us, after stuffing ourselves with sweets, would play several games of checkers while the adults passed their time sipping coffee and exchanging news of the latest events of the war and of their families and homes.

The checker games with Marek always ended in a heated altercation in which we accused each other of cheating and not playing by the rules. That is when our mothers stepped in and separated us before the argument became physical. We would part with a promise and a threat that next Sunday "I will show you!"

Correspondence with father seemed to stabilize but could not be done directly. Mother would send her letters to Ankara, Turkey and from there, they would reach his camp through the Red Cross. Father, on the other hand would send his correspondence to the Hotel Ferdousy, in Teheran, from where it would be forwarded to Isfahan. This meant that it would take about two months for the letters to come from one point to the other while being read by both Polish and German censors.

SEPTEMBER 1943
ISFAHAN, IRAN
My dearest Stach,

Many kisses for your letters. Lately news from you are reaching me. Not long ago I had a cable from Tarnasiewicz and a long letter from Florian. They are together. I was tremendously happy that they are concerned about us. He offered to help us but we have the essentials, so I thanked him for the concern and asked him to remember you. He wrote that he already has sent several parcels for which I am very happy.

I might be possible for me to be closer to Maria and Romek, but it is not certain yet. Terenia passed to third grade, she has a good report card, she is smart but she is such an imp. You would have hundred laughs if you saw how she behaves!

My dearest, I beg you don't worry about us, we will survive somehow. We live in good conditions but I feel bad that I am unable to help all of you. It probably is hard for Helen. I think about them all the time.

Dearest I end and kiss you dear, Jas, Helen and all
Your Ania and Terenia

Mother maintained contact with father's friends from his regiment who had managed to escape being captured by either the Germans or the Soviets by wending their way out of Poland to Romania and from there to France and eventually to England, where they joined the Polish Armed Forces. Besides Col. Tarnasiewicz, who had once been father's regimental commander, there was Captain Florian Zielinski, who later was in a regiment that took part in the battle of Monte Cassino in Italy. Father was reunited with him in 1945 when after the war they were assigned to the same regiment. All these friends not only remembered and helped their imprisoned comrades, but also were concerned about the welfare of their families.

It was during a night in September, when I was already living with mother, that a sensation of motion brought me out of my sleep. It was still dark and the silence of the night was disrupted by the distant barking of a dog. I was not fully awake while I tried to figure out whether it was a dream or something actually did occur, but my interrupted sleep quickly resumed and my last thought was that I must have dreamed.

Next morning I was awakened by my surprised mother, who wondered why our beds were askew and the picture frames on the dresser were lying face down. As we began to straighten up the room and push the beds into their former places, we concluded that we must have had a mild earthquake. Since there was not much one could do, I got dressed and was dropped off at my school as usual.

The school was buzzing with excitement, since the resident students and the staff had not slept through the episode but were told to evacuate the dorms in the darkness. Needless to say, the drill was full of confusion because some of the girls did not follow instructions and tried to take their belongings with them, which hampered the exit of others and resulted in falls and tripping. Following breakfast, we had a drill as to what to do in the event of the next quake, since tremors frequently occurred here but were not disastrous.

Class resumed as usual that day, the only difference being that we had to pick up some of the books that had fallen to the floor during the previous night's occurrence. I was in my second period of the day, a geography class, and I had been called to the blackboard to write the name of a river when the floor beneath me began to move. The chalk fell out of my hand as I tried to hold on to the board and instantly came the commanding voice of the teacher:

"It's an earthquake! Everybody outside! Quick! Quick! OUT!" With reassuring shoves she got us all into the garden where the other classes were assembling. There was a great deal of calling out for different people in order to make sure that no one was left in the building. In addition, some girls got panic attacks and were hysterically crying while the staff tried to calm us down by telling that the quake was over. No sooner had they said that when came a deep rumble and the earth began to shake beneath us. In unison came screams and squeals from the girls as we tried to hold on to the trees for protection. Though the shaking lasted only few minutes it seemed like an eternity, and by now we were all petrified with fear.

Wanting to avoid any further emotional traumas the staff decided that it would be better to have the rest of our classes outside where we felt more safe. So the rest of the day was spent outdoors, in anticipation of another tremor which never came. It was not until the next day that we found out how serious the quake was. Isfahan was evidently on the outer perimeter of the affected area and did not sustain any noticeable damage, but not too far from us whole villages were leveled with many casualties.

OCTOBER 1943
ISFAHAN, IRAN
My dearest Stach,

Thank you for the letter of 7-20 which I received. Terenia is waiting for your photograph, Dearest. I am sending our photo which was taken in May. Terenia came out well, I not so good but that's too bad. You see how big is our Terenia. That costume I made myself a year and a half ago when I was not working. I thank God for everything. I continue to work and it's not too bad. Terenia was ill and in hospital but now she is well. She often has bronchitis which worries me. In spring Luta was four months in hospital, she has chronic malaria and some other complications. She smokes a lot and eats little and I am helpless.

Florian wrote to me and I also received a cable from Tarnasiewicz. Do you get their parcels?

How do you feel my Dear? Be patient. How is Helen and the children and Bernard? Are they all well? How are they coping? I think about you all. Send kisses from me to Helen and the children.

I kiss you,
Ania

Mother does not go into detail concerning my illness, but for me it was an experience which started out as a childhood sickness and ended to be a seriously traumatic event. There was always some sort of illness in our school and the community, and we were vaccinated against smallpox, which was the dreaded disease of the time. So it was startling for the community to learn that one of our nurses came down with smallpox and was quarantined in the Armenian hospital. Her close friend volunteered to go into quarantine with her and nurse her, which resulted in both coming down with smallpox. Both women survived the illness but with devastation of their faces, which were left ravaged with pock marks.

Soon after this occurrence, I and five year old Wies, son of mother's friend Mrs. Zaydel, came down with high fever and other suspicious symptoms. We were sent to the hospital and quarantined.

Our room was in a long, one-story building separate from the main hospital. Our windows looked out into a portico that ran the length of the structure and opened into a colorful garden. While we had high fever and blisters we had constant care, but as soon as the crisis was over and we were better the close attention ceased and we were left to entertain ourselves. In the evenings we would have visits from our mothers, who brought us gifts of crayons, paper and treats.

Though we were told not to leave our room, one day when we got bored with drawing we decided to explore the adjacent rooms of the building since there was no activity. Being older I led the expedition, and Wies followed as we peered into several rooms and found nothing of interest until the room on the end. There was someone lying in that room. Face pressed against the dusty window, I tried to see who it was but the individual was not moving and was laid out on wooden, table-like structure.

"There's a dead person!" Astonished, I informed Wies, who immediately wanted to see the find. Our curiosity satisfied, we went back to our room not wanting anyone to find us wandering. Now we wondered what was to happen to the corpse; was it going to be taken away, and if so, when. We made a promise not to tell anyone what we had discovered next door since we were afraid of being reprimanded for leaving the room. When our mothers came that evening we never mentioned our find, but resumed our speculations after their departure.

Since I had seen *"Frankenstein"*, my imagination ran wild and I began to tell stories to Wies, who listened to them with great interest. The result was that by the time the nurse came to put the lights out for the evening, we were too petrified to sleep and continued to talk, afraid that the dead were going to get us at night. Eventually we did fall asleep, only to be awakened by any small noise. Needless to say, next morning we confided to a nurse about our find and wondered what the corpse was going to do. She was very sympathetic to our childish fears and explained that the dead person was no longer there and took us to the room to reassure us that there was nothing to be afraid of. For the next days while we were recuperating, the nurses kept a more vigilant eye on us.

Within days I returned home to mother and resumed my schoolwork. Her correspondence with father was occupied with trying to clear up a misunderstanding which evolved from one of her previous letters, in which she had been complaining.

> *NOVEMBER 1943*
> *ISFAHAN, IRAN*
> *My Dearest,*
>
> *Postcard from September 24 I have received. I am terribly sorry that I made you unhappy with my July letter. Stach, there are moments when one is taken over by apathy. But I would sin if I said that it is bad for us. Dearest, be reassured that we are well off and that work makes me forget things. I have now Terenia with me which was the realization of my dreams.*
>
> *Please send me blanks for the parcels. I kiss you warmly,*
> *Your Ania*

I kiss my Daddy warmly, Terenia

In addition, during this month of November our Polish community in Iran was closely watching activities in Teheran with great apprehension.

Teheran was hosting what became known as the Teheran Summit Conference, where the leaders of the Allied Powers came to discuss the future of post-war Europe. The city that already was the center of espionage activities during the war years now had to create extra-ordinary security, since Roosevelt, Churchill and Stalin came to the meeting.

Although the war in Europe was far from over, it was on the upturn from the Allied viewpoint; however, the outlook for Poles did not look promising. Poland was to have its boundaries changed and was to be put under Soviet domination. This situation put a grim prospect on our future, but everyone was hoping that there was still time for a change, since it was impossible to comprehend that Poland, being an ally and fighting for the same cause, could be so betrayed by her allies.

As Teheran was buzzing with the heads of states, the Polish authorities were still getting people out of the Soviet Union. It was towards the end of November when the last transport of Polish children came to Isfahan from Ashkabad, Turkmen Republic. The large group consisted of children that were left in homes, railroad stations or lost when their parents died. For them, since all schools were filled to capacity and they also needed added attention, two new schools were opened.

The Christmas Holidays were upon us and the anticipation of the joyful season was not dampened by the results of the Teheran Conference. It was going to be our second Christmas in Iran and the fifth in exile. Everyone was exchanging Christmas and New Year wishes that the next one would be in our homeland.

After Christmas, mother and I wrote a letter to father describing to him the latest events:

DECEMBER 28, 1943
ISFAHAN, IRAN
Dearest Daddy,
We are well. Thank you for a nice letter. The Holidays are over and we often mentioned you. We were sad. For sure the next Holidays we will spend together. I also had a Christmas tree. I got for

Christmas two dolls, a bed for them and crayons. Christmas Eve I finished the first semester. I had a good report card. I had two "goods", math "good" and Polish "good" and the rest "very good". I am already learning botany and geography and got "very good". I kiss warmly

Your very loving Terenia

My Dearest,

Your letter from October 6th I received and I already sent the attachment back. We have a very mild winter; the sun shines beautifully. As I already mentioned, I have Terenia with me and it is good to be together. In the morning, on the way to work, I walk her to school and in the afternoon we go together for a meal and then she plays with her girlfriends. Maria is going further away from us.

My dearest be only healthy and survive bravely. God again will let us have happy times together.

I sent embraces to Helen, Jas and kiss you warmly,

Ania

The reference to aunt Maria moving further away from us concerned the fact that she had completed her nurses' training in Palestine and received an assignment to the military hospital in El Kantara, Egypt. She remained there until 1947. She then was sent to England, where she settled permanently and remarried.

Chapter 23

Germany-Woldenberg

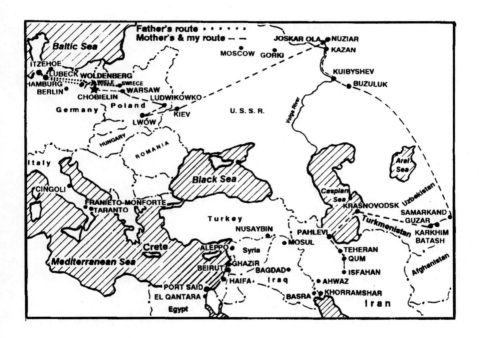

Several months had passed since father had written to aunt Helen. As has been seen previously in his letters, he repeats the main theme in order to make sure that, in case of loss of mail, the news would reach her:

OCTOBER 20, 1943
WOLDENBERG, GERMANY
Dear Helen,

I did not write for a long time because as you know all my correspondence is directed to Ania and not all the mail reaches her. But I always ask Jas to send my regards to you.

I want to let you know that everyone in Teheran is well. I received new photographs from Ania; they look beautiful and well, Terenia grew charmingly. Ania is working at the dentist office and lives together with Luta, and Maria is with Gabrysia again. She writes that finally now they have returned to a European look; they have clothed themselves suitably. Terenia has passed into the third grade. They are sending many hugs for you. They are thinking of moving to Syria since it would be closer to the homeland.

She has received the letter that you have sent through the Red Cross. I also receive cards from Terenia which move me deeply. She is now nine years old. Time passes quickly; October 28th is our 10th wedding anniversary. Their letters radiate happiness because they were able to leave Russia but at the same time they long for homeland and family. If I was not afraid that they would get lost I would send you their photographs, of course you would have to return them. Just so you could see them but it is a difficult procedure.

Winter is approaching and I have expenses in order to get a uniform, and that is why I was unable to send you any money; please forgive me, Helen. There is no reason to talk about the end of the war, since lots of water will pass under the bridge before it will end.

Ending now, Helen and I embrace Danuta and Maria, as well as the boys.

Stach

Two months had passed when father wrote to aunt but, as he mentioned, the end of their captivity did not appear in sight though the allies were making progress.

DECEMBER 15, 1943
WOLDENBERG, GERMANY
Dear Helen,

I again received several letters from Ania, as well as a postcard from Terenia. The letters are full of joy and they express contentment in their living conditions. Barbara is attending a high school, Terenia has passed to the 3rd. grade, and Romek is studying, just as Josef wished. Aniusia is telling me that she intends to move together with Luta, so they would be closer to Maria and all together.

I also received a photograph, they look very well and Terenia grew up very much and is happy and does well in her studies. Ania writes that she is her pride and joy. In the postcard, Terenia asks to send her hugs to Danuta and Maria, whom she always mentions. The only thing is that they long for the homeland and the heat bothers them. If I could I would send you their photographs to look at, but there are difficulties. From all the sisters I am sending you, Helen, embraces and regards.

There is no change with me. I am well and am able to survive some way. If only all this would end faster. Jas and I talk about all of you always and we remember the past moments that were and we spin our dreams.

With the coming Holiday I wish you, Helen, and the whole family a pleasant Holidays and that next year you would see Jas and all of our group.

Dear Danuta, I thank you fondly for remembering me, your every postscript brings me lots of joy. I embrace you all.

Stach

His fifth Christmas in captivity was approaching and father, though relieved that mother and I were safe, did not see any immediate end to his imprisonment. In spite of the news that Allied forces were making constant advances and winning victories, the news of the Polish situation that reached the camp was not good; a Polish Socialist Government had been created in Moscow, under Soviet tutelage and with Stalin's blessing. This news created a good deal of agitation in the camp since some officers who were pro-socialist, particularly the reservists who were teachers, started verbal attacks on the Polish government-in-exile in London.

As these rumors circulated and brought unrest within the camp, father was called in by General Czulowicz, the senior officer among the prisoners, and was asked if he would be willing to help the general to find the sources of the unrest. Father's task was to observe and listen and then to report the officers that were spreading anti-Polish propaganda. Since father had no love for the Soviets and Communism, the assignment was easy for him and he had no problem finding and naming the people that glorified the Soviets.

The political problems within the camp were compounded by added pressure from the Germans, who were systematically reducing existing prisoner privileges. Furthermore, so-called "tag inspections", where regardless of weather conditions the prisoners had to stand in rows for several hours while the camp officials compared the POW's photo tag and ID number with their own records, began to be more frequent.

Part Six

1944

Chapter 24

Iran-Isfahan

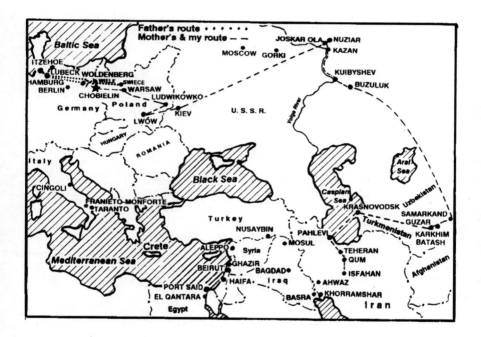

JANUARY 1944
ISFAHAN, IRAN

Our third Christmas Holiday in Isfahan was over and I returned to school after the short break. The weather was usually cold at this time, but this year it was also rainy, and everyone was waiting for the appearance of the blue skies for which the city was known.

In school I got a new English teacher, Mrs. Isabelle Wies, who was an American from Chicago. She became my favorite teacher and my English improved greatly. In addition to her, there were many wives of American soldiers who would come to visit Isfahan from the nearby military camp. The soldiers always brought excitement to the rather quiet city, as well as great amounts of chewing gum, chocolates and candies which they generously distributed to the children. The older girls and younger women were not overlooked, since there were a fair amount of rendezvous.

Mother continued her correspondence with father whenever she received the necessary letter blanks; the mail still could go only through the Red Cross in Ankara, Turkey. Her contact was limited to the POW camps and non-existent with the rest of occupied Poland.

FEBRUARY 1944
ISFAHAN, IRAN
My Dearest,

I have received your letters from November 3 and December 9, together with your photo. I was extremely happy my dearest, only you look very sad. I beseech you, please don't worry about us and continue to bravely hold up. I wrote to Florian since I am exceedingly grateful to him.

Stach, please send me the stickers for the parcels, do me that favor. About which Jadzia are you writing?

We are healthy, only it is not well with Luta, I am concerned about her.

Stach, I finally bought myself a watch, a sport one, "Orator" that has 16 jewels that runs well. What kind do you have dearest? I had couple pairs of shoes made for us, since I am afraid to be left without; that is why I always have a pair in reserve for me and Terenia. Terenia is finishing 3rd grade and is currently studying a foreign language and I think she will soon catch up with her mother. Stach, you should see how smart she is; she does extremely well but has a big mouth. I curb her the best I can. She is extremely lucky with other people and particularly the Hindu like her. As a sign of affection they pat her or give her chocolates. But she does not go any place by herself.

What is happening with your family? Is Jas still with you? How are Helen and the children coping? I would very much like to send her a parcel but I can't from here. I wrote to Maria. Is Bernard well? Is Barbara and children well? Maria sent us a photo, she looks very pretty. I end Stach and kiss you warmly, embraces for Jas.

Your Ania

Mother was finally earning some money which permitted her to get some luxuries such as the watch, since the one she previously had was long ago bartered for food when we were in the Soviet labor camps. At that time she also bought a watch for my father, in hopes that soon we would see him. The watch was finally given to him several years later when we were reunited. As for the shoes, it became mother's obsession that she would never again be left without them as in the Soviet camps.

My acquaintance with the Hindus, as mentioned in the letter, was an amusing friendship that continued for almost a year. Every day on the way to and from school I would pass a British military compound that had Indian/Hindu sentries at the gate. It did not take me long to make friends with the young soldiers who would give me chocolates and cookies as treats. Since I was now studying English in school I was able to try it on them, while the soldiers took delight in teaching me new words. There were two soldiers, in particular who went out of their way to stop and talk to me. One was named Kamal, who was a Catholic and gave me a rosary as a gift. The other was Joseph, who was a Protestant; his father, as he told me, was a minister in India. Both men were perhaps nineteen or twenty at most, swarthy and very good looking. They gave me photographs of themselves and asked me for mine, a request which I was only too happy to grant. These almost daily encounters had gone on for several months when one evening Joseph appeared at our apartment house, which was not too far from his post, and asked to see my mother. Surprised and mystified, mother invited him in and asked her friend Jadzia, who lived downstairs, to join us as an interpreter.

Joseph did not come empty handed, but brought gifts of chocolates, soaps and other goodies that mother accepted with a puzzled look. We wondered what the reason was for all these gifts, but no one had the courage to ask the guest. Then after an awkward minute or two of silence, Joseph stated the purpose of his visit.

"Mrs. Mikosz, I have come to ask you for permission to marry your daughter." At this point mother's face turned to startled amusement, but before she could say anything he continued.

"I know she is only ten years old, so I would want to send her to my parents in India where she could finish her school and then we would get married. Teresa would be well taken care of."

Mother seemed to regain her composure and said something to the effect that I couldn't go to India, while I was giggling and stuffing myself with chocolates.

Joseph continued to press and explain his cause, and mother with the help of Jadzia was trying to tell him that it is not our custom to choose husbands for daughters; besides, I was too young. He soon took leave; saying that he hoped that mother would think the matter over.

I was delighted with the attention and bragged in school of my first marriage proposal. I continued to see Joseph and Kamar at their posts, but within months they were transferred to Teheran. Both of the young men wrote to me from their new posts and I wrote back in my basic English. Joseph's father even wrote to mother from India on behalf of his son's cause and sent me a parcel that contained several yards of lovely blue Indian silk and a King James English bible. The gossamer silk was promptly sewed into a dress for me, while the book is still in my possession.

Since there was no interest from our side in Joseph's offer, eventually contact with him ceased. On the other hand, Kamar, who stayed longer in

Teheran, found me there the following year when we returned there—to mother's great consternation.

MARCH 1944
ISFAHAN, IRAN
My Dearest,

We received your two photos for which we thank you very much. Helen's Namesday has passed (March 2) and we send her best wishes. I wrote to Florian [in Great Britain] but there is also difficulty with letters reaching him. Terenia was very happy to receive your letter.

Stach, I am sending a parcel to you in addition to many parcels that Tarnasiewicz [in Great Britain], Maria and Wozimirski have sent. Do you receive them?

My dearest, we feel well and spring is here in full bloom. Write if Helen needs help and if so, what she needs and if it is permissible to send it. I am ending because Terenia wants to write. Don't worry about us. Keep sending the blanks for the parcels. I kiss you warmly my Dearest.

Your Ania

Dear Daddy,

Thank you for the letter and the photograph. I was very happy to get your letter. I miss you very much. But it is nothing, we will soon meet and be together. I am soon passing to the 4th grade. April 9 we have vacation and mommy promised to go to aunt Luta because it is out of town where the air is better and I will have a better appetite and it is close to the sanatorium. Is Daddy well? I kiss my dearest Daddy.

Your Terenia

As I mentioned before, our school years were very much shortened and the break between them would only be a week or two. During this time extra activities were set up. Besides spending a few days in Jolfa with aunt Luta and cousin Barbara, who was there in a girls high-school, I was to be confirmed in the Catholic faith with several hundred other children.

The festive occasion was supposed to be performed on the grounds of school #20 where an outside altar was erected. The Papal legate, Archbishop Marina, was going to officiate and perform the confirmation ceremony. After months of religious lessons, a new dress and of course new shoes, we were marched in twos from our school up the picturesque Chahar Bagh to join other participants in the festive event.

As everyone gathered and lined up before the altar, we stood singing hymns and listening to orations, which always referred to the war and reflected hope of returning to our homeland. The morning sun was beaming strongly and making the stay so uncomfortable that some children began to faint, among them myself, but we were revived with a cool drink and a rest under the shade of a tree, waiting there until our turn came to go up and be confirmed.

After the ceremonies most children dispersed to their schools, but mother took me to Jolfa to aunt Luta, with whom we had a celebratory meal in one of the restaurants there.

> *MAY 1944*
> *ISFAHAN, IRAN*
> *Dearest Daddy,*
> *Thank you for your card and that you write so beautifully to me. I passed to the fourth grade. Don't worry about us dearest Daddy. We are all healthy; aunt Luta, Barbara and I. We have such hot weather that it is difficult to wear a dress. Aunt Maria writes to us often. I kiss you very, very much.*
> *Your beloved Terenia*

Within weeks after our confirmation, it was announced to us that the Shah and his Queen would visit Isfahan and we would be able to see them. From the time of our arrival in Iran, I had seen photographs or paintings of the Shah in every shop, restaurant and often in shop windows. The young ruler came to the throne in 1941, when his father Reza Shah Pahlevi was forced to abdicate as the Allies occupied Iran, because of his sympathy toward Germany. Now the young Mohammed Reza Shah was the center of attention and adulation of his subjects. His consort was the beautiful Queen Fazia, the sister of King Farouk of Egypt, and they had one child, a lovely four-year-old girl.

The Polish community was very grateful to the Shah and the Iranian people for their hospitality, so when it was announced in school that the Shah would visit Isfahan there was great excitement. At last we would be able to see the handsome monarch and be able to express our appreciation personally, or at least as a group.

We were to visit the royal couple on the grounds of the Ali Qapu which was built by Shah Abbas I in the early 17th century. The Ali Qapu (Gate of Ali) was actually a monumental entrance to the royal compound, which consisted of several pavilions scattered throughout a vast park. The most striking pavilion which still existed was the Chehel Sotoon (Forty Columns), which lay in the center of the park with a long pool at the end of it. It is supported by twenty wooden columns that reflect in the pool; hence you have a Palace of forty Columns!

Since all the children could not go, each school was to select their representatives. I was fortunate to be chosen with three other girls to represent our school. We were rehearsed and drilled in how to curtsy when greeting the Shah. When the day of the meeting arrived, I was greatly excited. My companions and I put on our national Krakowski costumes, were spruced up and checked and double checked by the teacher, and then when finally deemed ready were taken by a landau to the gardens of the Palace to await the Shah's appearance along with the rest of the assembled children.

The beautiful fragrant gardens were now full of children of all ages, lined up in rows. The younger ones were in their national attire while the older wore their school uniforms. Our teachers were dressed in their best with the ladies sporting summer hats. At the far end of the park was the palace of several stories, with its wooden verandas that looked into the gardens; the higher ones overlooked the city.

There were to be several presentations of flowers and other gifts to the royal couple, and I was handed a flower bouquet that I was to present on behalf of our school. We waited patiently, peering in the direction of the palace for some sign of the upcoming great event, when people started to come out of the building. In a hushed tone, the word was passed:

"The Shah is coming!"

Silence fell over the gathering as each of us stretched our necks to see. As we peered out, the doors of the veranda opened and into the sunshine came the young royal couple which till then I had only seen in moving pictures and photographs. The Shah was in his dashing golden beige officer's uniform, and by his side was the dark-haired and slender Queen Fazia, dressed in an elegantly simple light dress.

The Shah was first greeted by the director of Polish schools in Isfahan and other people of the Legation, and then the presentation of various schools started. As our turn came we marched forward and presented our flowers to the Shah and his Queen with well rehearsed words and a deep curtsey. The Royal couple smiled and we returned to our places, from where we watched the rest of the ceremonies, after which the entourage returned into the interior of the palace building.

Needless to say, when our little group returned to school we were questioned by our classmates about the event, which I described several times over with great excitement.

Schoolwork continued throughout the upcoming summer with again a short mid- semester break at the end of June, when I wrote what was to be my last card to father in captivity.

> *JUNE 1944*
> *ISFAHAN, IRAN*
> *Dearest Daddy,*
>
> *We are well. We receive letters from aunt Maria, and not long ago even received a package. I attend fourth grade. Soon we will send to you Daddy a photograph of Mommy and me. Dearest, are you well? We live in a nice house with a garden. And how do you live Daddy? I kiss you dearest Daddy*
> *Your Terenia*

The news of the Allied invasion of Normandy, which included Polish forces, reached us through BBC news; we hoped that the end of the war was near. This month marked the fourth anniversary of our deportation from Poland and almost five years of war.

Chapter 25

GERMANY; IRAN

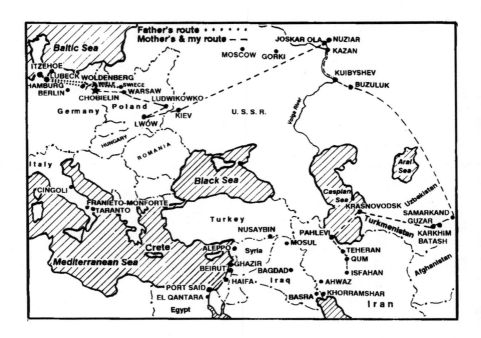

JANUARY 1944
WOLDENBERG, GERMANY

The Christmas season ended and the new year started full of optimism that this year could mean the end of war, since the POWs were able to receive encouraging news from both eastern and western fronts. The year started with many prisoners reassuring each other that "in spring" it would all end. But their spirits were dampened with an increase in the number of "tag inspections" which forced the POWs to stand for hours in the bitter cold of the snowy winter.

One of the more memorable inspections occurred on an early morning at the end of January, when the thermometer dipped well below zero and everyone had to line up in the snow. This time the camp officials were not in charge, as at previous times, but rather an SS unit that arrived with an empty truck in order to strip the prisoners of what they referred as "excess", which was destined for the German soldiers on the Soviet front. As the undernourished, dejected POWs stood outside on the bleak and cold winter morning, each was ordered to unbutton his worn-out overcoat for inspection. Then if the prisoner was fortunate to have a sweater or an extra warm coat lining he was quickly relieved of it, together with any other valuables which he might have been careless enough to leave in sight.

While the systematic personal search went on outside, another detachment of the SS was going through the barracks. Here they confiscated blankets; a prisoner was allowed to have only two, and they went on tearing up the bunks looking for any other clothing that they could find. When the several hour long ordeal ended, the SS loaded their trucks with "booty", leaving the shivering prisoners standing in the snow and their barracks in a shambles.

With the departure of the SS the officers were dismissed and headed for their barracks, which were without heat and now in addition had been almost demolished and stripped of any small comforts that the prisoners had managed to acquire in order to survive the elements. But, in a day or two life in the camp returned to the usual monotonous, bleak routine and father sat down to write a letter to aunt Helen:

> FEBRUARY 26, 1944
> WOLDENBERG, GERMANY
> Dear Helen,
> I am sending you sincere wishes on the occasion of your Namesday of the best things, health and that soon you may see Jas. Maybe God

will allow that the separation won't be too long and we will all be together and will again be able to enjoy life.

I am including a photo of Ania and Terenia that I have received a month ago. The photograph has been made in July of 1943. The dress that Terenia is wearing Ania has sewn for her herself because Terenia was taking part in a play. You understand, Helen, she seems to be a little actress.

I am not going to try to write about my happiness since it is indescribable since I know that they are living in peace and they have whatever they want to eat, but they do long for the homeland.

Ania complains about the problem with her legs but she said that now they are better. Luta is seriously ill with malaria. Both of them are sending you and the girls, as well as the boys, their warm regards and embraces.

I feel bad that you don't want to take the money which I can send you from time to time; but I will be contrary and will send it so you could buy the calf that you intend to get!

Dear Helen, please write back and tell me your impressions about Ania and Terenia. I was happy to hear about Danuta's health, for which I send her an embrace.

I repeat my Namesday wishes as well as best regards to Danuta, Maria and the boys, and see you soon.

Stach

It is the first time that father ends the letter with "see you soon", showing the anticipated end of the war. As the winter was winding down, the prisoners of Oflag Xa watched German transport planes overhead, heading east with supplies for the Soviet front. The progress of the war toward its end did not appear for some POWs to be in the immediate future and some opted for escape, even though none were totally successful and the fugitives would be caught sooner or later.

Nevertheless, one escape that occurred in March 1944 was a success. It was led by 2nd Lt. Przysierski, who was a reservist from the town of Naklo and spoke fluent German. He and two other POWs who joined him in the escape, after observing the German routine of taking sick prisoners to the nearby hospital in Szczecin (Stettin), decided that this would be the safest route by which they could leave.

Therefore, with the help of Polish soldiers, they managed to obtain a German hat, coat and boots. They had a fake rifle, artistically carved from wood and painted, that would pass for the real thing. Passes for the outside world were also forged, since one could not move around without proper papers which were continually checked by the military. Now they were ready to venture out and, as camp protocol required, Lt. Przysierski informed his senior officer, Maj. Paszota, that the escape attempt would be made on the following day.

That evening, the three men made their secret arrangements and moved themselves to a barrack nearest to the camp gate. In the morning they prepared themselves for the move; Lt. Przysierski donned his German uniform, pulled the cap over his eyes and pulled the coat collar up. The other two officers were in their Polish uniforms, but had civilian worker's clothes underneath them; they were to be the sick prisoners. Saying goodbye to their comrades, they set out for the walk through the two gates of the camp.

As the rest the camp held its collective breath and watched, the young Polish lieutenant, disguised as a German soldier, marched his friends in front of him and occasionally shouted orders in German. The threesome reached the first gate and entered the post house, stomping the wooden floor in order to shake the snow off their boots, while Lt. Przysierski was complaining to the German sergeant about his lousy assignment. In few minutes they were cleared and proceeded toward the outer gate of the camp. Here the guard, presuming that they had been cleared, opened the gate for them even before they reached it. Upon passing this last obstacle, the escapees headed for the train station and their destination in Poland.

Their escape went unnoticed by the Germans for several days, since the routine daily head count was camouflaged by the rest of the POWs in order to give them as much time as possible to get away. Then, on the tenth day after the escape, a "tag inspection" was executed, and whatever way the Germans counted they were short three people in one of the barracks. The camp officials were beside themselves and held the prisoners for over six hours standing in the snow, counting and re-counting them to no avail.

Finally, out of desperation the camp commander, a stout, retired German general by the name of Von Wachocki who lived on his nearby estate and every day would ride into the camp on horseback, confronted the Polish General Czulowicz, stating that he was responsible for his people.

"Sir," answered the Polish general, "you have the guards and you are supposed to guard the prisoners, not me."

Von Wachocki contained his rage and strutted back to his quarters, giving orders to dismiss the still standing prisoners.

Several months had passed when Maj. Paszota received a pre-arranged card from Warsaw that read:

"We are well and here in Warsaw. We wish to thank everyone for all their help and hope everything will end well."

There was no signature, but the major knew who sent it and he shared the news of success with the rest of the friends. Unfortunately, in July news reached camp that Lt. Przysierski had been caught by the Gestapo and was subsequently murdered by them. Nothing was ever heard about the other two officers who had accompanied him.

As always, the long winter came to an end and the wet spring which turned the camp road ways into mud trenches had arrived. Easter was soon to be celebrated, and with it hopes were raised that it would be the last behind barbed wire.

APRIL 4, 1944
WOLDENBERG, GERMANY
Dear Helen,

On the occasion of the Holidays (Easter) I am sending you, as well as the rest of the family, the best wishes. I have received the slippers from you and I am deeply touched by your thoughtfulness. I thank you very much. I am very happy that the photos of my dearest ones reached you. You see, dear Helen, how beautiful they look! In March I had two letters and a postcard from Terenia. She passed to the second semester and has a very good report card.

I kiss your hands Helen and I embrace Danuta and Maria.

Stach

The following month father wrote to his father and sister Maryla, who continued to live in Krakow and like the rest of the family tried to help the ones in camps in any way they could, though they themselves were in dire need of basic staples. Knowing how hard it was for them, father did not want them to send anything except the item that he really needed and could not get by bartering.

MAY 4, 1944

WOLDENBERG, GERMANY

Dear Father and Marylko [diminutive of Maria]

I received both of your cards and I thank you for the wishes [father's Namesday is May 8th] *Please do not send me any shoes since I have a good pair. I only need for the summer wooden sole sandals and nothing else besides that. I also do not need soap since I have satisfactory amount. In a word, I only ask you for things I really need and nothing else.*

I kiss Father and you and all the rest.

Stach.

In the beginning of June, uncle Jas came down with an attack of appendicitis and had to be taken for surgery to the hospital in Stettin, which was fifty six miles NW of Woldenberg. Since the hospitals did not have as strict isolation polices as did the camp, father hoped that aunt Helen could see him.

JUNE 20, 1944
WOLDENBERG, GERMANY
Dear Helen,
Many regards from Ania for you and all the family. I had three letters. Maria is where Ania was abroad before she married. Jas is [recuperating] after an appendix operation and in good health. He is in the POW hospital in Stargard, Prussia-near Szczecin (Stettin). His wife intends to visit him and he is looking forward to that.
Everything is the same with me, please write how you are doing.
Fondest regards to you and the young ladies.
Stach

This letter that would appear to the censors to be an innocent postcard, was full of family news. First the reference to aunt Maria's whereabouts meant that she was in Italy; mother had been there in a finishing school in 1928. The news was inaccurate, however, because aunt Maria never was transferred to Italy but instead went to an army hospital in Egypt.

Then father is telling aunt Helen that her husband is the hospital and that she should go and visit him. Getting this information, aunt Helen promptly arrived in the hospital and was able to see her husband after almost five years of separation. In addition to the family reunion, uncle Jas brought back scraps of fresh information to which father refers to in his next letter.

AUGUST 15, 1944
WOLDENBERG, GERMANY
Dear Helen,
Many regards from Ania and Terenia. I had three letters. They are well off and healthy and they are planning to move to Africa. Barbara is attending school, Luta is well. I found out a great deal of interesting things from Jas. What is happening with Bernard; it is a long time since I had any news from him. If only everything would end well.
Stach

Since the Soviet offensive began in June, the war had been taking a different turn and the fragile lines of contact were broken because uncle Bernard was living east of Warsaw and in the path of the German retreat. In addition, the news of the Allied landings in Normandy brought additional hope that the end of the war would be near.

Chapter 26

Iran-Isfahan

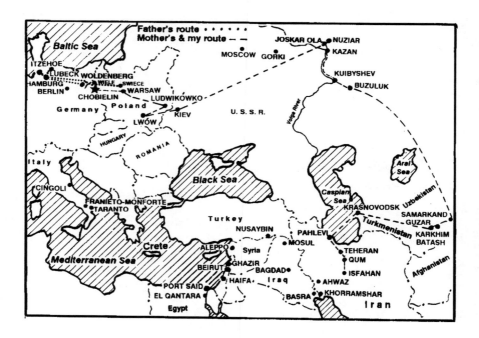

The news of the Allied offensive in Europe reached our enclave in Isfahan with regularity and was received with mixed emotions. Everyone looked to the day when the war would be over but the fear of casualties dimmed our view of the offensives' progress. In school we were taught about the sacrifices that our fathers, brothers and other countrymen were making to liberate Europe. The soldiers were included in our daily prayers, commemorated in patriotic songs and special assemblies. In addition we had another fear; that the Soviets, who were repelling their German invaders, were now about to enter Poland once again.

Watching the progress of the war, mother was concerned about losing contact with father who was in the middle of that turmoil. She wrote a letter which, unknown to her then, was the last one to reach him until the end of the war.

> *JULY 23, 1944*
> *ISFAHAN, IRAN*
> *My dearest Stach,*
>
> *I thank you very much for your letters. I am sending you my current photographs about which I was told they are not too good but I think they are all right. I will send some special (photos) of Terenia. I have sent a second parcel to you. What is going on with you, are you holding up bravely? How about Helen?*
>
> *Maria is leaving to where Florian is and Romek is there already. The hot weather is wearing us out, it is already the third summer that we have difficulty in coping with. It is time to change the climate and it will soon occur. What concerns me that there might be a long break in our correspondence, but that God only knows.*
>
> *As I wrote already, I received some money from Florian which I share with Luta. She doesn't feel well and Barbara suffers with malaria. Terenia is thin but healthy and I am returning to the former form and I am mindful of my health. Only you dear rest assured that we are well taken care of and that you must return to us so we can be together. Longing is great but one has to persevere.*
>
> *Ending, I kiss you my dearest and embrace Jas.*
> *Ania and Terenia*

Again the letter has several news items without spelling them out, so that it would pass through the censors, both Polish and German. Captain Florian Zielinski was father's military colleague who was now in the Polish

Armed Forces stationed in England. He not only helped father but also mother. So by saying that aunt Maria was going to join him, mother was telling father that she was going to England, which in reality did not occur at that time, but cousin Romek finished his cadet training in Palestine and joined the Polish Air Force in England.

As for the complaint about the climate in Isfahan, part of it was correct because the political climate was rapidly changing in Iran. The Soviets were pushing their communist propaganda through the press and some workers' demonstrations, which made our community uneasy. Slowly the Polish population of Isfahan began to be transferred to other places in the world. The first large group of about 200 people left for India in June and toward the end of September several hundred orphans were evacuated to New Zealand. In addition, there was active recruitment of women to the armed forces as well as of the youth to go to military cadet schools.

Furthermore, during the month of August when the Allies were making progress in the European front, came the news of the Warsaw uprising that we as a community closely followed while offering prayers for our suffering countrymen. Then the graphic communiqués came describing the brutal defeat and the devastation of the city, followed by memorials that we attended in order to remember the men, women and youths who perished in order to liberate our homeland.

SEPTEMBER 1944
ISFAHAN, IRAN

Towards the end of this month we experienced local celebrations that made us take our minds off the distant war. Though our Polish community basically kept to itself and did not have much contact with the Iranians, we evidently were an unwelcome nuisance to the fundamental religious Moslems. This is why when there was a Muslim religious holiday, all our schools were basically locked up and we in them. No one could venture into the streets, where groups of Iranians would demonstrate their religious fervor. The rule of confinement was enforced not only so as not to provoke the Muslims but also for our own safety. But the temporary lockup did not prevent me from satisfying my curiosity and peering into Chahar Bagh through a crack of the upstairs window of the dormitory. Since the mosque was nearby, the crowds of men would march down the avenue reciting together some slogans or verses, while some were scourging themselves in an ecstatic fervor. The sight of these ragged, fierce, angry and shouting men, some bloody from the scourging, was very unsettling. We stayed in the safety of our enclosed school, waiting a day or two until the holiday passed and we could resume our everyday life and I could go back to living with mother and resume my daily walks to classes.

With the heat of the summer over, our school excursions around the city resumed; one led us to the exploration of the ancient bridges of Isfahan, among them Sio-She Chehmeh (Thirty-three arches) south of the school, through which Chahar Bagh continued to Jolfa. This was still a main bridge that spanned the Zayandeh-Rud (life giving river); the bridge was designed by the architect of Shah Abbas in the 16th century and is about 200 ft long. Its many arches and niches now provided night shelter for some of the many poor that inhabited Isfahan. During the day the beggars sat in the shade with outstretched hands, asking for *bakshish*, while the deformed or diseased exposed their malady. It was not uncommon to find lepers among them.

Our lives had now been "normalized" in the sense that there was continuous school, with observance of all Polish national and religious holidays by a commemorative program of some sort, while at the same time we were made aware of the war's progress. The news that our community was receiving was not favorable to Poles, since the Soviet armies were retaking our homeland. Our previous contact with father had been cut off months ago, and the uncertainty of his situation made us very apprehensive. This lack of news from him dimmed the happy spirit of the upcoming Christmas holidays, our third in Isfahan. Nevertheless, the preparations for the holidays were made; mother and I went to Jolfa to have Christmas Eve supper with aunt Luta and Basia, where I received a new doll with several changes of clothing that Basia had made for it. The traditional sharing of *oplatek* (a wafer used during Christmas while exchanging holiday wishes) and optimistic exchanging of wishes was shared by all:

"In spring, the war will be over and next Christmas we all will be together in our homeland."

Chapter 27

Germany-Woldenberg

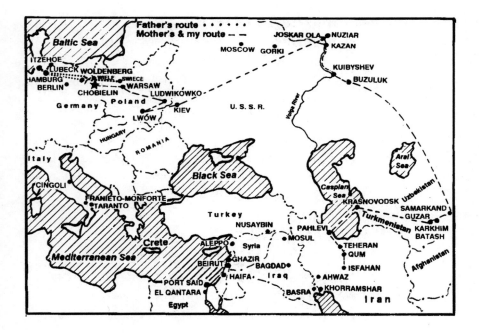

SEPTEMBER 1944
GERMANY

The German armies began their retreat from the Soviet Union and planned to make their stand against the advancing Soviets in Warsaw. The Soviet army was once again occupying Eastern Poland, the very same boundaries that they had seized in 1939. At the end of July 1944 Warsaw was the main and most important evacuation, as well as supply, center for the German armies. This was the time that the Polish underground army had been waiting for and it started its unsuccessful uprising, which lasted 63 days and subsequently was crushed by the Germans; four-fifths of the city of Warsaw was bombed out with such thoroughness that even the trees were cut down. The survivors were either executed or taken to concentration camps, or if an officer, to POW camps.

The Germans, besides killing people in the uprising, managed to take prisoners of war that were sent to the already existing camps. Some of these officers from the AK (*Armia Krajowa*-Polish Underground Army) were sent to Woldenberg and brought with them news of the brutal defeat, as well as news of the progress of the war in Europe. Though Warsaw's collapse overwhelmed the POWs, they were still hopeful that the end of war was near. These optimistic thoughts are expressed in father's next letter:

SEPTEMBER 25, 1944
WOLDENBERG, GERMANY
Dear Helen,

I thank you very much for the parcel received. I was very happy to receive it since with loss of contact with Bernard, I have lost a source (of getting parcels). Jas and I both received them and everything was all right. I noticed your change of address which I understand is due to technical reasons.

Do you know what is happening to Bernard? I have no news from him since June. From Ania everything has also stopped because of the difficulty of maintaining connections but I console myself that this will not last long or the war will end.

I yearn with my whole soul that the Christmas Holidays I will not have to spend imprisoned—there is a spark of hope but of course one cannot be sure of it. One thing is sure, that the war must end, and it is why one must be calm and trust in God.

Jas is happy now; looks younger and has returned to his old form after his stay in the hospital and his contact with family. We talk a great deal together, there is no shortage of subjects and that way one kills loneliness and the gray existence.

I am sending regards for Danuta, Maria and the boys.

Helen, I extend sincere wishes for speedy return to Chobielin and happiness.

Be of good thoughts

Stach

The POWs were of good thoughts and were anticipating their imminent liberation, which spurred them into preparations for it. They started to organize themselves, of course in secret since it was forbidden, for the eventuality of the coming battle in which they would find themselves.

Father was assigned to give classes on military topography to a group of junior officers. They would come to father's barrack where as a precaution several officers were strategically positioned as lookouts while the course was in session. For weeks the system worked without any problem, until one afternoon in November when father had spread out his illicitly acquired maps of Poland on the wooden table of the barrack and was explaining a point to his attentive group when, without warning, two German guards appeared in the doorway. Startled, father froze for the moment, knowing the severity of the penalty for this forbidden activity; the penalty was concentration camp. Thoughts flashed through father's mind:

"Oh God, this is the end...." then he noticed that he knew the senior guard. The man was a stout corporal Rudka, who was of Polish descent and came from Lodz and in addition spoke Polish. Furthermore, a few months ago Rudka had approached father and asked him if father could get him some coffee because he was leaving on a furlough to Berlin to see his family and he would like to bring them something. Father always had coffee and cigarettes from his Red Cross parcels. These items were treasured and used as currency. Father had parted with one of his treasured jars of Nescafe in exchange for a promise from corporal Rudka that he would bring father some provisions from Berlin, to which he happily exclaimed: "Its' a deal, Captain!" Two weeks later Rudka returned from his leave and under the pretext of checking the barrack, pushed into father's hands a brown paper bag that contained a ring of sausage and a bottle of vodka.

Within seconds, the corporal moved quickly towards the table and seeing the spread out map, reached for it.

"Corporal, these are my old maps" father started to explain, speaking Polish so the other guard did not understand. "As you see, these are not escape maps, they have no connection with the camp," father continued, as Rudka hesitated, looking at the map in front of him. He recognized that it was a map of the vicinity of Warsaw. Then glancing sideways at the waiting guard in the doorway, he said:

"Oh well, you are right, Captain, but you know you are not supposed to gather in groups in such a manner. So please disperse." With that he walked to the door and joined his waiting comrade, and they left, leaving the much relieved group of POWs behind them.

Next day father had to go to the camp office and ran into corporal Rudka, who took father to one side and in a low voice warned him:

"Captain, please don't do that again because if anybody else catches you, you won't be able to evade a concentration camp."

"Thank you Corporal, I understand." answered father, thankful that the matter had ended; although the training did not cease, the officers were much more careful and vigilant.

The activities of the camp continued as more news were reaching the POWs on the progress and advances of the allies. With several simultaneous war fronts, it is not surprising that the lines of postal communication were coming to a standstill. From mother, in the Middle East, father had no news since August. Contact with his military colleagues stationed in England came to a halt with the invasion of Normandy in June. Uncle Bernard was now cut off by the Soviet re-occupation of his area in Poland. The only person that father still had correspondence with was Aunt Helen, who was now the only source of badly needed food supplies.

NOVEMBER 16, 1944
WOLDENBERG, GERMANY
Dear Helen,
I thank you sincerely for the package and I kiss your hand. I have no news from Ania since August and that worries me very much.
I am very much afraid of the winter since it is the most difficult time of the year for you as well as for me. How are you doing Helen, is your and the rest of the family's health good?
Many fond regards for Danuta, Maria and the boys.
Stach

Once again aunt Helen came through with much needed assistance, supplementing the basic needs despite the fact that she herself had barely enough to make ends meet. The following letter of father's is his last until 1946, when contact was renewed.

DECEMBER 4, 1944
WOLDENBERG, GERMANY
Dear Helen,
Thank you very much for the card. I am touched by your concern for me and I am very grateful for it. I am sending the sticker [for a parcel]. I did not send it before because I know that it is also hard for you. Everything stopped for me since July when Bernard was left on the other side. If it is possible to send anything, then I would ask for such products as: bread, barley, flour and onions. In any event, nothing else. Happy Holidays.
Stach

There were more letters sent to aunt Helen that month but none reached her since the Soviet front was moving fast towards the west; Bydgoszcz and Poznan fell to the Soviets and Woldenberg was only 20 miles from the Polish border, so the battle was coming to their doorsteps.

The bleak weather of winter and apprehension for the future made this holiday very tense. Nevertheless, the best efforts were made by the POWs to make this Holiday special and to be of good spirit in the belief that it was only a matter of months before Germany would have to surrender.

The rooms were decorated with branches of evergreens and some barracks even had Christmas trees. Permission was given by the camp commandant to have lights on until 1 o'clock on Christmas Eve. The Christmas midnight mass was celebrated, together with singing of traditional Polish Christmas carols, while outside the German guards marched with leashed watchdogs.

Holiday wishes were exchanged, and everyone felt that this had to be their last Christmas in captivity.

Part Seven

1945-1946

Chapter 28

Iran-Isfahan, Qum, Teheran, Ahwaz, Khoramshar

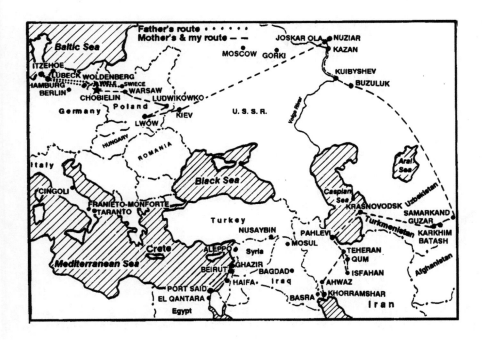

JANUARY 1945
ISFAHAN, IRAN

The start of the new year brought several changes in our lives. First, my school year ended this month; I completed fourth grade. In addition, because of the political changes in Iran, where the Soviets were stirring unrest, the Polish community in Isfahan slowly continued to disperse its operations, having started to do so the previous year. The dental office where mother worked was to close in March and its personnel to be transferred to Teheran. This meant that in the following month mother and I would leave Isfahan, after spending three memorable years there. Aunt Luta and Basia were to remain behind, but only for a few months, because they would join us in Teheran in July.

As for me, I was parting from the friends, classmates and teachers who had been an essential part of my life for the last three years and had made our stay here a fascinating experience. With our departure date set for March, I again took out my autograph book and asked my friends to write in it. Some of the inscriptions were standard verses, but one is more poignant:

Jan. 26, 1945
ISFAHAN, IRAN 5th Grade

> *When you leave the wall of Isfahan,*
> *And depart into the far world*
> *Don't forget a friend of former years.*

FEBRUARY. 1945
ISFAHAN, IRAN

The war news from Europe was optimistic and everyone assumed that the end was near. With great interest we followed news of the Yalta Conference that was held at the beginning of February and was attended by President Roosevelt, Prime Minister Churchill, and Stalin, but it was a devastating blow to our Polish community when the outcome of Yalta was made public. The three powers decided that Poland was to be part of the Soviet zone of influence and the US and Great Britain agreed to withdraw recognition of the Polish Government in London and to accept the legitimacy of the new Soviet-controlled government of Poland. The prospect for us, who had escaped Soviet captivity, of returning back to Soviet domination did not look feasible or even possible. In addition, everyone had families in Poland and were concerned about what would happen to them.

APRIL 4, 1945
DEPARTING ISFAHAN, IRAN

Since mother and I had only a few material possessions that fit into two suitcases, packing was simple. The goodbyes were long and tearful, particularly with aunt Luta and Basia, since we had not been separated throughout all the ordeals of the last six years.

It was early morning when mother and I arrived at the assigned place in front of the Legation building in order to join the departing trucks, which now had seats and were used as passenger transport vehicles. There were several other families that were going to Teheran with the same transport and who were to make the 200-mile journey with us. With little commotion, the trucks were loaded and began to pull out.

As the vehicles moved north on the Chahar Bagh I peered back in order to get a last glimpse of the beautiful blue domes of the Mosques that were the trademark of the city of Isfahan and watched the camel caravans heading to the local bazaars. Soon the trucks left the perimeter of the city with its gardens and many trees, and within a few miles the terrain became merely a monotonous road that continued until our first stop, in Qum.

APRIL 1945
QUM, IRAN

After half a day on the road, we were approaching the Holy City of Qum. From a distance the golden dome and the massive minarets were visible, and the road was cluttered with pilgrims heading for the Holy shrine.

The city's fame dates back to the 8th century, but settlement of this site probably dates back much further. It is one of the major Shiite religious centers. It is here where Fatima, a sister of Iman Reza, died and is buried in the Mosque which was built by Safavid rulers in the 17th century. The tomb attracts thousands of pilgrims, in particular women who pray for favors. As non-Moslems we were not allowed to enter the compound, but through the massive portals saw the picturesque facade of the mosque.

Here near the mosque we stopped for a meal at some nondescript post, and then entered the city where we were able to explore a little and stretch our legs for an hour before continuing the journey to Teheran.

The next 100 miles of road continued north on the dry vast plateau on which here and there one could spot the remnants of some former caravansary. The road was dusty and tiring, so we were relieved to reach our destination late that evening, where a meal and bathing facilities were waiting for us.

APRIL 1945
TEHERAN, IRAN

We were assigned provisional quarters on the outskirts of Teheran in what was known as Camp #1, which consisted of several one story brick structures and some Quonset huts. This was only a transit facility and mother was to remain here until more suitable quarters were to be found, while I was to go to a Polish boarding school and again visit her on the weekends.

As we waited several days for assignment orders to be implemented, the spring weather played havoc. While a few girls and I were playing hopscotch in front of our building the skies started to get darker and the winds increased, so we decided to go inside. It started to rain and in no time the rain turned into hail. As we watched with fascination from the doorway the huge ice balls, the size of eggs, pounded the rooftops, broke windows and covered the ground, creating a thick icy carpet. The storm subsided as fast as it came but left a great amount of damage to the housing complex. My playmates and I darted out to play with the icy deposits before they could melt.

Within a few days I went to the assigned school, which was in the city proper. The coeducational school was housed in a large one-story villa-like building with spacious grounds containing an abundance of trees and a small stream running through it. The stream was often utilized for frog hunting by boys, who then would chase the squealing girls with their trophies. Here we had our dormitories, dining room and recreational space, but classes were held in another location in the city. The central school complex served not only the children who lived in the boarding school but also pupils who lived with their parents. So, every morning we would take our shuttle transportation from the boarding school to the classrooms and would be returned there at the end of the day.

In the meantime mother was assigned to the dental office, located not too far from where I attended my classes, which enabled me to come and see her at lunch breaks. Though the school was very nice and pleasant, I was always wanting to be with mother and did not want to live apart from her. On several occasions, feeling terribly homesick, I would evade the return shuttle bus to school and march the few blocks to mother's office in the hope that I could stay with her. Needless to say, after mother finished her work she would take me back in a taxi to the school, where I would bid her a tearful farewell and impatiently wait for the weekend.

It was here in the boarding school that Kamal, my Hindu friend from Isfahan, found me. One Sunday evening when I returned to school after a weekend with mother, I found candy, several cakes of Lux soap and a cake on my bed. I looked at the items quite puzzled, in particular at the cake which had a large segment missing. But before I could inquire further, the head mistress came to the room and informed me:

"Oh, these are the gifts of a Hindu soldier that came here this morning looking for you. He said that he knows your mother and you from Isfahan. Kamal was his name. Do you know him?"

"Oh yes! They always give me candies" I replied, inspecting the cake, "but why is there a piece of cake missing?"

"Well..." the head mistress started hesitantly, "we wanted to make sure that it was all right, you know...that it was not poisoned. So we sampled."

I was very amused at her concern, in that she was so willing to "sacrifice" herself for such a large piece. I gathered my treasures and took what was left of the cake "after sampling," and shared it with my playmates.

As for Kamal, he came to school once more bearing sweets and some stuffed animals for me, and told me that he was being shipped out.

MAY 1945
TEHERAN, IRAN

Within few a weeks mother was given new housing in a small apartment complex near the hospital on the other side of town, and I was now able to come and live with her. Mother was now attending nursing training at the hospital while I continued to commute to the same school, as a day student with other children from the building.

The apartment building would be primitive by to-day's standards, or , for that matter, by ours in pre-war Poland, but for us at that time it was very nice and better than what we had previously. The quarters consisted of a large room on the first floor with a balcony overlooking a garden courtyard that had a small pool. The toilet was down the hallway for the use of ours and the other four rooms. For water, one had to go to the cellar where there were also facilities for doing laundry; i.e., a tub. We had electricity, which in those days was not always a norm. Like everyone in Teheran, we had an open water ditch that ran past the house; it served many purposes, including replenishing the garden pool. In summer, when we saw that the water was reasonably clean, we would open the "lock" to the house and fill "our pool" with it so we could bathe. On very hot nights many of the residents, as well as mother and I, would take our mattresses to the courtyard and sleep in the garden beside the pool, enjoying the balmy air under starry skies.

Not far from our new home was the Soviet Embassy. The huge complex was spread out over several blocks, surrounded by armed guards who loomed over the neighborhood, reminding us of the Soviet presence. It was here that less than two years ago, in November 1943, Stalin, Churchill and Roosevelt met for their Teheran conference. Now only a several-story-high banner picture of Stalin hung on its facade.

I always scrupulously avoided coming even close to the building or near Soviet soldiers, still remembering the years of our Soviet imprisonment. So it was one day when mother and I were returning from town that we stopped at our favorite ice cream parlor, which was several blocks away from our house and in the vicinity of the Soviet Embassy.

The colorful shop was brightly decorated, and it was renowned for its varieties of ice creams and ice milks and other sweets. As we sat down and waited to give our order, in walked three Soviet soldiers, presumably to have some ice cream. The sight of uniformed Russians struck panic in me, because there was always a fear in the back of my mind that they would get us again.

"Mother!" I pulled at her hand and pointed "look! They are here!"

"It's all right, don't be frightened, they just came for ice cream." Mother tried to reassure me.

"No, no! Please let's leave. I don't want any ice cream!"

Mother tried to calm me down, but I was close to bursting into tears of panic, so she thought it would be wiser to leave. Grabbing her hand tightly I pulled her out of the parlor, forgetting my appetite for ice cream. All I wanted to do was to get away from the soldiers as far as possible, to the safety of our home and my friends.

I had several friends of my age in the building but my constant companion was one of my classmates, named Dana, and whose father was also a POW of the German's. She lived with her mother and the mother's Iranian army officer boyfriend, on the next street. I always looked forward to be invited by Dana to stay for a meal because they ate in the traditional

Middle Eastern style, where you sit on the floor covered with thick and colorful Persian carpets and enjoy a variety of mouth-watering dishes.

Each school day morning Dana and I would take a shuttle bus to the cross road of the Shah Reza and Pahlevi Avenues and then wait on the corner for the next bus that would deliver us to our school. One day, when we were waiting at our customary spot, an Iranian officer was waiting there for someone. As our truck/bus pulled in and Dana stepped off the curb to get into the back, while I was still on the sidewalk, an Iranian military truck came roaring by and was hailed down by the officer. In a split second everything exploded as the screeching truck ran into our vehicle, pinning screaming Dana in between. Everyone around was trying to help and called for assistance, while the Iranian officer was yelling at the soldier-driver, smacking him on the face.

Dana was quickly taken to our hospital, and after many anxious weeks there recuperated, mainly due to being able to get penicillin, which at this time was a new drug and scarce.

From our house, mother and I would make excursions down town on the local overcrowded busses, where everyone would literally hang out of the windows. The reason for the overcrowding, which often resulted in accidents, was that the busses were privately owned and the more people they squeezed in the more profit was obtained.

Our trips would take us to restaurants and cafes where mother would meet her friends; we also would often go to the Red Cross recreational facilities at the Hotel Ferdousy. Here at the hotel were not only Poles but many British and, in particular, American military personnel. Whenever the Americans were in town the place would be bustling with activity and I would reap many benefits. There were not many children at these gatherings, so the American soldiers would play with me and indulge me with gifts of chewing gum and chocolate and buy me dolls from the gift shop. I would usually receive so many sweets that my class would be well supplied with goodies the following day.

This place exploded with jubilation when the news of the end of the war reached us. The Poles watched the joyful celebrations in a very subdued mood, knowing that we had no free homeland to which to return. In addition, mother, who had not heard from father since July 1944 and did not know his whereabouts, was very apprehensive about his situation.

JUNE 30, 1945
TEHERAN, IRAN

The long awaited news of father's liberation finally reached us via the Welfare Center for Iran that read as follows:

> *WELFARE CENTER FOR IRAN*
> *re: locating Capt. S. Mikosz*
> *to: Mrs. Anna Mikosz-Teheran*
> *I am informing that your husband, Capt. Stanislaw Mikosz, according to information received by us on May 25th, 1945, has been liberated from a prisoner of war camp in Germany. He is at present in the Polish Centre for Ex-Prisoner of War, Murnau, ober Bayern, Base Censor A.P.O. 887 U.S. Army.*
> *The information is based on a communiqué from military welfare, Dept. for Military dependents dated June 15, 1945.*
> *Centre Director*
> *Capt. Stefan Jezewski*

In fact the news of father's whereabouts were brought to mother by me. The school day ended and I came to mother's office; as I entered the building I met the lady from the Centre carrying the dispatch to mother. Seeing me, she said with a big smile:

"You take the good news to your mother," and handed the piece of paper to me.

I read the communiqué with momentary disbelief and made a dash for mother's office, bursting through the door yelling:

"Daddy is free! Daddy is free!"

Having father's address, I was able to write to him for the first time in a year, and also on regular paper and not on the required POW forms.

JULY 1945

TEHERAN, IRAN

To: Capt. Stanislaw Mikosz

Most beloved Daddy,

I was very happy when I received news that you are free. I can't wait the moment when we will again be together. Mommy was afraid that you are where uncle Jas is. The last day of the school, 30th of June, I ran to the office where Mommy works, with news that Daddy is liberated. Mommy almost went crazy hearing the news, as well as I.

At the end of the school year in front of the entire school in Teheran, the Consul (Polish) presented me with my report card as the best student in my class. Now I have vacations. I go to the swimming pool every day and I am learning to swim. Mommy bought me a chair in which I sit and read books. I read 32 books. Now I am reading a book titled "Rycez bez Skazy" (Virtuous Knight).

We have a surprise for Daddy, a very pleasant one, but I will not tell.

Write to us and tell us how you feel. Now I kiss my dear Daddy many, many times.

Your loving

Terenia

At the bottom of the letter I drew a picture of a mosque with two minarets. Beside the mosque sit two Iranians with turbans on a carpet. Towards them is walking another Iranian in local garb, with a donkey. In the background are high mountains.

In addition, I mention in the letter that mother was afraid that father was where uncle Jas was. Mother did receive news from aunt Helen that uncle Jas was liberated by the Soviets and returned to Poland to be with his family.

The same month, July 6th, news reached us that the Communist Government in Poland had been recognized by the British and that we, as Poles, were under their jurisdiction and they would be responsible for our welfare. Rumors erupted that we would be forced to go back to Poland and be under the Communists, from whom all of us had escaped with such difficulty.

Under such uncertain circumstances, the Polish authorities in Tehran started to search for alternative places where we could reside. Also, on the last day of the month aunt Luta and Basia arrived with a transport from Isfahan and were put in transitional camp #3. The camp was located in a hilly park, with large tents strewn throughout it that served as living quarters.

AUGUST 1945
TEHERAN, IRAN

In the first week of the month mother finally received long-awaited news in the form of a letter from father through the Polish Red Cross in Egypt. The letter was written from Italy and told of his whereabouts. Immediately mother responded by telegram to the Red Cross, confirming our place of stay, before writing personally to father.

At the same time, preparations were being made for the Polish population to evacuate Iran to several different locations. We, that is mother and I, together with aunt Luta and Basia, were to go to Lebanon. The route that we were to take was through Ahwaz, Iran, and Basra, Iraq, and then through Baghdad and Mosul, skirting southern Turkey, to Syria, and then to our final destination, Beirut, Lebanon.

Some logistic problems arose since Syria and Iraq did not allow any Jews to enter into their country, even to pass through. Therefore, all who were to travel that route were issued the following papers:

ROMAN CATHOLIC
CHIEF CHAPLAIN-IRAN
TEHERAN August 4, 1945
CERTIFICATE

I certify here-by that Mrs. Mikosz-Anna with daughter Teresa is
of Roman Catholic faith.
   This certificate is issued at the request of Iraq Consulate.
   Ks. Goralik Aleksander
   R.C. Chief-Chaplain
   Iran

There were some Poles who were Jewish and were in the same transport; the Catholic Chaplain issued them the same certificates in order to
facilitate their move. In addition, mother, being anxious to be reunited
with father, went to the French Consulate and obtained a visa on her own,
which read as follows: (translation from French)

Consulate of France in Teheran
Entry Visa
   Good for crossing the borders until October 20, 1945
   Good for single trip and stay in Syria and Lebanon for six months.
   Reason for trip: evacuation of Poles

The closing of the Polish facilities was accelerated and since several people from our apartment were transferred to transit camps in the city or had
left for other destinations, the decision was made to close the building.
Mother was now attending a nurses' training course at the nearby British
hospital, so we moved to the housing facilities on the hospital grounds.
Here we spent our last weeks in Teheran, and from which I continued to
commute to school.

It was not until the beginning of November that we were assigned to
leave Teheran with a group of medical evacuees from Isfahan. Aunt Luta,
who never regained her health after her years in the Soviet camps, and
Basia were on the same train, but not with us since the transport contained also American military personnel in addition to Polish civilians and
some hospital personnel. Since mother had completed her nursing course

she was assigned to this group. We departed the Teheran station in the late afternoon. Though the train was quite crowded, we were fortunate to get a compartment, which mother and I shared with a friend of hers from nurses' training and a British officer.

As the journey progressed, mother and her friend were conversing in Polish while the officer read his newspaper. After an hour or so, and presumably getting bored, the two women began to make comments, not entirely complimentary, to each other about the British officer. He was not paying any attention to them but could hear their chatter. The train made a stop at Qum station and as the officer got ready to leave, he nodded his head to the women, who smiled back at him, and then in flawless Polish said:

"It was very nice traveling with you; goodbye." leaving them with their mouths open in astonishment.

Before they could utter a word and regain their composure, the officer left the train. For the rest of the train ride the two were trying to figure out how a British officer could speak Polish so well. Also, they agreed that they would be more cautious when making comments in the future.

It was getting late; we were all tired and ready to settle down for the night and the rest of the journey that was to last almost twenty-four hours.

NOVEMBER 1945
AHWAZ, IRAN

When I awakened in the early morning, the terrain of the evening before had changed. We were now traversing the green Zagros Mountains where the trains were continually going in and out of a maze of tunnels. The mountain peaks were snow covered and along the rail road track was a fast flowing river that sped in the same direction as our train. As the train was emerging from the mountain range in the foothills, we passed a small station with the name of Shush.

Shush, better known as Susa, is now just another Moslem Shiite devotional center where presumably is the tomb of the Prophet Daniel. But to historians it is a place with more than 4000 years of history, best remembered as the splendid winter residence of the Achaemenian Kings which was captured by Alexander the Great in 331 BC. The city had a comeback during the time of the Sassanian Kings, only to be destroyed soon after, and from then on it slowly sank into decline.

The train now chugged through the low lying plain of the province of Khuzistan to its capital, Ahwaz. Because of the town's low-lying location the climate is hot and humid. In spite of its climatic drawbacks, Ahwaz had been gaining importance since 1930 with the rediscovery of oil in this area.

It was early evening when our train stopped at the Ahwaz station, and we began to disembark and be loaded into the waiting trucks that took us to the transit camp.

We were quartered in what was once an Iranian military camp, which in 1942 the British authorities had designated as a transitional place for the Polish armed forces and civilians that were coming from the Soviet Union and in turn, were sent from here to Iraq. At that time, thousands had come through this camp and a field hospital was still in existence. Now, the only reminder of those who had passed through Ahwaz was a large Polish cemetery, a grim reminder that many never made it any further.

After the hot and tedious train ride we reached our communal quarters, which consisted of large rooms with lines of bunk beds. The heat was suffocating and all everyone wanted was a cleansing shower. Fortunately, the showers were plentiful and refreshing, making one once more feel cool and clean.

In the meantime, mother had to get our transit papers in order and obtain permission from the hospital to travel to Lebanon. Here she encountered difficulties because the chief of the hospital, a British doctor, wanted to retain mother in the Polish hospital in Ahwaz. She tried to get out of the assignment by saying that she was not a nurse (although she did finish the course), but a dental assistant. Peeved, the doctor gave up his demands, but said that mother would not travel as one of the hospital personnel, but as a civilian. Though it was a less desirable mode of travel, she was happy to get permission to leave for Lebanon.

After a couple of monotonous weeks of endless humid heat and watching movies in our camp, our only source of recreation, the word came that we were about to leave on the next leg of our journey.

It was a late November evening when we boarded a passenger train for a relatively short trip of about 75 miles south to the port of Khoramshar.

NOVEMBER 26, 1945
KHORAMSHAR, IRAN

We arrived at the station with the early rays of dawn. The port is the border between Iran and Iraq, located at Shatt al Arab, which is the joint flow of the Tigris and Euphrates rivers that flow into the Persian Gulf. Here, as at all our other stops, military personnel were waiting for us with breakfast before we continued further by truck. There was no train connection between Khoramshar and Basra, Iraq, though Basra is only about 15 miles northwest on the Shatt al Arab.

After breakfast of coffee and rolls, we scrambled into the tarpaulin-covered trucks, with their sides rolled up, and I looked around for the last time at Iran, where I had spent three and a half memorable years.

Chapter 29

Germany-Woldenberg, Hamburg, Murnau

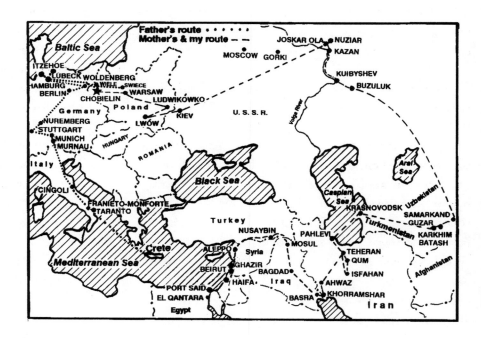

JANUARY 1945
WOLDENBERG, GERMANY

The end of the war was now imminent, but the fate of the POWs was not yet determined since news had reached the camp that the Soviets were occupying terrain not far to the east; the German camp command was very uneasy but was not making any moves. Then on January 23rd another communiqué followed—the Soviet army had broken through the German front near Schneidemuhl (today Pila, Poland) situated only 37 miles away; therefore, all prisoners were to evacuate the camp on the next morning. That afternoon a general alarm was sounded in the camp and the food magazines were opened so everyone could take what they wanted. The hungry POWs descended in a mad fervor on the unexpected bounty, grabbing anything in sight. Father also made a run in order to supply himself; he managed to get his hands on two loaves of bread, a large tin can of margarine, a bag of sugar and two cans of meat. He returned to his barrack with the newly acquired supplies and started to prepare himself for the upcoming march. From his extra shirt he made himself a knapsack into which he put the new provisions with his two blankets, a new pair of shoes that he was saving and his extra military jacket.

Next morning at 4:00 AM reveille was sounded and the POWs with their meager belongings lined up in three columns, each approximately 1500 people, and in the darkness of a snowy winter morning marched out of the camp heading west, each column taking a separate road in the destination of Krzecin, towards Stettin. Left behind in the camp were the sick in the infirmary, together with their doctor and a Polish Chaplain.

Father's column was situated on the western most spearhead of the three columns, which proved later to be his salvation, resulting in his not being captured by the Soviets. Heavy snow continued falling, covering the already snow-laden roads and making the march exhausting and difficult, so it wasn't long when the underfed and weak POWs began to fall down in the snow from exhaustion and cold. But the German escort guards did not bother to pick them up or force them to march, just left them in the snow, since the objective was to move as fast and as far as possible away from the oncoming battle front that was fast approaching from the east. As the slow trekking unit moved on, the darkness of the winter morning dissipated, giving way to daylight that brought out Soviet planes. The planes circled in the gray skies and sprayed the POW column with bullets, but were repelled by the German escorts who were well equipped with machine guns. Fortunately, there were no casualties and the march continued in the heavy snow without a stop for the rest of the day through Krzecin and Barlinek, when at dusk, around 5PM, another small village was sighted.

As the short winter day was rapidly coming to an end and there was no let up of the falling snow, the prisoner column was halted and ordered to disperse for the night; meaning every man for himself to find a shelter for the night. Father and his companion Capt. Dulski managed to find a pigsty which, though odorous, was out of the winter cold and snow. The two men glanced around the new found shelter and realized that the only place to lay down was manure covered ground. Reluctantly, Capt. Dulski produced out of his bundle a quilt that his wife had sent him and which he had treasured for several years. Gingerly the two men spread the covering over the smelly and damp floor and, exhausted, fell asleep without removing any clothing.

At dawn, awakened by the reveille, father and Capt. Dulski reluctantly stretched their stiff limbs and gathered their knapsack and bundle. The prized quilt had been soaked through and now was unusable and so they reluctantly had to part with it. They once again stepped out into the cold and joined the forming column of POWs. There was no attempt on the part of the Germans to feed the prisoners; they were left to their own ingenuity. So, while waiting for the next order, father took one of his loaves of bread and shared it with Captain Dulski.

It was not long before marching orders were given and the unit moved out of the village onto the snow laden road. The march continued through the day into the evening without any event, except for the constant falling out of exhausted prisoners and being hampered by refugees that were also trying to get away from the Russians.

The daylight was quickly diminishing when father's unit came upon another group of POWs from Woldenberg that was standing in the middle of a small village. As the men passed each other they exchanged greetings, when suddenly father heard a familiar voice:

"Stach! Stach!" It was uncle Jas. The two embraced and reassured each other that each was well. "Stach," continued uncle Jas, "why don't you stay here; then we would be together."

"Oh, but you know I can't, since I am registered in the other column...they will shoot me if I do that!" explained father, and reluctantly said his farewell since his group was continuing further. This was unfortunately the last time the two friends would ever see each other, since soon after that encounter uncle Jas was captured by the Soviet army and returned to Poland to be reunited with his wife, aunt Helen, and his children. It was at the beginning of March when he, reunited with his family, decided to go back to Chobielin. By that time the manor was devastated and ransacked by the Russians. The nights were full of fright, since roaming bands of Soviet deserters roamed the countryside with remnants of Germans that had managed not to get caught. Therefore, for safety they would barricade themselves in one of the rooms for the night. After some time it was apparent that the communist regime was about to throw them out, so uncle Jas took the family back to nearby Naklo, where the girls returned to school.

As the two groups parted, father's column continued further west for another mile. It was getting dark and there was still no letup of the falling snow, when the houses of a village were spotted nearby. The small hamlet was perched on a rolling hill that lay on the east bank of a narrow, now frozen river. A road that divided the village continued over a bridge and headed further west.

The guards in front gave the order to halt and then told the POWs to find a place for the night. Quickly, father and Capt. Dulski made a run for a nearby barn in order to appropriate a space for the night, since the village appeared to be deserted. The doors of the large barn opened with a creak as they peered into the darkened interior. In the far corner they spotted some hay and headed for it, thinking themselves fortunate to find a dry and relatively warm spot for a much needed night's rest.

As father dropped to the ground he started to take off his shoes, which were wet through from the day's march. No sooner had he removed one shoe when the village came under a barrage of artillery fire from approaching Soviet tanks. In no time some houses exploded under direct hits from the shells, then ignited into bright flames that lit the dark winter sky. Both German soldiers and Polish POWs were running for shelter in confusion and chaos. General Von Wachocki, the commandant of the Oflag, was making a dashing exit out of the village in his horse carriage, heading west. Among the screams of the frightened or those actually hit, Polish voices were heard shouting instructions:

"Gentlemen! Don't run away...freedom has come! We are going back to Poland!" These were the voices of officers who were socialists and staunch supporters of the Polish People's Republic (i.e., communists) whose numbers were many at the camp.

Captain Dulski stood in the doorway listening to the calling and hesitated, not being sure whether he should stay and return to Poland or escape to the west.

"Zygmunt!" father yelled at him; "Zygmunt, are you coming or staying here?," but since he did not get an answer from his friend, father started running away from the barn and was joined by other officers as they headed for the cover of the ditch that ran the along side of the road. Here, under the cover of darkness, with exploding artillery shells above, father made slow progress in waist deep snow, heading west. They continued their trek until they were sure that they were out of the immediate battle zone.

With the initial danger eliminated, father's small group sat in the snow in order to take a rest and catch their breath. As he sat, figures of men emerged from the darkness—they were more Polish officers who followed the same route as father and among them was Captain Dulski. Reinforced in numbers and glad that they were able to escape the battle and capture by the Soviets, the group of now fourteen officers started up again, trying to put as much distance as possible between them and the Russians. They now thought it was safe to scramble out of the ditch and onto the road heading westward.

The trek on the snow-laden road under cover of darkness continued through the night without encountering either Soviet or German troops or even any other settlement. Then, as dawn was starting to break, a cluster of houses became visible on the near horizon. There was no sign of life or visible military forces of either side. The eerie silence made them cautious as they neared the village. The group approached the first building slowly, noticing that the settlement grouping was of about ten farms that at present appeared to be abandoned. The door of the farm buildings were ajar and the chickens and pigs roamed the yards as well as the road at large.

Upon careful inspection of the first open house, to their astonishment, the weary and hungry group found larders full of food. In no time, the officers proceeded in preparing their much needed meal and in minutes the aromas of roasting sausages and bubbling soup begun to permeate the kitchen. Within an hour the hungry POWs sat down to a sumptuous meal that they consumed with eagerness. As the last morsel of prepared food disappeared, the early dawn sun was peeking through the snow clouds. It was daylight.

Father looked over the men and saw that he was the senior officer of the group and thus in charge. The men were all weary and exhausted from the last 24 hour march and badly in need of sleep.

"Gentleman, it is obvious that we can't go any further at the moment, but we can't stay in this house since it is at the entrance of the village. This would not be safe. Let's go further in the complex and find a safer place to rest." All agreed to father's idea and took their shirt "knapsacks" which they replenished with the food from the pantry and started to walk out in search of safer quarters.

In the middle of the village they spotted a hay barn which had a high loft. There in the loft, behind hay stacks and out of the cold, the weary officers fell into a heavy sleep. They slept all day until the sound of vehicle motors in the courtyard of the farm woke them up—it was evening. Through a crack in the barn wall they could tell it was some army unit, but could not tell whether they were Germans or Russians. Every so often someone would come into the barn and scan the inside with a flashlight and then leave. Father and his group sat motionless, high in the hay loft, not daring to make their presence known until the soldiers could be identified. Under this pressure and tension they sat until dawn, waiting for the daylight.

Finally the darkness started to fade away and the smatterings of the early rays of dawn came through the winter clouds. Gingerly, father got up and with the help of Captain Dulski loosened a couple of the roof shingles; through this opening he could see the silhouettes of vehicles in the courtyard, but it was still too dark to see their insignias. The few soldiers that were around the vehicles wore unrecognizable get-ups, since by this time in the war German soldiers wore all sorts of fur coats and coverings that were given to them from donations and confiscations, even coats made of their blankets; the German soldier now looked as ragged as Soviet soldiers normally did.

Time dragged on. Minutes seemed to last for an eternity while they waited for full daylight, which in winter of course comes late; in addition, it was snowing again. Then finally with daylight a tank arrived into view, and to their great joy and relief, father saw German insignia on it. The soldiers piled out of the tank and they wore German uniforms. After recognizing the soldiers' nationality, the decision of the group in hiding was to come out and make contact with the unit. Curiously, soldiers of their longtime bitter enemy were clearly to be preferred over those of their self-proclaimed ally.

Cautiously, one by one, they made their way down from the loft hiding place into the courtyard, coming closer to the group of German soldiers that were gathered around a field kitchen consuming their breakfast. The soldiers did not make any move; engrossed in eating, they ignored the small POW group. Father now spotted, a short distance beyond the field kitchen, a young German officer who had one arm in a sling and in his other had a cigarette. The officer sighted the Polish officers and languidly moved toward them. The POWs tensed up. Then, to their great surprise, the officer smiled and in perfect Polish said:

"Gentleman, are you officers from Woldenberg? We have already encountered several groups like yours on the road." Seeing the astonished look on the faces of the Polish officers the German officer decided to further explain:

"I see you gentleman are surprised that I speak Polish fluently. I am from the Poznan district and I attended high school there; in addition, I was an officer cadet in the Polish 57th Infantry Regiment in Ostrzeszow. But since I was German, I was drafted into the German army. " Now the puzzle was solved and the POWs felt relieved. The young German officer showed genuine concern for the Polish group. He asked if they had any mess kits, which they didn't, so he ordered his NCO to issue some to them and told the POW's to go the field kitchen to have breakfast and then get hot water in order so they could wash themselves. In addition, he sent a soldier who had a razor so all of the group could shave themselves. There were no restrictions put on them, so the POWs moved around the square freely and conversed with the officer who further expounded on his experiences. Father learned that the young officer, a Captain Frank, had already spent three years in the front lines and was eager for the war to end. Then, toward the end of the day, Frank approached father and informed him that the Soviets were progressing further west and that he had orders to stay here and defend the position. Further, he added:

"I am expecting supplies to arrive here in the morning, so I will send all you to Stettin in the truck in the morning. Please be ready."

As promised, in the morning a truck arrived with ammunition and food. It was promptly unloaded and was ready to take the rested POWs who were issued by the German officer appropriate papers that the German police would request. For the journey the POWs were also issued field rations. Father thanked Captain Frank, gave him a pack of cigarettes that he had saved from his Red Cross packages, and wished him the best.

The truck, with the Polish POWs supposedly under guard by two youthful German soldiers, headed north-west in the direction of Stettin, about 45 miles away, but could not go all the way. The prisoners were supposed to walk the last 15 miles, so when the truck reached the appointed crossroad the guards told them to get out. The aspect of walking in the deep snow did not look too appealing, so father and his group decided to strike a bargain with the German soldiers.

"Do you like cigarettes?" father asked.

"Of course!" was the quick answer as the two soldiers exchanged glances.

"Well..." father started again "We will give you American cigarettes if you take us a little further."

The two Germans again looked at each other and nodded in approval, but said that they wanted fifty cigarettes. After some haggling the price was set at thirty cigarettes.

"Ja, ja." They all hopped back into the truck and continued nine miles further, where they came to a final stop. The Germans explained that this is was far as they dared to go because the Gestapo would get them. Reluctantly the POWs unloaded. Father gave the two soldiers their promised cigarettes and the truck sped off back to the crossroad.

Offloaded, father and his group had sat down by the roadside while they decided what would be the next step when the roar of tanks was heard. A German tank column was lumbering towards Stettin, taking no notice of the group of POWs by the side of the road. It took the tanks about twenty minutes to pass and then the wide road was clear again. The officers resumed their trek on the snow covered highway that now had been made easier to walk on since the tanks had compressed the snow. They walked for two hours without encountering anything, when in the distance a cluster of buildings surrounded with trees appeared. As they neared them, several armed soldiers in German uniforms jumped out shouting and ready to shoot. But they were yelling in Russian and not in German! The Poles came to an abrupt stop and waited as the soldiers neared them, holding their bayonets in ready position. When they came close one could see the insignia which read "*Frei Rusland*" (Free Russia), which solved the mystery right away. They were a part of a German army formed from Soviet prisoners of war under the leadership of Gen. Vlasoff, and of course they did not speak German but only Russian. Fortunately, there were a couple of Polish officers in father's group who spoke Russian and who quickly surmised that the soldiers were going to rob the POWs. This contingent of the army under Gen. Vlasoff had already a reputation as cutthroats, thieves and murderers who only a few months before had helped the Germans to liquidate the Warsaw Uprising. Therefore, a Polish officer who spoke Russian refused to show them the POW's papers but demanded to see their commandant, for whom he had the necessary documents. The Russian soldiers hesitated a while but, fearing German authority, soon led them a short distance to one of the houses which actually had a sign identifying it as some sort of headquarters. The Russian soldier then exchanged some words with the guard at the front door, who went inside and soon emerged with a German Major, to the relief of the Polish POWs.

Now another Polish officer, but one who spoke German, stepped up and explained to the Major the groups' predicament and showed him the papers that they received from Captain Frank. He added that their orders were to go to Stettin. The Major looked over the papers and then asked when was the last time the group had something to eat. Learning that their last meal had been breakfast, he gave orders to have the POWs fed, after which he would explain the situation. Within the hour the Poles reported back to the commandant, who said:

"You know, gentlemen, there was another group of Polish officers that passed this point. They were from Grossborn camp. Now, I must send you to the gathering center for POWs that is on the west side of Stettin where the remnants of four Oflags from Pomerania are being consolidated. Unfortunately, I have no vehicles to spare so you will have to walk across Stettin to the other side of the Oder River. Not only have I no vehicles, but I don't have soldiers available to take you over. I will give you papers with instructions where to go, and my orders so you would not be stopped on the way. " With that he stamped the already made-out papers and drew a map showing how to reach the city and cross the bridge. Father and the officers thanked the Major for taking care of them, and the fourteen POWs departed for the city.

Soon the group entered the city limits of Stettin. The towns-people as well as military personnel were all around, but no one was taking notice of them. They were on their own after so many years of incarceration and it felt good. Now, as they passed a cafe, some person suggested that it would be a good idea to stop for some coffee and warm up.

"Good idea!" and "Why not." and then "Let's go" was heard, so the group cautiously entered the premises.

There were several people at the tables who, seeing Polish uniforms, mistook them for Russians and were panic stricken. Some started to dart out and the proprietor did not know what to do, whether to run or stay. Again the officer who spoke German came forward and went to the owner, explaining:

"Sir, we are Polish POWs, officers, and all we would like is some coffee. We are not the Russians." The proprietor sighed with relief as looked the straggly group over, but was still hesitant.

"Sir," continued the Pole, "we don't want it free, we will pay for it with American cigarettes."

Then a smile appeared on the innkeeper's face; he gestured to them to sit down and took the order and the whole establishment was most friendly and hospitable. They not only got their coffee but were showered with all sorts of pastries, delicacies that they had not seen in five years. They ate and drank the aromatic brew with relish. After they "paid" their bill and were again ready to depart, the proprietor and the guests bid them farewell as if the Polish officers were their old friends. One young man even offered to take them to the bridge, for which of course he received a few cigarettes.

Before the group reached their first bridge, an air raid sounded. Everyone scurried for nearby shelters, but fortunately the raid was a light one. The air attack was done by Soviet planes, which were quickly dispelled by the persistent anti-aircraft fire without doing too much damage. When the all clear sounded, the POWs resumed their approach to the bridge. Here, father noticed an anti-aircraft battery that was totally manned by women. The officers encountered their first sentry, who after checking their papers waved them on. The scene repeated itself at the second bridge, since the river Oder has three branches at this point and they had to make all three crossings. At the third and last bridge a German sergeant, after inspecting the papers, asked them their nationality and then waved them on. On the other side of the bridge was yet another check point, which consisted of two tables manned by German military who looked over their documents and told them to go another two miles to an estate where the Polish POWs were to meet. The German gave them a paper with a name of the place and drew a simple map. Father later found out that each nationality had a different gathering center.

Within half an hour father and his group reached the manor house of the appointed estate, where they found a lone, aged sentry who pointed out the office where they were supposed to report. The office was run by a Polish POW, Col. Kaczmarek, who was designated to be in charge of the arriving prisoners. There were no guards, since the Germans knew that the POWs who had managed to escape the Soviets were not going to go anywhere. The Colonel informed them that the only living quarters available here were in the barns, but if they could find something better, go for it.

So, father and his companions headed towards the barn, which turned out to be even than less what they had expected because there was nothing but bare ground. Being the middle of winter and they having no bedding, they decided to go to the nearby farm and buy some hay, which they soon brought back. Now, at least they were content to have a roof over their heads and were out of the snow while they waited while other POWs from different camps kept trickling in.

Within several days the numbers of stragglers grew to around 600 Polish soldiers, mostly officers but also a number of NCOs. With the gathering center now overfilled, the Germans decided to move them out. In came two German officers with an escort and announced that they were going to march out and provided the POWs with rations of bread.

FEBRUARY 15, 1945
EAST GERMANY

At the assigned early morning hour the POWs assembled on the road, forming a lengthy column that was lead by a supply vehicle on which rode the German commandant with several soldiers. In the rear of the unit was another supply truck on which the rest of the German soldiers rode. The march started toward western Germany under the most arduous conditions, on icy winter roads crowded with military personnel and the escaping German population who wanted to get away from the battle zones. The next two weeks were a continuous march from 8AM to 5PM, six days a week, where if conditions permitted the column would make 10 miles a day. In addition to the crowded roads there were several allied air raids, which shelled the unit not knowing that these were POWs. The number of sick and weak prisoners was increasing, and they were put on the rear supply truck which soon was filled to capacity. But unfortunately, not all were sick because many wanted a free ride. The Germans soon caught on to the gimmick, and one day when the truck was full of supposed sick they transported them to the nearest concentration camp where they were left and never heard from again.

Needless to say, for the rest of the grueling journey that took them to Waren, Parchin, and toward Hamburg, there was no faking sickness among the marchers. Their chaotic progress westward lasted almost six weeks with many casualties, and when it came to a stop they were in a settlement near Hamburg.

END of MARCH 1945
NEAR HAMBURG, GERMANY

The exhausted POWs were quartered in a village on the outskirts of Hamburg, from which the city was visible in the distance. The Germans took a head-count of the prisoners, whose numbers had dwindled to about 450. They were then put up in different farmhouses, wherever there was some space, and the farmers were ordered to give the prisoners soup. Father, like most of the POWs, had cigarettes and soap saved from his Red Cross parcels which he used as currency and so was able to eat quite well. At that point in the war, the Germans did not see cigarettes, particularly American ones, so for a pack he was able to eat well for two days.

The stay on the outskirts of Hamburg lasted ten days while additional POWs arrived, swelling the ranks to approximately 700. It was at that time when a Red Cross commission arrived to check on the welfare of the POWs and take the sick and the disabled. Captain Dulski, who had been with father through the march, announced that he planned to report as sick since his feet were rubbed raw from the long march. On the other hand, father had no such problem because he had managed to keep his feet dry and had a good pair of American shoes that he had at one time received from the Red Cross.

"You know, Zygmunt, reporting as sick is not a good idea. Really, it is foolish, because you don't know where they might take you," Father tried to convince his friend, " it is safer to stick with the group."

Captain Dulski did not heed father's advice and reported as sick. He was promptly rejected and returned into the ranks, where father did not pass the opportunity for friendly ribbing. There were only 50 POWs who considered themselves well, but the commission started to weed out the fit from the "sick" group. Half of the so-called sick were disqualified and returned to the ranks to await the next order.

The next day a German sergeant informed the "well" group that the healthy ones were going to continue marching while the sick ones were going to go by train.

"Where are we marching?" father inquired, but the Sergeant shrugged his shoulders and said that he did not know.

"Oh, Stach! We are really stupid." said Captain Dulski after hearing the plan; "if we could have passed for sick we would not have to walk!"

"Zygmunt, whatever you say, it is safer to walk than to ride a train. You are a sitting target since the trains are constantly being bombed." Father was trying to justify his decision.

Then the next morning the sergeant appeared again and told each to take a bundle of hay, since they would go by train.

"What is happening with the sick?"

"They are staying here and you are going south," was the short answer from the sergeant.

While the fit were transported by train, the sick who were supposed to stay in place were later dragged from one place to another on foot. They were shelled and bombarded, so that many died. Then finally, at the end of the war, they were liberated by the British.

APRIL 1945
HEADING SOUTH IN GERMANY

The 200 POWs who were pronounced fit to travel by the Red Cross were marched to the nearest Hamburg train station, each carrying a bundle of hay, and loaded into five waiting freight cars. The cars were locked and the train headed south. The cars were so packed that one did not have room to lie down but could only sit, and the cramped prisoners were let out only once daily to stretch and be given some food. In such confinement they were kept for almost two weeks while the train shuffled through Germany amidst constant allied bombardment. They first went to Dusseldorf, then headed south to Stuttgart and then back north to Nuremberg where a bombing raid caught the train standing in the station.

Here, the German guards left the helpless prisoners in the locked cars while they ran for shelter. The train rocked on its track from the impact of the exploding bombs.

After a while, realizing that no one was going to release them, one of the smallest men in the car was hoisted up and was able to squeeze out through the train car window. He then quickly unbolted the doors of all of the five cars while the POWs darted out, heading for the shelter of the nearby train tunnel. Here they a found a multitude of people of different nationalities, both civilian and military, including their surprised German guards, who inquired how they managed to get out.

The devastating bombing raid lasted almost three hours but their train escaped any damage. It took some time before the tracks were ready, when the POWs again returned to their cars to resume the journey south and reached Munich. The train made a stop at the station, where finally the POWs were told that they were going to an Oflag in Murnau, which they reached the following day.

APRIL 15, 1945
MURNAU, BAVARIA

It was a beautiful countryside, nothing devastated by war, fresh air among the snow covered Alps. Only a short distance from here was Hitler's mountain retreat of Garmisch-Partenrkirchen, now abandoned by him.

Father and the rest were happy to be let out of the confines of the train and marched several miles to the camp, and were placed in the modern barracks of a German artillery unit. It was one of four Polish officers' camps in Germany and it was known as Oflag VIIA. There were two in Pomerania-Woldenberg and Arnswalde. The third was in Desel, and Murnau was the fourth. Since the camp was close to the border it served as a show place for various Red Cross delegates that the Germans were trying to impress by showing how well they treated POWs. Here the prisoners slept on beds with mattresses and had shower facilities and well organized medical care. The camp contained over 5000 officers, including almost all

Polish Generals who had been taken prisoner. The Murnau camp was also the only POW camp that was untouched by battle, and once imprisoned here the individuals remained for the duration of the war. Proximity to Switzerland resulted in easier communication with other countries, as well as in receiving more food parcels. With excellent climate and cleanliness, the camp appeared to the worn-out prisoners to be a normal army camp with the exception of the poor food that was like all POW's rations. At present, father and the new arrivals were quartered in what at one time had served as garages, due to overcrowding.

Every day news of the war's progress received through various sources made the POWs optimistic that any moment they could be freed by the advancing American Forces, but they grew impatient when the battles for Munich took longer than anticipated. They watched the wide road that ran along the camp, on which there was constant vehicle traffic heading for Switzerland. They even watched as an entire Hungarian division was making a hasty retreat to that country. The Germans took precautions so as not to have the camp bombed by constructing large "POW" letters on the ground of the center courtyard. These signs came handy when two American reconnaissance planes circled the camp several times, dropping leaflets with announcements that they were going to be there soon. The Germans by this time were aware that the end was near and did not even bother shooting at the planes. Then on the April 25th a communiqué reached the camp regarding the imminent capture of Berlin.

APRIL 28, 1945
MURNAU, GERMANY

That morning the General commanding the camp summoned the senior Polish General Rummel to his office. The German commandant informed Gen. Rummel that he had received orders from his commanders to be ready to transfer his command to the SS Staffel who were already on the way to Murnau. He then added:

"As you probably know, General, this creates a very dangerous situation since they have already liquidated several Soviet camps and they might do the same here." He continued as Gen. Rummel listened to his frank explanation. "Because the Americans are not far from here and the three story barrack buildings are brick with strong doors, tell the officers to barricade themselves in and not to come out if such orders are given through the loud-speakers. What is important is to create at least half a day's delay, by which time the Americans should be here."

The news was passed to the POWs and preparations were made with speed. All the officers that were located in the garages, including father, went to the main buildings, where from the third floor they were looking for their liberators. Noon passed. The camp grounds were deserted as the tense prisoners waited and there was nothing in sight. Then, when it was almost 2 PM, on the road to Murnau a slow-moving American tank column was spotted. The German camp command announced that the Americans were approaching. Two of the tanks did not stop, but just rode through the barbed wire without firing a shot, since the camp tower guards did not fire but came down with hands raised to surrender while the rest of the tank unit was proceeding towards the town of Murnau. Then, as father continued to watch the unfolding scenario from the upper window, from behind the bend, from the direction of the town of Murnau, coming towards the camp, appeared German panzer vehicles and three trucks full of SS soldiers. The Americans, without hesitation, unanimously opened fire on the SS, who started to dart out of the trucks, but to no avail; there were no survivors left. A jubilant cheer rose from the watching POWs, who watched the scenario with disbelief, knowing well that if the Americans were delayed any longer this might have been the end for them.

A group of POWs, throwing caution to the wind, ran out to greet the American liberators, waving a flag, when a German sniper's bullet hit one of them. It was a sad ending for the Polish officer who died at the moment when after so many years, he had gained his freedom; he was the last casualty of the camp.

The joy and jubilation of the freed POWs was ecstatic as they began to pour out of the buildings toward the two American tanks. The American soldiers were smiling and exchanging greetings, and one young soldier was shouting in Polish:

"I am a Pole! I'm from Chicago!" giving the officers cigarettes and chocolate.

In the meantime, the American tank commander rounded up all of the German camp crew and guards, disarmed them, and locked them in the garages where the POWs had been before. Then he told the Polish officers to guard them till the American MP's could come and take them off their hands. In addition, the Americans opened the food storages so the former inmates could help themselves to the abundance of spoils. The command of the camp was now turned over to the Poles, and within two days the Americans brought further supplies which became needed since many different people, former inmates from neighboring concentration camps, work-camps started to drift in.

The day after the liberation father and Captain Dulski, basking in their new-found freedom, decided to go into town where the German population expressed fright at seeing them. They would get off the sidewalk when they saw the Poles walking in their direction. Ignoring all, the two walked into a nearby cafe and enjoyed being free.

Life had turned around for father and his fellow officers; the guards had disappeared, the camp loud speakers were silent and they were not subjected to the Hitler propaganda. Nevertheless, he started to wonder what was going to be next. What was going to be his future, since as the Allies had given Poland to Soviet rule there was no home to go back to? What was happening with mother and me and how would we be able to be together?

Suddenly after several days of silence, the loud speakers resumed:

"This is BBC, Polish Language station; we are reporting the latest news to our countrymen...." The impact of hearing a program, in Polish, with factual news of the world and Polish affairs was tremendous. The news broadcasts were heard daily, together with news from the "Peoples Republic of Poland" i.e. Communist Poland, that resulted in the departure of several officers, who were reservists, without permission in order to return to Poland.

MAY 1945
MURNAU, GERMANY

Within days of liberation, information was given to the ex-POWs as to who they should contact in order to find their families, and father took advantage of the opportunity to search for mother and me. In addition, the US military was now in charge of the camp and issued new ID's for the ex-prisoners.

The closest Polish unit to Murnau was the Polish Second Corps that had fought the battles in Italy and was now part of the occupying forces there. The commanding officer was no other than the three-star General Anders, who had brought most of his soldiers from the Soviet Union, as well as all of us civilians that were now in the Middle East.

Within two weeks arrived official representatives from 2nd Corps, HQ to take stock of the situation, bringing with them a theatrical group. The temptation to leave the camp was great but the latest orders strictly forbade anybody to leave on their own without official papers of transfer. Therefore, father was surprised when he heard a call through the loudspeaker paging him to report to the commandant's office; he immediately went to answer the call, still wondering what would be a reason for this urgent summons to him. As father entered the office a pleasant surprise was waiting for him. Two young lieutenants reported to him officially and it was then that father recognized them as his former officer cadets from Grudziadz. Formality was quickly dispensed with as they all embraced each other. They said that they had spotted father's name on the POW list and came to Murnau get him to come to join the 2nd Corps, where they were in the Carpathian Lancers Regiment. They also explained that in 1939 they had managed to escape the Germans, going through Romania and then joining their unit in Syria which later took part in the battle of Tobruk, north Africa; they had fought at Monte Cassino.

They brought with them several large jugs of Chianti to celebrate, so father invited some of his closer friends to join. Needless to say, it did not take long for the officers who had not had alcohol for almost five years to feel no pain.

The following day the lieutenants were ready to return to their unit and were trying to persuade father to come with them. Although father was greatly tempted to take them up on the offer, he declined because he did not want to go against the orders of the camp.

It turned out that father did the right thing, because at the beginning of June came an order from the Polish 2nd Corps. Out of the 5000 officers in Murnau, there were selected 150 career officers who received assignments with the Corps in Italy, and father was one of them.

Before father's departure, two letters reached him bringing the awaited news of our whereabouts. One read as follows:

Polish Welfare and Education Department
Military Families Section
Brook Green-High House, London, England
June 15, 1945
To: Capt. Stanislaw Mikosz
Polish Centre for Ex-Prisoners of War
Base Censor A.P.O. 887, US Army
Murnau o/Bayern/Germany
Former Oflag VIIA
In regards to your letter of May 25, 1945, I inform you that I informed your wife Anna and your Sister-in-law Maria Stankiewicz about your release.
Both ladies probably are in Isfahan, Iran.
You can write to the following address: c/o/ Polish town Mayor, Military Families Section, Teheran, Iran.
I requested a search for Romuald Muslewski.

Capt. Florian Zielinski is in London, who at one time showed interest in your family and wanted to send them help. His last known address was: 12-13 Grafton Street, London W.I.

I have sent him news of you.

Chief Military Families Section

Lt. Col. Sikorski

The information sent by London was not up to date, since at that time both mother and I were in Teheran and aunt Maria in Egypt, but close enough to enable us to renew contact. The other short note came from Paris, from the Consulate General of Poland that a search for mother and aunt Maria had been undertaken.

Reinforced by the news that we were alive and well, father bid farewell to his officer friends whom he left behind, including Capt. Dulski, with the hope that the Captain might be assigned to 2nd Corps with the next group. There was no next group, and Captain Dulski went on to Great Britain where he worked for a time and subsequently migrated to Canada.

Chapter 30

Iraq-Basra, Bagdad; Syria-Alleppo; Lebanon-Beirut, Ghazir

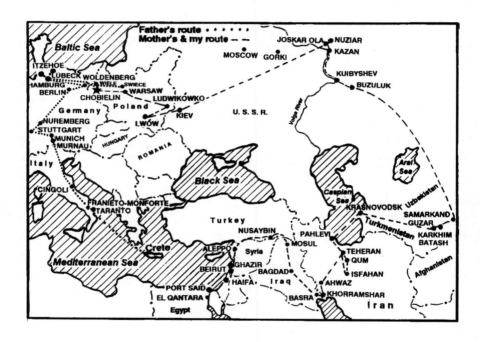

NOVEMBER 1945
BASRA, IRAQ

As our convoy neared Basra the terrain was transformed into a lush green land full of slender palms which not long ago had been laden with heavy bunches of dates. This was almost the end of the harvest season that

338

began in August and had brought many nomads from the surrounding area to help in harvesting.

Beyond the city lay marshes that were sparsely populated by Marsh Arabs, who lived in woven reed houses that looked like giant elephant tusks set up as arches. They presented a great contrast to their desert cousins, who roamed the sandy expanse on the backs of camels.

We made another stop in a British Military camp, where again we were fed before being taken to the Basra train station in order to continue to Baghdad. The train was an old rickety relic of days gone by, and we were crammed into cars that consisted of rows of wooden seats and windows which had no glass, but only wooden jalousie shutters. Since it was over 300 miles to our next destination through desert country, the cars were supplied with cans of water and sandwiches for our journey. It was early evening by the time the train was loaded and ready to leave the station, heading northwest through the ancient lands under whose sands still lie buried remains of the old empires of Mesopotamia. The narrow gauge train bumped monotonously through the desert and as I tried to peer through the slats of the wooden shutters that failed to keep out the gritty sand, all I could see was sand dunes and occasionally a few camels with their nomad riders. In spite of the crammed and inconvenient facilities, people in the train settled down and some were even sleeping. It was getting late; the sun had set and the desert air abruptly cooled. The railroad tracks made a definite turn to the north, closer to the Euphrates River, when someone pointed out that were passing through the area where the ancient city of Ur had stood. Curiously, I looked into the falling dusk outside but all I was able to discern were large tells and some vague outlines in the sand.

With the coolness of the night, sleep overcame me as I huddled in my seat covered with a blanket. When I awakened the train tracks were running along the Euphrates and to the east, in the desert, I saw on the horizon a large golden lake. As I wondered why the reflection of the water was so bright, the "lake" slowly inched up to the horizon and then to my astonishment a golden ball rose into the sky. It was then that I realized that I was watching a desert mirage, which became sunrise in the desert. The phenomena of this occurrence was etched in my memory forever.

Now the train passed more inhabited areas that contained scattered settlements and villages situated amidst palm groves and a variety of exotic fruit trees. About 50 miles before Baghdad, we passed through the town of Hilla on the river; this was the ancient Babylon. The only remnant that now remained was the outline of the walls of the palaces that almost 2500 years ago boasted of the Hanging Gardens that were one of the seven wonders of the world. The City was overtaken in turn by the Persians and later by Alexander the Great before falling into a secondary position. Most of the city's fantastic Ishtar Gate and processional way that survived millennia under the cover of the sands was excavated by the Germans in the early twenties and dismounted brick by brick; it now is set up in the Berlin Museum.

In the early morning the train pulled into the Baghdad station, where a convoy of trucks was already waiting in order to convey us to the transit tent camp on the outskirts of the city.

NOVEMBER 1945
BAGHDAD, IRAQ

The city was and is the capital of Iraq and was originally built on the western bank of the Tigris River; through time with constant growth it has expanded to the eastern side. With the coming of Islam in the 7th century AD, the Middle East became the center of Islamic civilization. But it was not until 750 AD, when the Abbasid dynasty became dominant with the help of the Shi'a of Iraq' that they transferred their seat of power to the new city that they had built—Baghdad. The Caliph encouraged the

Arabic culture and under him it flourished; he is still remembered in the stories of the "Thousand and One Nights". The Abbasid palace with several gold domed mosques still remains from the golden era of the city.

In the 13th century Baghdad was invaded by the Mongols and lost its power and importance; in the 16th century it fell to the Turks and became part of the Ottoman Empire until its demise three centuries later. Now it was a British mandate and a city which served as a transit point for allied military and civilians.

As our convoy wound its way through the streets of Baghdad, I observed with a certain disappointment that the dusty city was not at all like the city of Hollywood's "Thief of Baghdad". The Arab men were dominant on the streets, wearing a variety of colorful costumes while the women, who were seen only occasionally, darted in and out of merchant's stalls completely covered by their dark *chadors*.

We arrived at our transit quarters, a tent camp that had been used by the military during the war. The large tents stood in orderly rows; each contained several individual cots where we were to stay a day or two until the next transport and accompanying travel papers would be ready for our group. As we settled down after breakfast and some excursions to the city were planned, a sudden downpour came. In minutes the rain transformed the dry camp into a virtual lake of standing water that almost reached the bottom of our cots. I sat cross-legged on the bed and watched the waters rise; it reminded me of the Biblical deluge. Then, as suddenly as the rain had started, it stopped. The sun came out, and in no time the earth was parched again as if the downpour had not occurred.

The "day or two" planned stay, for some reason of transportation logistics, extended to ten days. There was not much to do here since the weather was turning into the rainy season, with constant downpours and then cold nights. But mother and I, whenever it was possible to get a ride to town, would go to look at the local bazaars which were but a pale shadow of what we had seen in Isfahan and Teheran.

NOVEMBER 1945
LEAVING BAGHDAD, IRAQ

The day of departure finally arrived and once again we were taken to a railroad station and in the late afternoon boarded our train. It consisted of cars of various classes but this time was a standard gauge train. Our car was reasonably comfortable but filled to capacity. It was already dark when our train finally left the station and the illuminated city of Baghdad, heading north for Mosul and our final destination of Beirut on a journey that was to last forty hours.

Tired after the day's waiting and shuttling about, I settled in for the night snuggled in my blanket and fell asleep. The next morning I awakened to the bustle in the car where food for the rest of the day was being distributed. Mother and aunt Luta, who was traveling with us, went to get our quota while I, not quite awake, peered out the window at the new terrain. The train tracks ran along the west bank of the Tigris River, which at this point seemed to wander through the flat terrain.

At a steady speed the train kept going north as we passed oil pipe lines on the fertile plain of Mosul, which in ancient times was the center of the Assyrian Empire. Around here were the cities of Nineveh, Nimrud and Khorsabad, whose ruins lay in the surrounding hills. By evening the train crossed the Turkish border and came to a stop.

NOVEMBER 1945
NUSAYBIN, TURKEY

The small town's importance now was only its location on the Baghdad train line but like most settlements here it can boast of its existence as far back as the first millennium BC, when it was known as Nisibis. Here the train was detained until almost midnight and was boarded by Turkish military guards, who stationed themselves in each train car. We really did not know the reason for all this security; it made all of us very uneasy.

Our guarded voyage continued throughout the next day west along the Turkish-Syrian border, until evening when we reached the border crossing and continued several miles to Aleppo, Syria.

DECEMBER 1945
ALEPPO, SYRIA

The busy Aleppo station was all lit up when our train pulled into it, and the Syrian and French authorities who boarded the train began to check our papers with the assistance of the Polish personnel that were on hand. After the laborious process had been completed we were told to leave the train and come to the platform where a kitchen was set up and we were fed a hot meal. After two days and two nights confined to the train car, it was a relief to stretch our legs and inhale the cool night air of this ancient city. Unfortunately, it was dark and all I could see of the town was its lighted buildings and the mosque domes shimmering in the moonlight.

After several hours, fed and more relaxed, we were once again put on a train, but this time in freight cars with hay strewn on the floor. This was to be the last leg of our journey to Beirut and I welcomed the unconventional mode of transportation because at least I could lie down and sleep comfortably. Sleep came to me quickly, and when I awakened it was light and we were about to cross the Syria-Lebanon border, where we had another short stop; we then headed south for Tripoli and along the coastal plain of the Mediterranean Sea to Beirut. To the east were visible the mountains of Lebanon, their foothills covered with deep green vegetation.

DECEMBER 5, 1945
BEIRUT, LEBANON

We entered the Beirut rail station sometime in the afternoon; the Polish authorities were waiting for us, and after a meal we were packed into waiting trucks to be taken to our assigned quarters.

Since the beginning of the war Beirut had served as a transit point for many Polish military personnel, as well as civilians. But it was not until now that the Lebanese Government agreed to receive several thousand Polish refugees; for that purpose, centers were set up around the city which housed them and provided schools for children of various ages.

The city of Beirut was the capital of the Lebanese Republic, which at one time was a part of the Phoenician League and had commercial and cultural ties with Greece and the Mediterranean world. For two centuries, from 1099 to 1291, the Crusaders and Arabs fought for the control of the city, but it was not until 1920 that Beirut became the capital under French mandate.

The country was a mosaic of races, but the majority were Arabs speaking Arabic and Aramaic, while French was the language of business and government. Religious diversity splintered the population even further; they were roughly divided into Muslim and Christian, but each of these in tern had subgroups of their own. The largest Christian group were the Maronites, who came from the north in the 7th century escaping persecution in Syria.

Now our truck convoy passed through a wide promenade planted with tall green palms and lined with shops and bustling crowds. The city appeared curiously continental, interlaced with Middle Eastern enchantment; Christian church steeples and Moslem minarets were silhouetted together against the sky.

Mother and I, together with aunt Luta and Basia, were to go to the first established settlement, Ghazir, a short distance of 15 miles to the north of the city.

DECEMBER 1945
GHAZIR, LEBANON

Ghazir was an enchanting place. The small town was a summer resort precariously perched about 2000 feet above the sea level, with panoramic views of the two bays of Joune and St. George. Our house, which was typically Lebanese, square and made of large chiseled stones, was on the outskirts above Ghazir. Since everything was on tiered plateaus, the building was just below the main road so that its roof was level with the road that continued to climb upward to the mammoth statue of Christ which was erected by the Jesuit fathers. The gardens that surrounded the house were full of fig trees, banana palms laden with fruit, and African violets that grew in abundance. Below the house were the terraced fields of the villagers which I began to explore, finding several cascading streams which were hidden among the bends.

The house itself was spartan, with a large central room that had windows overlooking the distant bay and the valley below. From this room doors led to small cubicles that served as bedrooms which contained plank beds with straw mattresses. We shared the house with aunt Luta and Basia and two other friends of mother's who had also come from Iran and now were on the staff of the Polish Ghazir administration.

The Polish school was already operational when we arrived, so I was able to continue classes without much interruption. I was in fifth grade and made my daily morning trek down the winding road to the village where the school was located. Every day, coming and going seemed an adventure to me because there were always different discoveries, be they shops or churches. In addition, we had school excursions, and one in particular was very memorable. It was to the nearby monastery of St. Anthony, which looked like a huge medieval castle perched on a hill with massive walls extending into the hillside. According to its chronicles and history, the Polish romantic poet Juliusz Slowacki stayed there in 1837 while journeying to the Middle East. Here he wrote the poem "Anhelli" and, before leaving Lebanon, the Poles put up a plaque commemorating his stay.

Mother had already notified father of our new whereabouts and resumed correspondence with him, from which she knew that he was trying to get the necessary papers to come and see us. We hoped that he might make it for Christmas, but as the holidays grew closer it did not look promising.

Our small "house family" spent Christmas Eve together, having the traditional Polish Christmas supper and exchanging the wafer together with wishes and hopes for the coming year. This was our sixth Christmas on foreign soil and the first without war. This was the Holiday that we had all presumed would be celebrated back in Poland. But instead we could not return to our homeland even after six years in exile, with half of the family losing their lives in the process. The remaining family members were scattered; aunt Maria was in Egypt working in the military hospital in Cassasin, Romek was an airman in the Polish Air Force in England, and father was stationed in Italy trying to reach mother and me.

Furthermore, since I was now eleven years old, mother agreed to let me go to midnight Mass together with Basia and her girlfriend, who had joined us for the supper. It was an exiting evening with presents and sweets, which soon tired me out so I decided to lie down and rest before venturing to Church. I extracted a solemn promise from Basia to wake me up if I should fall asleep.

I lay down fully clothed on my cot, and the next thing I remember was waking up very refreshed and ready to go. I looked around; mother was asleep in the next bed and it was getting light. I walked out of our room and went in search of Basia, who was fast asleep in her bed. I nudged her shoulder.

"Basia, is it time to go?" She opened her eyes, squinting, and grumbled

"We already went. I tried to wake you up but couldn't. Go back to sleep and I'll talk to you later."

Disappointed that I had missed my big chance, I went back to bed since I did not want to wake up the rest of the household.

The last week of the year was uneventful, as I continued to enjoy my Christmas break and the wonderful warm weather for which the area was known.

Chapter 31

Italy-Franieto Monforte, Taranto; Greece-Crete; Egypt-Port Said, El Qantara; Palestine-Haifa

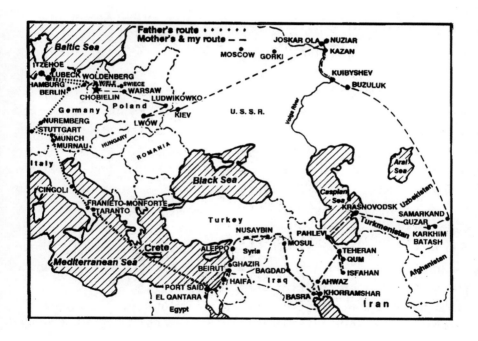

JUNE 1945
ITALY

The journey from Murnau lasted two days as the transport wound its way to Innsbruck, Austria, through the Brenner Pass of the Alps, and down to Verona where the former POW's had a chance to rest for a while before continuing to Ancona, a port on the Adriatic Sea. Ancona was now the location of the Headquarters of the Polish 2nd Corps, where the released officers were to report. The commander himself, Lt. Gen. Anders, was on hand to welcome them and that evening hosted a splendid party at the officers' club in their honor.

At the party father was reunited with several other friends with whom he had served before September '39, among whom was Major Garbacki, who informed father of his new assignment. Maj. Garbacki told father that he was going to the 12th Podolian Lancers Regiment stationed in Cingoli, where the major was second in command.

Thus next day father left with Maj. Garbacki for Cingoli, thirty miles southwest of Ancona. The small medieval hamlet was nestled on a hilltop among the mountains. It was walled and could be entered only through its several massive gates. From its ramparts, on a clear day one could see the sprawling countryside, the winding roads below and even the distant seashore.

Upon his arrival father again was warmly greeted by his fellow officers; he was the first former POW officer assigned to this Regiment. Here again he was welcomed by two of his former cadet officers from Grudziadz, Capt. Dziekonski and Lt. Kolotko, but was sad to learn that the third one that had been with them, Lt. Rejmanski, was killed in action at Monte Cassino. Being among men that he had known for many years made father's transition back to active duty easier.

As father was settling into his new surroundings, correspondence caught up with him and he received two letters in answer to his previous inquiries:

JULY 30, 1945
CINGOLI, ITALY
Dear Captain,
I am sending you a letter with news and address of your wife. So far, I have not received any information about the address of Mrs. Stankiewicz.
Helena Lasko
Polish Forces C.M.E.550

With the note came the copy of the following notification from:

Polish Red Cross in Middle East
Missing Persons Inquiries Office
July 19, 1945
   To: Headquarters 2nd Corps
         Chief Medical Officer-Head Nurse
   In regards to your letter of July 1945 L>dz.318/ms/45 Center for Inquiries informs that according to information of April 15, 1945 Mrs. Anna Mikosz lived in Teheran. At the same time we are informing her of her husbands, Stanislaw Mikosz who was liberated from German imprisonment, search for her.
   All correspondence for Mrs. Anna Mikosz should be addressed to:
   c/o Polish Red Cross, Teheran, Iran
   Chief of Missing Persons Office

Now all the agencies that father contacted were replying to his inquires and this reassured him that we were indeed safe and in Iran. Then at the end of the month came another communication, with further news of our whereabouts.

POLISH RED CROSS
Delegation For the Middle East
Cairo
2, Kadi el Fadel
>   *August 22, 1945*
>   *We received a telegram from Teheran with news that your wife*
> *Anna and daughter Teresa received your letter of July 29, 1945.*
> *They are well and soon they are leaving for Lebanon.*
>   *We presume that soon you will receive news directly from them.*

Father tried to get a leave and come to Teheran as well as to get permission to bring us to bring us to Italy, but the Allied High Command in Caserta refused to grant it because of difficulties in sea transport.

SEPTEMBER 1945
CINGOLI, ITALY

In the meantime, father was appointed as commander of the 4th company of his regiment and in conjunction with that was go to Polish/English staff officer training in Franieto-Monforte, which was in the vicinity of Naples. He was scheduled to leave the following month but in the meantime he tried to cut through the red tape and bring us to Italy by writing to different agencies and individuals who were in a position to help.

Father did receive two replies, which were not positive but gave further instruction how to proceed with this matter.

> *From: Col. A. Konczacki*
>   *Polish Forces ME 281*
>   *Sept. 15, 1945*
> *Dear Captain,*
>   *In an answer to your letter of August 25, 1945, with great regret*
> *I have to inform you that the quest of bringing your wife and daughter to Italy as you were informed, is not that simple. It is true, that*
> *chief of PCK (Polish Red Cross) attached to the 2nd Corps needs sev-*

eral people to work in Italy, but unfortunately you need more than that in order to get permission which has to be given by the Command of the 2nd Corps. And for bringing a child you need permission from the British. At present there are 20 persons in Egypt waiting for that kind of permit, of whom a few have been there several months and despite many written requests and telegrams nothing is accomplished.

Bringing your wife from Teheran to Egypt, at present is also almost impossible, particularly with a daughter. Presently, the chief of PCK (Polish Red Cross) in Teheran is here and we came to the conclusion that the best would be to get a Syrian visa and send your wife and daughter to Lebanon (Beirut) from where it would be easier to eventually get permission to leave for Italy. The permit to come to 2nd Corps will be easier for you to obtain on the spot at the office of the Military Welfare of 2nd Corps. After getting such permission, then we will try to put your wife on the waiting transport and we can get it all moving.

I think it would be best that you first know that your wife is already in Beirut and have received the permission from 2nd Corps for them, that you come here personally to take them back.

Experience teaches that such personal interventions have better chances of succeeding.

Sincerely yours, Col. A Konczacki

P.S. We have information that several hundred military dependents will be evacuated from Iran to Lebanon. It would be recommended that you write to the Polish Legation In Beirut (Mr. Gilar in charge of military affairs) so they place your family on the list of persons recommended for departure to Lebanon as military dependents. On my side, I will do all in power to obtain speedy departure once the evacuation starts.

P.O. Delegate PCK (Polish Red Cross) for Iran
T. Bielski

OCTOBER 15, 1945
FRANIETO-MONFORTE, ITALY

Father left Cingoli for the training course, still not being able to obtain the necessary papers so mother and I could come to Italy. He made arrangements to have his mail and other regimental correspondence to be brought to Franieto on regular basis. So it was not a surprise when within a week after his arrival there, he received an answer from Egypt to his inquiry.

Polish Red Cross
Delegation for the Middle East
Cairo, October 15, 1945

> *To:*   *Captain Stanislaw Mikosz*
> *Polish Forces CMF 156*

> *I am confirming receipt of your letter of Sept. 29, 1945 and in response we would like to inform you that we would like to help you with the request of bringing your wife and daughter to Italy. We already wrote about this request on Oct.9, 1945 to Lt Jerry Lipowski and Capt. S. Skupinski and we are enclosing copies of the responses. At the same time we are informing you that in order to bring anyone to 2nd Corps, we have to have an individual permission from the Quartermaster of 2nd Corps. Otherwise, persons brought to Palestine or Egypt have to wait there months for such a permit. Lately we brought 20 nurses of PCK from Iran, who are in Egypt for the last three months and still did not receive the permit to come to Italy. On one hand this overextends our budget and on the other it creates discontent for the waiting persons.*

> *So, in order that your wife's case would move forward from the start, please get the permission to bring them while you are at 2nd Corps. Also, make sure that the permit is sent to us as soon as possible. Then we will make sure that your family will be brought to Egypt from where they would be able to leave immediately for the 2nd Corps.*

*Ending, we want to reassure you that we want to give you help
fully knowing that you want to be reunited quickly with your wife
and daughter.*

Sincerely

Inspector General of PCK (Polish Red Cross)

With the above letter came a response from the Polish Consul in
Beirut, whose son was a junior officer in father's newly assigned company,
and who took personal interest in trying to help father.

Ministry of Labor and Welfare
Beirut, Lebanon

October 19, 1945

Dear Captain,

*I am responding to two of your letters of Sept. 29, and Oct.2,
1945 that I received today. As soon as I received the letter from my
son Jerzy, I started the procedure to bring your family from Teheran
to Lebanon as soon as possible.*

*Because, in the meantime the Lebanese authorities are question-
ing the arrival of persons who received visas from the French authorities on their own, to which your family belongs, I am trying anew to
get them a visa from local Lebanese authorities with the help of the
Polish Legation in Beirut. I will try to telegraph these visas to
Teheran.*

*At the same time I am requesting the delegate of Ministry of
Labor and Welfare in Teheran that, upon receipt of the visas, your
family be immediately attached to the transport of refugees from
Isfahan who are presently being evacuated to Lebanon.*

*I am happy to reassure you that, after your family arrives to
Beirut, I will immediately contact you. I will try to do all I can so to
help you to be reunited with them.*

Sincerely yours,

Delegate, Ministry of Labor and Welfare

E. Kocuper

Mr. Kocuper's work to get the system moving had positive results, because soon a dispatch reached father that read as follows:

Polish Red Cross

Delegation for Middle East, Cairo, Egypt

> *Oct. 31, 1945*
>
> *To: Capt. S. Mikosz*
>
> *Polish Arm Forces, CMF 156*
>
> *We are cordially informing you that we have received news from PCK Delegation for Iran, that your wife and daughter have visas to go to Lebanon. The departure will probably be in mid November.*

Not wasting any time, father contacted the Quartermaster as he had been previously instructed and received the required documents, which were radiogramed to Teheran immediately.

> *Quartermaster of 2nd Corps*
>
> *Office of Military Welfare*
>
> *Nov. 7, 1945*
>
> *Please send the employee of PCK, Anna Mikosz and her daughter Teresa, who are now residing in Teheran-English Embassy, Polish Section of Civil Hospital, Iran to Italy.*
>
> *Quartermaster 2nd. Corp.*
>
> *Col. Skowronski*

NOVEMBER 1945
FRANIETO-MONFORTE, ITALY

The training course was set to last eight weeks and father found it most interesting after the long years in prison and being out of contact with the military. In addition, he now was able to put his English, which he had started to learn in the camp, into practical use.

Having secured the necessary papers from the military authorities, father was anxiously waiting for further developments from Iran. The anxiously awaited news came toward the end of the month.

Delegation de la Crois Rouge
Polonaise en Iran

Teheran, Nov. 13, 1945

Dear Captain,

I received your letter of Oct. 2, 1945 ten days ago but I did not hurry with the answer since I was waiting for the resolvment of leave for your wife and daughter for Lebanon.

In fact, no one was able to depart from Teheran for the last several weeks because of technical reasons; there were no roads for Polish transports.

Though over hundred persons came to Ahwaz (town in the south of Iran) but no one left from there for Lebanon.

I advised your wife, with whom I am in constant contact, not to go to Ahwaz yet, until the road from Ahwaz to Bagdad and then to Lebanon is going to be opened.

Today the prospects of departure of all Polish people looks much better than a few weeks ago.

We are almost sure that all people will leave by rail. Your wife with daughter will be attached to one of the transports as a Red Cross nurse.

According to our calculations it should occur between 1-15th of December or maybe sooner; it all depends if the transport scheduled for Nov. 20th will leave Teheran, which the British are confirming and in whose hands are all the transports.

I also advised your wife not to leave on her own since it would ruin her financially and the result would be eventually the same if she went with the group at the Welfare cost.

Therefore, please wait patiently for my notification of your family's departure; I will notify you by telegraph.

For your reassurance, I would like to inform you, that having a
visa at this point has no practical purpose, since all transports are
issued visas while in transit without any problems.
  Your family has exit and transit visas.
  Sincerely yours,
  T. Bielski
  p.o.Delegate P.C.K. for Iran

DECEMBER 1945
FRANIETO-MONFORTE, ITALY

In the beginning of the month, shortly before the training course was
to end, father received news that his request for furlough to go to the
Middle East was approved. Now, he was waiting for the final notice that
we were able to leave Iran. Then on the 15th the long awaited telegram
came from Mr. Kocuper in Beirut:

NOTIFICATION

I am confirming that Mrs. Anna Mikosz, wife of Capt. S.
Mikosz C.M.F. 159, as well as daughter Teresa Mikosz, b. 1934,
came from Iran to Lebanon on December 5, 1945 and are residing
in the Polish community in Ghazir.

Mrs. Mikosz is not employed by any government institution or
private Polish section and is not receiving any help from Delegation
MP. & OS. in Beirut.

Mrs. Mikosz receives from Delegation MP. and OS. in Beirut
military dependent subsidy from the day of arrival to Lebanon in the
amount of LL 101.20 per month.

This confirmation is issued in order to obtain additional
Military dependent subsidy.

  Delegate
  Min. of Labor and Welfare, Beirut
  E. Kocuper

With all the necessary paper work done, his leave secured and the training course finished, the next step was for father to secure transport to the Middle East. Fortunately, father had made a great many preliminary inquiries beforehand. He now had only to make a couple of phone calls to get results. The orders came; father was to go immediately to the Port of Taranto where there was a place reserved on a ship which was going to Port Said, Egypt

Father came to the training course with his staff car and a driver, who now was told to pack up and get an extra supply of gasoline since they were going to leave right after lunch. The distance to Taranto was close to 350 kilometers (about 220 miles) and over winding roads still difficult to travel; father wanted to make sure to be there by morning.

But when on the   following morning father reported to the British transport officer in the port he was informed: "Captain, the ship left four hours ago. We were looking for you but to no avail." The British officer related to my disappointed father.

"When is the next ship sailing for the Middle East?"

"I can't really say, Captain, since sea transportation is not yet regular and the ships that are going from Gibraltar to India stop at various Mediterranean ports taking on passengers and military cargo. My suggestion is that you should go to the transit camp here, and telephone me each evening to see if there is any ship with space available"

Not having any other choice, father took the transport officer's advice and, after finding quarters in the transit camp, he sat down and wrote a letter to his regimental commander explaining the situation.

DECEMBER 25, 1945
TARANTO, ITALY

Father spent his first Christmas in freedom quietly with other military personnel that were in transit and did not make it to their destination before the Holidays. Though disappointed that he was not with us, he was knew that it was just a matter of a short time before he would reach mother and me.

That evening father telephoned the transport officer at the port, as he had been instructed to do, and was informed of the latest news.

"Captain, there is a ship that just left Gibraltar; it will stop in Marseilles and Genoa before it arrives in Taranto. I managed to secure a place on for you. But it is hard to say when the ship will be here; it might be three to four days."

For the following days father waited, ready to go at a moment's notice; on December 29th he received the welcome news:

"Please be in the port tomorrow at 6 A.M."

Needless to say, father was there long before the assigned time since he did not want have any more complications. The large, 45,000 ton ship, which at one time had been a passenger vessel, was now painted in military battle gray and was waiting for the noon departure. It was full of various military people; a Scottish Battalion with their all-female band heading for Sudan, Hindus going to Bombay, and some contingents returning to Palestine, as well as a few Polish officers. The ship's first stop after leaving Taranto was Crete, where it was to pick up another Hindu unit that was heading home. Father was assigned to share a cabin with three Hindu officers who made the voyage very congenial.

DECEMBER 31, 1945
CRETE

The ship docked in the harbor in the early evening. It was the first New Year's Eve after the end of the long war, and the island was illuminated with colorful displays of fireworks. On the ship, all the passengers gathered in the largest hall to celebrate. The women's band, attired in Scottish garb, provided continuous and joyous music while the wine flowed freely.

Then at midnight the toasts began, starting with one to the King. After several of them, the British Brigadier who was the transport commander stepped to the microphone and quieted the jubilant crowd, saying:

"Gentlemen, we have among us several Polish officers, the best allies in arms who with their blood and sacrifice contributed to the victory. They were brave and paid dearly for the hope of attaining independence. Their whole nation suffered greatly but their suffering and sacrifice did not bring them freedom because a political sellout robbed them of the opportunity to return to their homeland. In honor of Poland and our Polish officer friends present here, I raise a toast: Long live free and independent Poland!" Cheers rose from the crowd as the orchestra burst forth with Chopin's *Polonaise Militaire*. In the morning the transport ship departed for its next destination: Port Said, Egypt.

JANUARY 2, 1946
PORT SAID, EGYPT

The transport ship sailed into the harbor of Suez greeted by an imposing statue of the Suez Canal's builder, Ferdinand de Lesseps, and docked to disembark its military passengers who represented many nations, among them a Palestinian detachment which was heading for home. The Polish officers with whom father had shared the voyage were returning to their camp situated south of Cairo, leaving father with a Captain who like himself was going to see his family, in his case in Tel Aviv.

The two of them took a taxi to the train station, where they reported to the British transportation officer and received detailed information about local customs and what to look out for. Since they had five hours before the train's departure, father and his companion decided to explore the town.

The port of Suez lies on a barren strip of land and owes its existence to the Suez Canal, at whose north end it is situated. The completion of the Canal in 1869 made Port Said the link between the Mediterranean and the Gulf of Suez, thus also making it a very important strategic point in World War II and now in transporting troops.

It was father's first look at the Middle East and he explored the streets with curiosity. The variety of colorful garb as well as the overabundance of vendors, shops and street crowds overwhelmed him; it was nothing like Europe. The sellers of goods, which ranged from aromatic herbs and tourist souvenirs to gold, lined every street. Time passed quickly, and father had to put a stop to his sightseeing and go back to the railroad station in order to catch his train for the Polish Military camp in Qassasin where he was to receive his movement orders for further travel in the Middle East.

The railway between Port Said and Ismalia to the south runs parallel to the west bank of the Suez Canal, and as the train sped along he watched the giant ships glide through it. The distance of 50 miles to Ismalia was soon reached and then the train headed west for another hour before reaching the station of Qassasin, where father got off and made his way to the nearby camp. Again, he reported to the camp authorities and stayed here for the night. Next morning his orders were ready; they read:

> *POLISH TRANSIT CAMP M.E.*
>
> *Requisition for train ticket Nr. 706285*
>
> *MOVEMENT ORDER*
>
> *This is to certify that the bearer Capt. Stanislaw Mikosz of Polish Transit Camp M.E. is to leave by train, road from Qassasin via to CAIRO, LEBANON-BEIRUT and back.*
>
> *Authority for move HQ Base 2 Pol. Corps No. 10638/Tj/Kwat.Ruch?45 of 31 Dec 45.*
>
> *All Military Authorities are kindly requested to grant him the necessary assistance in the case of need*
>
> *Valid: From Jan. 6, 1946—To Feb. 10, 1946*
>
> *Signature of holder- S. Mikosz*
>
> *O.C. Polish Transit Camp M.E.*
>
> *Commandant O.P. J.W.S.W*
>
> *Col. R. Niementowski*

Since father had a few days before he could take his assigned train, he took advantage of the time and went to visit aunt Maria, with whom he was in contact, and who was stationed not far from there.

JANUARY 3, 1946
EL QANTARA, EGYPT

In the morning father headed back to the station and took the train back to Ismalia and then on to El Qantara, where the 8th Polish General Hospital was located on the east bank of the Suez Canal. It also was the starting point of the Palestinian Railway, which had been built during World War I.

There are no bridges across the Canal in El Qantara and one has to take a felucca to be ferried across by the enterprising locals. The Canal lies in the middle of fertile lands, a crossing point between Egypt and the Middle East and therefore a quarantine center and border crossing throughout the ages for people who wanted to enter Egypt. Here on the east bank, in the 19th century, the Polish poet Slowacki, after leaving Lebanon, paused for a while and while there wrote an epic called "*Ojciec Zadzumiony*" (Father of the Plagued). It is a tale of a bedouin who came here and waited weeks in the quarantine camp for permission to cross while his family died of plague, one by one. Now there only were remnants of the old cemetery, which told tales of ancient sufferings.

Father had a joyful reunion with aunt Maria, who filled him in about some of our journeys and he in turn told her about uncle Jas. The two days he spent there passed quickly and father was anxious to continue his journey to Beirut. He also told aunt Maria that he had the necessary papers and would bring mother and me back with him to Italy. But he promised aunt Maria that we would come back this way in a few weeks and stay with her for a time before boarding the ship for Italy.

JANUARY 6, 1946
FROM EL QANTARA TO BEIRUT

Father's train left the east El Qantara station in the evening heading northeast through the desert to El Arich, where it made a stop to replenish its water supply. It arrived early the next morning at Gaza, where the military passengers were given breakfast before going on to Rehvot, where many had to change trains. Since father was continuing to Haifa, he remained on it throughout the night without any further interruption.

JANUARY 7, 1946
HAIFA, PALESTINE

Arriving in the early morning at Haifa without any problems, all military personnel had their documents checked by the British Military Police since it was only 25 miles from there to the Lebanese border, which was in a different military district. The transportation officer who accompanied the MP looked at father's destination and shook his head, saying:

"Captain, I am sorry to inform you that you can't go any further today. The rail tracks north of Haifa were destroyed last night and I cannot tell you when they will be operational." It was the result of constant warfare between the Arabs and Jews, making travel in Palestine tedious as well as hazardous.

This unexpected obstacle momentarily set father aback but, seeing his dilemma, the transport officer suggested an alternative.

"You know, Captain Mikosz, that it is only 100 miles from here to Beirut and it can easily be reached by taxi. There are several of them that have taken passengers there but you have to be careful so as not to be taken in by them. The cost is approximately 10 pounds." As he continued to explain, he looked through his papers and told father that there was another Polish officer, whom he pointed out, who was going to Beirut.

Father thanked the British officer for his concern and went over to the Polish captain. Together, the two began to search for a vehicle to complete their journey. Within an hour they found one willing driver, who had an old Ford that did not inspire much confidence in its reliability. Nevertheless, not having much choice, after some negotiation father and his new found companion set out on the road north heading for Beirut.

As they ventured north along the road that skirted the ancient Phoenician coast they took advantage of their opportunity and stopped in Sour, which was the ancient Tyre. The once busy port was now a pleasant village, where they had lunch and explored its picturesque harbor.

Thirty miles further north was the town of Saida, known in ancient times as Sidon, where the olden days of its past glory lay buried under the modern town. The present town was rich in remnants of the Middle Ages. Now, only the foundations and one tower remain of the once mighty Sea Castle where the Crusaders held out until 1291. Father and his companion took the opportunity to look around while the driver took a short rest before going further. As the road meandered along the rocky coast, they spotted a plaque placed high above the road on the cliff side. They motioned the driver to stop and the two men went out to read it. The inscription was in three languages, English, French and Arabic. It stated that in 1799 Napoleon's army reached this point after defeating the Mamelukes of Egypt.

After finally reaching Beirut and saying good-by to his traveling companion father tried to find the Polish Military Command, where he had to report before he could go any further. After unsuccessfully trying to get some information, because the people that he approached spoke only French and no English, rain began to fall, and father took refuge in a cafe. He was tired and thought that he needed a bit of time to rest and regroup. As father sat at a table near the window and sipped his coffee, observing the crowd of pedestrians, he saw a military person walking in his direction. As the man came closer, father recognized a Polish uniform. Quickly he paid his bill and went to catch the individual, who turned out to be a Polish NCO and who, spotting father's rank, saluted him.

"Sergeant, I am looking for the Polish Command Headquarters. Could you tell me how to get there?"

"Captain, I am going there myself since I work there. Please, we can go there together." replied the smiling sergeant.

Delighted with this stroke of luck, father followed the NCO to the Headquarters, where he reported to the officer on duty and explained his situation. Since there were several Polish settlements around Beirut, the officer pulled out a large log of names and confirmed that mother and I were in Ghazir. He also added that the last lorry for the day would be departing for Ghazir in ten minutes, adding:

"Hurry, since the next one won't be until tomorrow afternoon." With that he personally took father to the already filled-up truck, which served as a shuttle bus between Ghazir and Beirut for the Polish community.

The occupants of the truck were mostly women and father was the only person in uniform, which aroused some curiosity on their part as to whom he knew in Ghazir. The truck wound its way up the mountainous road and then turned into a side road before reaching the first grouping of houses, where all the passengers got off. As father wondered what was next, an elderly man who waited at the stop approached him and introduced himself as the senior administrator of the settlement. When father explained to him why he was there, the man called the driver of the truck back and told him to drive father to our house, which was another three quarters of a mile further up the road.

As the truck pulled up to the house and father left the vehicle, many thoughts ran through his mind. How would he find us? It was six years and four months since he had last seen us. I was five years old when I said goodbye to father and was now eleven, grown, and in school.

Gingerly, he knocked at the door and saw that someone looked through the window before the door was opened. I was in my room when I heard a great commotion, so I went out to see what was going on. There by the door were aunt Luta, Basia and mother's friends, while my mother was hugging and kissing some man in a uniform. I stood toward the side, wondering who the person was, until mother noticed me and motioned to me:

"Come, Terenia. Give a kiss to your Daddy."

The winter that had lasted for more than six years was over. Spring had come at last.

Afterword

After our reunion with Father, the three of us proceeded to Egypt to see Aunt Maria before boarding a ship for Italy, where father was stationed and where I subsequently attended school in Rome. In September 1946 Father's regiment was transferred to England, where we lived for two years. During that period I learned English and went to an English boarding school. In 1948, not being able to return to Poland because of communist rule, as well as not being able to come to the United States, my family emigrated to Canada. My parents and I lived in Canada until 1953 when we finally were able to come to the United States.

At the time of this publication, my mother is still living, aged 92. Father died in 1998 at the age of 94. Other members of my family who survived the Soviet Union took various routes out of the Middle East. After the war Aunt Maria came to England, remarried and had a daughter. She died in 1985. Aunt Luta with cousin Romek and Barbara also went to England. Aunt Luta died in 1971. Romek married, had two daughters and died in England in 1981. Barbara presently lives in England with her family.

The Slawinski family stayed in Poland and were reunited with uncle Jas. Both aunt Helen and uncle Jas lived well into their eighties. Their daughters Danka and Marysia are both widows but have extensive families.

As for me, I have tried to revisit some of the places of my past with some success. In 1999 I returned to Uzbekistan and searched in vain for the grave of my cousin Krystofer in Samarkand. But I did go to Kharkim Batash and Guzar. I found the madrasa where I lay when I had typhoid, and found the Polish cemetery with 670 graves.

In 2001 I am returning to Lebanon and Ghazir to see the enchanted place of my childhood.

Chobielin is still standing. It survived occupation and Soviet pillage, and then was taken by the Polish communists. The manor house was sold by the Polish communist government to an opportunist who after the fall of communism is now in the government. The present government is not returning the vast lands of the estate to our family. I returned to Chobielin for the first time in 1983. It was then a pale shadow of its former proud past. There were some village people who remembered and asked about the family. Chobielin is a reminder of a time and a society that is gone forever.

December 2000

About the Author

Teresa Mikosz-Hintzke came to the United States with her parents in 1953 and lived for many years in Detroit. Now a longtime resident of the Chicago area, she graduated from Northwestern University majoring in art history but professionally is a technical illustrator.

She keeps in touch with many former Isfahan students living in the Chicago area, as well as others who are scattered around the world.